EVANGELISM: Christ's Imperative Commission

Revised

Roland Q. Leavell

Revised by Landrum P. Leavell II and
Harold T. Bryson

BROADMAN PRESS
Nashville, Tennessee

4225-34

ISBN: 0-8054-2534-9

All Scripture quotations marked TEV are reprinted from *The Bible in Today's English Version*. Old Testament: Copyright © American Bible Society 1976. Used by permission.

All Scripture quotations marked Moffatt are taken from *The Bible: A New Translation* by James Moffatt, copyright 1954.

Dewey Decimal Classification: 269

Subject heading: EVANGELISTIC WORK

Library of Congress Catalog Card Number: 78-059983

Printed in the United States of America

Preface

Evangelism and Christian education are the alternate heartbeats of the Christian enterprise. This book is submitted with the prayer that it will make a contribution to both of these causes. The pages reflect the belief that evangelism is the sublimest activity of the human soul. Christian service offers no more heavenly experience than that of pointing one to God through the Lord Jesus Christ. To do this service is the imperative commission of the divine Son of God to every follower of his.

The greatest need of the world today is for Christians to render this service of soul-winning. It is the hope for winning the lost men of the world. It is the hope for a better social order and a better world. It is the hope, under God's Spirit, for the answer to the prayer of our Lord: "Thy kingdom come. Thy will be done, as in heaven, so in earth" (Luke 11:2). Personal soul-winning, evangelistic churches, and a worldwide missionary enterprise constitute the challenge with which the Christian forces must meet the needs of the world today.

This volume, as originally written, was a product of the brilliant mind and warm heart of Roland Q. Leavell. Its revision is being offered by two men who share teaching responsibilities in evangelism at the New Orleans Baptist Theological Seminary today, both of whom sat under the teaching of Dr. Roland Leavell. Parts I and II of the original have undergone minor revisions. In Part III, chapter 12 on city-wide simultaneous evangelistic campaigns has been eliminated; and a new chapter entitled "Planning and Promoting a Church Revival" has been inserted. Chapter 13 in the original, "Evangelism in a District Association," becomes "Training Lay Persons for Evangelism" in the revision.

Parts I and II attempt to tell something of the scriptural authority of evangelism, of the present-day need for evangelism, and of some vital historical background for evangelism. This material could not be treated exhaustively in one volume. Some outstanding evangelists have been chosen because they illustrate the various types of evangelism prevalent or possible today. Their spiritual successes should instruct and encourage; their weaknesses should warn.

Part III is intended to be intensely practical. It outlines various methods used in different approaches or programs which have been successful in winning souls. Every program discussed in this part of the book must be adjusted to the immediate situation where it is to be promoted. It is the idea throughout that the churches may experience a high, continuous plateau of perennial evangelistic success, rather than only occasional mountain peaks of victorious revival.

Part IV deals with the fine art of helping others to become Christians through a person-to-person approach. Large portions of this section of the book have been taken, by permission of the publishers, from the author's book *Winning Others to Christ*. We express our gratitude to the Sunday School Board of the Southern Baptist Convention for permission to draw freely from this material. Deep appreciation is expressed to Miss Kathryn Harper for her excellent work as typist.

Dr. Harold Bryson and I have undertaken this project with one prayer—that this book will bless the lives of others in the future as it has blessed and challenged us in the past.

LANDRUM P. LEAVELL II

CONTENTS

Introduction

The gospel of Christ is eternally timeless and is always timely. It is the hope of the world today. It was in the heart of God from the beginning; yet it falls each day upon mankind as a gift fresh from the Creator's hand. Throughout all ages it has been the power of God unto salvation to all who believe. History's pages are both numerous and luminous as they reveal the power of evangelistic fires to purge the dross of sin from individual lives and from the social order.

Our Lord Jesus Christ stood upon the peak of his resurrection glory and gave to his followers for all time to come the great evangelistic commission: "All power is given unto me in heaven and in earth. Go ye therefore, and teach all nations, baptizing them in the name of the Father, and of the Son, and of the Holy Ghost: Teaching them to observe all things whatsoever I have commanded you: and, lo, I am with you alway, even unto the end of the world" (Matt. 28:18-20).

His apostles and the early church members took him seriously. They taught men publicly and from house to house. They testified for Christ, both to the Jews and to the Gentiles. They took the "good news" of the truth in Christ to all the known world. Since apostolic times, wherever the church has maintained an evangelistic, missionary zeal and a soul-winning fervor, the Holy Spirit of God has given his blessings to the church. Wherever the church has lost its missionary zeal and soul-winning fervor, God has moved on.

The center of the Christian enterprise during the first half of the first century A.D. was in Jerusalem. The apostles sought to obey the commission of Christ. "Ye shall be witnesses unto me both in Jerusalem, and in all Judaea, and in Samaria, and unto the uttermost part of the earth" (Acts 1:8). But the Judaizers, certain Christian Jews, did

7

not want the Gentiles to become Christians unless they became Jewish proselytes. This antimissionary spirit conquered the Jerusalem church. Their evangelistic zeal was chilled, and their soul-winning fervor was killed. God moved on!

The center of the Christian enterprise during the second half of the first century A.D. was in Antioch of Syria. Paul, Barnabas, Silas, and others worked there and went out from there. Worldliness and sensuality, seeping in from the sordid environment of Antioch, poisoned the life of the churches. Their evangelistic zeal was chilled, and their soul-winning fervor was killed. God moved on!

Strong centers of the Christian enterprise during the second and third centuries were established in Ephesus and Alexandria. The gospel was preached throughout the entire Roman Empire. But the gnostic heresy, denying the essential deity of Jesus, crept in. Their evangelistic zeal was chilled, and their soul-winning fervor was killed. God moved on!

A strategic citadel of the Christian enterprise from A.D. 330 until the close of the sixth century was in Constantinople. Missionary activity radiated from there into Ireland and Scotland and among the Germans. But Constantine united the church and state. Formalism became the order of worship. The liturgy usurped the place of spirituality. Finally the inroads of Islam killed the already waning power of Christianity there. Their evangelistic zeal was chilled, and their soul-winning fervor was killed. God moved on!

The center of the Christian enterprise in the West from about A.D. 600 until A.D. 1050 and beyond was in Rome. There was much missionary activity at first. They evangelized the Anglo-Saxons, Irish, Scotch, Germans, and Scandinavians. But very few could read the Bible, which was available only in Latin. Monasteries grew up. Unscriptural beliefs crept in. Infant baptism was practiced more universally. Biblical theology decayed. Preaching and religious instruction were neglected. Their evangelistic zeal was chilled, and their soul-winning fervor was killed. God moved on!

The Christian enterprise flourished in France during the twelfth, thirteenth, and fourteenth centuries, especially when the papacy was located in Avignon (1309-1377). The believers' passion for Christianity led them into the Crusades, which lasted for about two hundred years. But the power of the pope was greatly strengthened at about the same time, and a mighty struggle developed between the church and the state. Schism rent the church in twain and led to internal stagnation. The Crusades led to war and bloodshed. Their evangelistic zeal was chilled, and their soul-winning fervor was killed. God moved on!

The center of evangelistic and evangelical Christianity during the middle of the sixteenth century was in Germany. Luther's Reformation began in 1517. Fervent preaching of salvation by grace through faith in Jesus Christ, rather than through ecclesiastical ceremony and sacrament, spread the gospel through Germany, Denmark, Sweden, Norway, Poland, Bavaria, Bohemia, Moravia, and elsewhere. But bitter controversies between the reformers arose concerning their theological interpretations. They forgot the souls of men. Their evangelistic zeal was chilled, and their soul-winning fervor was killed. God moved on!

A mighty center of Christian opportunity for evangelism during the exploration of the western world was in Spain and Portugal. Missionaries went into Central America, South America, the Philippines, and the southern parts of North America. But the gold which they found ushered in an age of materialism. Their greed for gold supplanted their passion for souls. Their evangelistic zeal was chilled, and their soul-winning fervor was killed. God moved on!

The center of the Christian enterprise during the period of the colonization and development of the western world was in England. Missionaries won far-reaching victories in Canada, Australia, New Zealand, and India. But bloody religious wars were fought. The age of skepticism came. An ungodly rationalism flowed out of France and Germany into English thought. Religion was paralyzed. Their evangelistic zeal was chilled, and their soul-winning fervor was killed. God moved on!

The center of the Christian enterprise during the first half of the nineteenth century was New England and the states along the Atlantic seaboard. The so-called "Revival of 1800" began about 1785 and continued in power until about 1812. The educational institutions were saved from the grip of infidelity and were transformed into mighty evangelistic agencies. The crime wave was wiped out. Liquor was brought into disrepute. Homelife was saved. Prosperity was ushered in. The churches were immeasurably strengthened. The foreign missionary movement in America was born in the midst of this revival. But after some years, Unitarianism swept over the churches, denying the deity of Jesus and doubting the inspiration of the Scripture. Materialism absorbed their interests. Their evangelistic zeal was chilled, and their soul-winning fervor was killed. God moved on!

We quote a passage of K. S. Latourette's *History of the Expansion of Christianity—Advance Through Storm:*

> Although the kinds of Christianity which spread were not always the same, the ones which had the largest continuing share were . . . those which found their centre in Jesus and declared that in Him God had once for all bridged the gulf between himself and man, that He was fully man and yet that in Him God was incarnated. Those, like the Gnostics, who minimized the historical Jesus or, like the Jacobites, exalted his divinity above His humanity, flourished for a time, but had no long continuing place in the expansion of the faith. Those who, like the Arians, tended to stress his humanity and to make Him something less than of the very essence of the eternal God also had no persistent part in the spread of the faith. The more extreme representatives of this view, Socinians and Unitarians, had scarcely even a fleeting share in the expansion.[1]

Today Christian expansion circles the globe, with special concentration in the United States. The lessons of history are clear to him who would learn. American Christians must evangelize, or else God will move on. God's hand is upon the Christian forces of America, thrusting them forth into the ripe fields of evangelism. The United States offers the richest, ripest, and most extensive opportunity for soul-winning and for missionary aggressiveness to be found in the wide, wide world. Present world conditions demand evangelism. Christ's commission commands evangelism.

> Give us a watchword for the hour,
> A thrilling word, a word of power;
> A battle-cry, a flaming breath,
> A call to conquest or to death;
> A word to rouse the church from rest,

To heed the Master's high behest.
The call is given: Ye hosts, arise,
Our watchword is Evangelize!
. . . .

To dying men, a fallen race,
Make known the gift of gospel grace;
The world that now in darkness lies,
Evangelize! Evangelize!

—*Henry Crocker*

Note

1. K. S. Latourette, *History of the Expansion of Christianity—Advance Through Storm* (New York: Harper and Brothers, 1937-1945), vol. 7, pp. 484-485.

PART

I

The Imperative Need for Evangelism

1
Evangelism Is Central in Scripture and Experience

All authority hath been given unto me in heaven and on earth. Go ye therefore, and make disciples of all the nations, baptizing them in the name of the Father and of the Son and of the Holy Spirit; teaching them to observe all things whatsoever I commanded you: and lo, I am with you always, even unto the end of the world (Matt. 28:18-20, ASV).

The Great Commission is the Magna Charta of evangelism. It is the marching order of the supreme Commander. It is the proclamation of the King of kings to all his kingdom citizens. It is Christ's imperative for all who name his name.

In this commission there is one dominant and controlling imperative, while all the other verb forms are participles. The central part of Jesus' commission is found in the imperative: "Make disciples." In the original Greek this verb is formed on the noun for "disciple" and should be translated "make disciples." The other three verb forms of the Great Commission are participles: "going," "baptizing," "teaching." The first part of the commission begins with the participle "going." It could be translated, "As you go, make disciples." Students of the Greek New Testament know that a participle can have a imperatival force. Therefore, the various translations are not wrong when they translate the participle as an imperative: "Go."

Christ commissioned his disciples to go to "all the nations." For the Christian, the field is the world. This means that soul-winning is central, that evangelism is the divine imperative, that worldwide missionary endeavor is the very heart of Christ's commands to his disciples. Going with the gospel to all the nations comprised a unique mission. No other religion in Jesus' day aimed for that goal. Existing religions were believed to be merely the products of national instincts and aspirations. Each religion was considered to be the furniture of the particular culture. Jesus believed that Greeks, Barbarians, Romans, and Scythians, bondmen, and free men were targets for the gospel. Jesus commissioned his disciples for all the nations to be made disciples.

Those who become disciples are to be "baptized" into the name of the Father and of the Son and of the Holy Spirit. "Baptizing" is a present participle in the original Greek. To be baptized means that a person has identified openly with Christ. The other present participle is "teaching." Baptism is the ceremonial and initial act of obedience to Christ. It should be followed by a lifelong obedience to all of the commandments of Christ. The person who is discipled and baptized has only started in a course of Christian living. The people who become disciples need to be baptized, and they need to be aware of the duty of obeying Christ in all things.

Evangelism comes as an imperative commission from the living Christ. Because of his authority over all powers, Jesus can command disciples to go to the world with the good news. The disciple of Christ should dare to ask four soul-searching questions about the Great Commission: (1) How seriously do I take the command of Christ? (2) How much do I pray about fulfilling the Great Commission? (3) Will I share Christ wherever I go? (4) How much will I dare to share the good news with the nations?

Evangelism has its compelling urge within an obedient, loving heart. The lack of compassion for people is the greatest tragedy of Christians and of churches throughout the world. Christians need to take seriously the commission of Christ. Evangelistic results will never come until disciples obey the command of Christ to go to the nations and make disciples. Great evangelistic harvests have and will come when disciples obey the orders of the King.

The Authority of the Scripture

The Bible is the essential authority and the perfect source of instruction in evangelism for every Christian. The Bible records God's profound concern for lost people. The Scriptures disclose how God feels and how God acts to bring alienated humans into a proper relationship with himself. If one accepts the authority of the Bible, then he will accept the imperative commission to tell others the good news about Jesus Christ.

Evangelism in the Old Testament

The Old Testament records the beginning of God's evangelistic concern. When the first persons rebelled against God, they sought to hide from the presence of the Lord. God was not content for them to be away from him and to be miserable. Instead, God began a search for Adam and Eve. God's question "Where art thou?" (Gen. 3:9) indicated God's desire to restore. After the Lord found the rebellious pair, he promised a redemption. "And I will put enmity between thee and the woman, and between thy seed and her seed; it shall bruise thy head, and thou shalt bruise his heel" (Gen. 3:15). The declaration of the victory of the woman's seed over the serpent has been called the *Protevangelium*, the first gospel, the first good news. Evangelism had its beginning when the first human being rebelled against God. It means that God did something to restore the relationship.

A concentrated evangelistic effort can be seen in God's call to Abraham. When this call came, it meant that God was choosing a method to reach all of the nations with the good news. Abraham's call was the initial act in the great drama of redemption that reached its climax in the incarnation, death, and resurrection of Jesus Christ. This was the beginning of what theologians refer to as "salvation history." The call of Abraham, recorded in Genesis 12:1-3, is deeply significant for the understanding of God's redemptive mission. Abraham was elected by God to be blessed not as a mere favorite of God, but as a medium of God's blessing. "I will bless you, . . . so that you will be a blessing" (vv. 2-3, TEV). Abraham and his heirs, the members of Israel, served a universal purpose. Through Abraham and his offspring "all the families of the earth will be blessed." God selected one man to found a new nation. Its members were to reach the nations.

Later the Old Testament records Israel's significance as the people of God in Exodus 19:3-6. At Mount Sinai by God's election, God made a covenant with Israel. He invested Israel with a holy vocation which was to have universal significance. Israel was to be a "kingdom of priests" serving in the courts of the divine King and representing the whole of mankind. Israel was to be a "holy nation" manifesting the holy character of God to the world.

Throughout the story of Israel recorded in the Old Testament, there is the evangelism story. God's holy character was to be manifested in the life of the nation. Israel was to be the medium by which all the nations of the world would be evangelized.

The Divine Example of Jesus

The Scripture tells how Jesus searched for the lost. He came to seek and to save those who were lost (Luke 19:10). Jesus wanted to reach the multitudes. To reach the masses of people, Jesus selected twelve men. The Master trained these men and sent them to seek the lost and to share the good news about Jesus with them. On one occasion Jesus sent these men on a mission two by two. Later Jesus sent seventy people on an evangelistic mission. Jesus enabled others to go and to fulfill his orders. To reach the multitudes of lost people in today's world, the church needs to study how Jesus sought to win the multitudes by training small groups.

The twelve and the other groups learned much about soul-winning from the example of Jesus. They learned about the broadness of Christ's concern. Jesus sought to win Pharisees, Sadducees, Herodians, and Zealots. He interviewed rulers of the Sanhedrin, Samaritans, Galileans, Greeks, Romans, and other Gentiles. His incessant soul-winning led him to deal with common people, wise men, publicans, harlots, lechers, little children, soldiers, thieves, beggars, fishermen, and tax collectors.

Jesus met people where they lived. He won several disciples while they were fishing. Matthew, the Gospel writer, was won while collecting taxes. A woman was won when she went to draw water at Jacob's well. A lawyer was won in the highway, and another person was won in a Pharisee's house. Zacchaeus was won on the street. The thief was won while he was dying on a cross. These examples furnish us the insight that Jesus identified with people. His example teaches that a close identity and relationship needs to be established. When relationships are established, the lost person will listen and trust our word.

The Master utilized various techniques, becoming all things to all men that by all means they might be saved. He capitalized on social contacts—eating in the houses of sinners, attending wedding feasts, worshiping in the synagogues. He utilized the quietness of private conferences—with Nicodemus, the young lawyer, Mary Magdalene, Zacchaeus, and others. He preached with mighty power to the multitudes, and he taught God's truth. From the beginning to the end of his public ministry, Jesus was about his Father's business of soul-winning.

One cannot seriously study the life and ministry of Jesus Christ without concluding that Jesus sought to reach people. Jesus committed the task of evangelism to his followers. While Jesus was standing on the Mount of Olives before his ascension, his last command concerned the Christian's duty to witness to lost men: "But ye shall receive power, after that the Holy Ghost is come upon you: and ye shall be witnesses unto me both in Jerusalem, and in all Judaea, and in Samaria, and unto the uttermost part of the earth" (Acts 1:8). He promised to direct his disciples where and why, to what and to whom they should bear witness. Having spoken his last word, Jesus vanished from their sight. Henceforth they would carry on the ministry of evangelism, sustained by his presence.

The early disciples took seriously the command of Jesus. They went to Jerusalem and to Judaea. They went to Samaria; to Asia Minor; to Macedonia; to Achaia; to Rome; and to the uttermost parts of the world. The early Christians were motivated by Christ's Great Commission: "Go ye therefore, and make disciples of all the nations" (Acts 1:8, ASV). When persecutors sought to stop them, the early Christians obeyed Christ's command. Peter and John said to the rulers in Jerusalem, "Whether it be right in the sight of God to hearken unto you more than unto God, judge ye" (Acts 4:19). The apostles acted under the authoritative command of Christ the Lord.

The apostle Paul obeyed Christ's Great Commission. He interpreted Christ's command as heaven's authority. He said, "Now then we are ambassadors for Christ, as though God did beseech you by us: we pray you in Christ's stead, be ye reconciled to God" (2 Cor. 5:20). Ambassadors for Christ misrepresent grossly their Sovereign if they do not love souls, yearn for souls, and plead with people to come in a right relationship with God. The authority for evangelism is no greater than in Christ's authoritative command, "Go ye therefore, and make disciples" (Matt. 28:19).

The Witness by Early Christians

John the Baptizer represents an effective witness for Christ. He pointed people to the Lamb of God. He preached about Jesus, whom he declared "is much greater than I" (John 1:15, TEV). When people heard John the Baptizer preach, they were directed to Jesus. "The two disciples heard him speak, and they followed Jesus" (John 1:37).

Andrew can be cited as an exemplary soul-winner. Wherever Andrew is mentioned in the New Testament, he is found working with others. He began his witness for Jesus at home by telling his brother Simon about Christ. Like many a soul-winner since that time, Andrew brought to Christ a man more capable in other areas than himself.

The New Testament records the experience of Andrew with a boy who had five loaves and two fish. Andrew persuaded the boy to put all his resources in the hands of the Savior. Also, when some Greeks sought to see Jesus, Andrew broke through the bounds of race prejudice and took them to the Master.

The discerning Bible student understands that it was not Peter's sermon alone which won 3,000 to the Lord at Pentecost. Before Peter preached, 120 prayerful, Spirit-filled, soul-minded Christians testified all over the city about Christ. The personal work of those Christians, soul-minded after ten days of prayer, was as vital a part of the victorious results of Pentecost as was the preaching of the evangelist.

The New Testament cites numerous examples of lay persons who shared their experiences in Christ. Philip and Stephen were two deacons who had a vibrant witness for the Master. Stephen testified to the Jews about Christ. His witness resulted in death by stoning. Philip was so ablaze with love for people that he conducted a city-wide revival in Samaria. With equal ease, Philip went to the desert to lead persons to Christ and to baptize a high court official of Ethiopia.

The book of Acts records numerous soul-winning exploits. The conversion of Saul of Tarsus and his work for Christ occupies most of the book of Acts. Paul used preaching, teaching, personal conferences, house-to-house visitation, miracles, and every possible method of winning people to Christ. Paul made his way into a cosmopolitan city, obtained work as a tentmaker, built relationships with people, attended the synagogue, and as a result led Jews and Gentiles to faith in Christ. With the torch of truth he freed the hearts of some here and some there, then went on to other fields. His boundless energy of body, mind, and spirit came from his love for Christ and for lost souls. "I say the truth in Christ, I lie not, my conscience also bearing me witness in the Holy Ghost, That I have great heaviness and continual sorrow in my heart. For I could wish that myself were accursed from Christ for my brethren, my kinsmen according to the flesh" (Rom.9:1-3). This is obedience to Christ's imperative commission and sincere compassion for lost people.

Evangelization by First-Century Churches

Jesus committed his ministry to the church. "Thou art Peter, and upon this rock I will build my church; and the gates of Hades shall not prevail against it. I will give unto thee the keys of the kingdom of heaven" (Matt. 16:18-19, ASV). Without a doubt the Lord told Peter that he was committing to Peter and to other disciples the task of evangelizing along with other ministries. Every regenerated member of every New Testament church has access to the keys of the kingdom; that is, every Christian can win people to the King.

The book of Acts records the remarkable growth of the church in Jerusalem from a few into thousands. The task of evangelism was accomplished primarily through vibrant, alive local congregations that sought to reach people and to nurture them. The churches at Antioch, Ephesus, Philippi, Rome, and elsewhere enjoyed spiritual power and rapid growth as long as they maintained their soul-winning efforts at home and their evangelistic enterprises abroad. When other things in these churches supplanted or destroyed their fervent zeal for leading souls to Christ, these churches began to wane.

Evangelism is central in the Scriptures. If one accepts the authority of the Bible, one cannot deny the task of evangelism. The task of soul-winning began in a garden, continued in the making of a nation, came to clear focus in the life and ministry of Jesus Christ, and prospered in first-century churches. Wherever one turns in the Bible, there will be the direct or indirect passion for people to come in right relationship with God.

The Continuous March of the Kingdom

Christians did not cease to obey the imperative commission of Christ. The history of the progress of Christianity since the first century is the history of evangelism in the churches. Almost every age since the time of Christ has experienced revivals of evangelism. Spirit-filled prophets of God have continuously led the people of God in soul-winning and church growth. Evangelism is central in Christian history.

The Light that Has Never Gone Out

In 1914 there was an all-night debate in the British House of Commons before it was agreed to declare war on Germany. Lord Grey was in the Foreign Office at dawn, watching through the window as an old-fashioned lamplighter with a pole extinguished the streetlights below. He said to an aide nearby, "The lights are going out all over Europe; we shall not see them lit again in our lifetime." But the one true Light that shines in every man has not been extinguished. "The light keeps on shining in the darkness, and the darkness could not put it out" (John 1:5, Roland Q. Leavell's translation).

Evangelism in Jerusalem soon broke out from the narrow confines of Jewish nationalism and spread to the Gentiles in Syria and Egypt. Unable to be restrained, the gospel was received by the people on the islands of the Mediterranean and in the heart of Asia Minor. The Holy Spirit led Paul and his companions into Macedonia and Achaia, provinces of Greece. The evangelists were beaten, stoned, imprisoned, and scorned. Yet they continued to obey Christ's commission. Paul went to Rome as a prisoner in chains, but even his imprisonment continued to advance the gospel. From Rome the word of Christ went in all directions, until the areas of Western Europe, Babylon, North Africa, and the islands of the sea heard the call to repent and to believe in the gospel.

Recurrent Revivals of Evangelism

The history of Christianity records numerous revivals of evangelistic zeal. The evangelistic fervor lasted continuously and extensively throughout the first three centuries. At the beginning of the fourth century, the emperor Constantine made Christianity the religion of the state. Great outbursts of religious fervor came under the leadership of many men, such as Augustine of Hippo (354-430), John of Antioch (345?-407), who was called Chrysostom, Justinian (527-565), Gregory, who became bishop of Rome in A.D. 590, and John of Damascus (700-753).

The time of the Crusades was a time of impulsive zeal and fervor for evangelism. The days of the Middle Ages were dark, but occasionally the light of the gospel broke through the darkness under the leadership of men like Francis of Assisi (1182-1226), John Tauler (1290-1361), Savonarola (1452-1498), and others too numerous to mention.

The Protestant Reformation, beginning in the early part of the sixteenth century, was a flame of evangelism which spread throughout all Western Europe, under such intrepid and dynamic leaders as Luther, Zwingli, Calvin, Knox, and numerous others. Likewise, the eighteenth century was a period of mighty evangelistic fervor under the leadership of John Wesley (1703-1791) and many worthy contemporaries. The nineteenth century began under the power of a great revival in America. The twentieth century is difficult to assess because of our closeness to the time. Within the twentieth century there have been numerous recurrences of evangelistic fervor.

Looking over Christian history causes one to conclude that the flames of evangelism have never gone out. Evangelism has had its bright times and its dark times, but the light has never gone out. Because of the historical legacy of disciples who obeyed Christ's commission, we can make evangelism central.

The Benefits of Evangelism

Evangelistic efforts have brought numerous blessings to the world and to individual lives. Those who are evangelized experience a new life. "Therefore if any man be in Christ, he is a new creature: old things are passed away; behold, all things are become new" (2 Cor. 5:17). Changed lives being grouped together results in a better and more pleasant world.

The people who engage in evangelistic activity share a joy and personal growth. No tongue or pen can describe the satisfaction, joy, and glory which comes to a Christian when he leads another to Christ.

Paul had a deep sense of happiness over his evangelistic efforts in Thessalonica. "For what is our hope, or joy, or crown of glorying? Are not even ye, before our Lord Jesus at his coming? For ye are our glory and our joy" (1 Thess. 2:19-20, ASV). No endeavor that a person can attempt will bring more benefit than going with the good news and attempting to make disciples. Evangelism is central because of the enormous benefits that it yields.

The Transformation of Lives

One of the rich rewards of the soul-winner's work is to see the lost saved, to see the dead in sin come into eternal life in Christ, to see degraded men changed into the image of Christ "from glory to glory, even as by the Spirit of the Lord." Sinners can experience a personal transformation when they receive Christ. Nothing satisfied the Savior more than to observe transformed lives. Study the Gospel records and observe the difference that Jesus made in a person's life: a woman at Jacob's well; Zacchaeus; Simon Peter; Matthew; Nicodemus; Mary Magdalene; an adulteress about to be stoned; James, the Lord's half-brother; and numerous others.

Search the Scripture for confirmation about changed lives. When Paul came to Corinth he found a secular city. The Corinthians engaged in sensual idolatry. Listen to Paul's description of the converts in Corinth. "Know ye not that the unrighteous shall not inherit the kingdom of God? Be not deceived: neither fornicators, nor idolaters, nor adulterers, nor effeminate, nor abusers of themselves with mankind, Nor thieves, nor covetous, nor drunkards, nor revilers, nor extortioners, shall inherit the kingdom of God. And such were some of you: but ye are washed, but ye are sanctified, but ye are justified in the name of the Lord Jesus, and by the Spirit of our God" (1 Cor. 6:9-11). The apostle Paul knew the life-style of these people before they opened their lives to Christ. Paul was convinced that the reception of the gospel could change a person's life.

Look through Christian history at Christian conversions. Sinners have been changed to saints. Monica must have been convinced that Christ could make a difference when she saw her profligate son Augustine transformed into the most influential Christian of his generation. Nothing makes a better motivation for evangelism than to collect and to share accounts of how Christ has made and is making a difference in a person's life.

The Purification of Society

The soul-winner has the exalted consciousness of helping to build a better social order. Christian people alone can make a Christian society. Think of the hopeless degeneracy and sinfulness the world would have without the presence of "born again" people. Christians are the salt of the earth. This means that God's people serve as an antiseptic against corruption. Christians are also the light of the world. This means that believers show the world a better way of living. A better society can be ordered with regenerated people.

The Satisfaction of the Christian

In addition to benefiting the convert, soul-winning brings a joy and satisfaction to the one who shares the good news. Nothing could have satisfied the Savior more than to make someone else happy. Study the fourth chapter of John. The Master was weary and thirsty when he came to Jacob's well. At the well he met a sinful and socially despised woman. This woman saw God in his gentleness, in his gracious words, and in his holiness. Something wonderful happened to the Master. He expressed satisfaction to his disciples when he said, "I have meat to eat that ye know not of" (John 4:32). He taught them, saying, "He that reapeth receiveth wages, and gathereth fruit unto life eternal; that both he that soweth and he that reapeth may rejoice together" (John 4:36).

The apostle Paul must have grown because of evangelistic results. Nothing pleased Paul more than to see self-righteous Jews and sensual Gentiles come into relationship with the Lord. Paul was not able to see the converts from Antioch, Philippi, Ephesus, and numerous other places.

Fred Kimball must have rejoiced over the far-reaching power of D. L. Moody. A layman, Kimball led Moody to Christ in a shoe store in Boston. This one convert reached thousands for Christ. A humble mountain preacher named J. G. Pulliam must have been gratified over his part in leading George W. Truett to Christ. The mind cannot assess the benefit one receives when another comes to Christ through his ministry.

The Population of Heaven

Jesus exhorted his hearers to make for themselves friends who would receive them into eternal tabernacles (Luke 16:9). One of the most glorious experiences of heaven will be that of having a host of redeemed souls there who will testify in the Savior's presence, "You helped me to find and to follow my Lord."

Dr. John A. Broadus, former president of Southern Baptist Theological Seminary, was a pastor in Virginia during his early ministry. There was a half-witted boy whom he tried diligently to teach the way of salvation. Because of his mental condition, the boy was slow to grasp the message. Friends often said to Broadus, "You are wasting your time. He will never be able to understand." Eventually the message got through to the boy. He trusted Christ. Thereafter, wherever the boy saw the pastor, he would put out his hand and say: "Howdy, John. Thank you, John!" At the church, in crowds on the street, or wherever he saw the pastor, he would say: "Howdy, John. Thank you, John!"

The boy fell mortally ill. Dr. Broadus hastened to the humble home to see him. Among the last words the poor fellow said were: "Howdy, John. Thank you, John!" When Dr. Broadus became president of the seminary, he often related this story. He said that one of the bright expectations of heaven for him was to see that boy and to hear him say, "Howdy, John. Thank you, John!" The boy whom he led to Christ was his joy here and his hope for the hereafter.

The Glorification of Christ

The loving Christian heart normally desires to be everything possible for the glory of the Lord Jesus Christ. The soul-winner's most priceless possibility is to add glory to Christ through leading others to love and to obey him. Every additional person who accepts Christ has the possibility of glorifying the Savior in this life and will live forever in the presence of God. The great benefit of evangelism is that converts give additional opportunity for the world to see their good works and "glorify the Father which is in heaven."

Suggestions for Advanced Study

1. Try to find the justification for evangelism in the Old Testament, in the life and ministry of Jesus, and in the book of Acts.
2. Using books on Christian history or on evangelism, make a close study of one particular era of evangelism.
3. Seek to determine the positive benefits which could enhance your evangelistic efforts.

References for Further Study

Borchert, Gerald L. *Dynamics of Evangelism.* Waco, Texas: Word Books, 1976.
Coleman, Robert E. *The Master Plan of Evangelism.* Old Tappan, New Jersey: Fleming H. Revell Company, 1963.
Dobbins, Gaines S. *Evangelism According to Christ.* Nashville: Broadman Press, 1949.
Green, Michael. *Evangelism in the Early Church.* Grand Rapids: William B. Eerdmans Publishing Company, 1970.
Scharpff, Paulus. *History of Evangelism: Three Hundred Years of Evangelism in Germany, Great Britain, and the United States of America.* Translated by Helga Bender Henry. Grand Rapids: William B. Eerdmans Publishing Company, 1964.

2
Evangelism Is Urgent in Incentive and Need

There is none righteous, no, not one. For all have sinned, and come short of the glory of God (Rom. 3:10, 23).

Today Christian disciples need to obey Christ's imperative commission. Vast hosts of people need evangelizing. This is a sin-sick, morally bankrupt, heavyhearted, and hungry-hearted world of people among whom we live. Multitudes of people long for an answer to their guilt, their loneliness and boredom, their futility, their fears, and their anxieties. To look at the distortion of human lives should convince the Christian disciple that the task of evangelism is urgent. Put together multitudes of lost people and you have a social order dominated by deadly evils. Only the gospel of Christ can bring new life to an individual and new order to a society. The changing power of the gospel gives an incentive to go and make disciples. Because people hurt and society wastes away, the task of evangelism is urgent.

The World's Need for Evangelism

The silly notion that people can get along well without God has brought the world into a time of unprecedented revenge, hatred, and strife. Modern man has come to think of himself as the most important creature. Religion is optional to this kind of thinking. Materialism is the philosophy of multitudes, and the god of gold is the god of millions of people. Greed and godless pursuit after material things indicate a lack of concern for spiritual things. Because of the grasp for material and sensual gain, crime continues to increase with murder, robbery, rape, and numerous other forms of dissipation. The Christian prophet of today needs to pray with Habakkuk of old, "[O Jehovah,] revive thy work in the midst of the years" (Hab. 3:2).

28

The Universal Malady

The entire world is affected by sin. Rebellion is no provincial matter that is restricted to a certain racial or cultural class. "All have sinned, and come short of the glory of God" (Rom. 3:23). In every city, village, or rural community, lost souls can be found. They are lost to God's highest and best purposes for them in life. They are lost while they live on the earth, and they will be lost throughout eternity unless they are won to Christ.

Everyone can look about and notice that our world is in serious trouble. No country or social group is immune from tragic rebellion against God. The whole world suffers from rising crime and from gross inhumanities to other human beings. One has only to read a newspaper in any city of the world or to listen to a global news report. One reads and hears of murders, rape, robbery, revolution, and numerous other atrocities around the world. The problem of sin plagues all classes, colors, and culture groups.

Most people would agree with the universal malady of sin by looking into their personal lives. One does not have to look around to see the malady of sin. Observe the inward part of your life. Face the reality of your ungodly thoughts. Acknowledge the presence of your secret sins. The apostle Paul confessed his confrontation with sin in his life. After examining his thoughts and actions, Paul said, "O wretched man that I am! who shall deliver me from the body of this death?" (Rom. 7:24). If one is honest with himself and with God, he will acknowledge his sinfulness.

A Tragic Degradation

A Christian was being guided through one of the more degraded districts of New York City. His guide, a worker from a rescue mission, was in tears when the tour of inspection came to an end. The Christian visitor heard him sob, "Oh, the sinfulness of sin!" It was this knowledge of the degrading effects of sin upon life that made this worker give his life to the soul-saving task among the lowest type of sinners.

Sin has caused a tragic degradation to the human race. It has left in its slimy trail a sinning, saddened, suffering world. God intended a high and noble purpose for every person. Instead of attaining this high purpose, every human being has decided to manage life by himself. Living life dominated by selfish interests degrades character. Sin separates a person from fellowship with God. It causes one to disregard others in preference for self, resulting in apathy toward and injustice to other human beings. Sin destroys the inward person. God intends for a person to live in fellowship with him. The Lord gave laws to safeguard a person. Disobeying God's commands destroys the person and degrades the person to a status lower than God intended.

The character of people is constantly collapsing because of sin. No one can measure the depths to which a person might sink if not rescued by the Savior. God grants a person freedom. There is the freedom to be oneself in Jesus Christ, and there is the freedom to destroy one's authentic self outside of Christ. Because so many have refused to open their lives to the Lord, individual degradation and corporate corruption abounds.

The Critical Need

No thoughtful Christian would deny that the world's need for Christ is urgent. The prevalence of people without Christ shows how critical the need for evangelism really is. The world population has grown to over four billion people. There are more unsaved people in the world today than when Christ trod the hills of Galilee. Each minute 144,000 people are born into the world. The pagan population of the world is annually increasing faster than Christians are winning pagan people to Christ.

Even America is not becoming Christian at any rapid rate. Of the 220-plus million people who live in America, only 84 million people attend any kind of religious service. Approximately eight persons out of twenty-five in the United States have no religious affiliation whatever—neither Evangelical, Catholic, Jewish, nor otherwise. Every year millions of children are born who will never receive Christian training.

Statisticians say there are numerous villages in the United States without a church, hundreds of villages and towns without a resident pastor, and close to twenty million children who are receiving no religious education.

The world's need for Christ is critical because of the rapid rise of new foes of Christianity. For many years the major opponents of Christianity were Islam, Hinduism, Buddhism, Confucianism, and other ancient religions. Today the aggressive foes are godless communism, avid nationalism, proud humanism, and materialistic secularism. Numerous other alternatives to Christianity are given in the names of the Bahai World Faith, the Unification Church of Sun Myung Moon, and numerous other groups. Add to this list nonsystematized religions. For example, the religion of many people today is a new economic order. The religion of others is the totalitarian state. Great areas of the world's population are turning away from their idols and are turning to a stark unbelief in any form of religion. In some nations where once there was a nominal type of Christianity, now an absolute atheism is being substituted.

The situation is critical because of the state of many churches. Some professing Christians do not emphasize evangelism. In one year in the Southern Baptist Convention, almost 20 percent of the churches did not report a single baptism. Other matters have held priority over the task of evangelizing a lost and needy world. Richard Niebuhr has said: "A liberal modernism is seeking to tell the people that a God without wrath brought man without sin into a kingdom without judgment through a Christ without a cross." Sin sickness grows with an exploding population. Inadequate philosophies appeal to people, but they do not satisfy. The situation is too critical for a church not to give priority to reaching a sin-sick, guilt-ridden world.

The Christian's Concern for Lost Souls

The tragic lostness of people will stir a Spirit-filled Christian with love, zeal, and compassion. Studying about the reality of lost souls will motivate one to share the good news about Christ to the lost. Looking through one's life heightens the concern for others. When one identifies with what Christ has done for him or her, the convert is eager to help others have what they have found.

A Legitimate Reason for Concern

The best picture of God and of man is found in Luke 15. The shepherd seeking a lost sheep depicts the intimate concern of God for strayed, rebellious beings. The woman searching for the lost coin denotes how God wishes to recover the value of the coin. The father yearning for an intimate relationship with both his sons portrays the Lord as a compassionate Father. With these simple parables Jesus demonstrated his gracious concern and loving action for lost people. A child of God, with God's nature, will love lost souls. One true evidence of being a child of God is to have a loving concern for the lost.

The Scripture could not be clearer about the plight of human beings. The three parables paint the portrait of lostness. A sheep wandered from the guidance of a shepherd through sheer stubbornness. The carelessness of another caused the coin to be lost. Neither son, though they used different expressions, was in relationship to the father. The Bible depicts the condition of persons as lost. This means that they are misplaced. They are not where they belong.

God's word teaches that people without Christ are without God and without hope in this world. They are aliens and enemies to God. They are estranged, gone backward, sick of head, faint of heart, standing in slippery places. Oftentimes the emphasis for lostness in today's church seems to be delegated primarily to the life beyond the grave. The Bible describes lostness in terms of life here and now as well as life beyond the grave.

When Robert Louis Stevenson lay ill in Samoa, he received a note from a clergyman who asked if he would like a minister to talk to him "as to one in danger of dying." Stevenson declined, but he said he would be very glad to have the clergyman talk to him "as to one in danger of living." It is dreadful to think of anyone missing for even a single day the wonders of life in Christ. The purpose of evangelism is not just to save people from dying without Christ, but to save them from living without him. Lostness is a condition on earth of a life apart from openness to God.

The Bible also speaks of a person's lostness beyond this life. Jesus described the place and experience of the unsaved with the graphic picture of the Valley of Hinnom. In Jesus' day this was a garbage dump where people brought worthless articles. The picture is graphic. People who refuse to open their lives to Jesus Christ throw their lives away. They destroy life. The Bible also described the place of the lost in the hereafter as a prison (1 Pet. 3:19), a place of chains or pits of darkness (2 Pet. 2:4), and a place of retention until the judgment of punishment (2 Pet. 2:19). Jesus, the merciful Lord, spoke of the rich man as being in "torment" and "tormented in this flame" (Luke 16:23-24). Lost people go after death away from the presence of God into the presence of Satan, the archdeceiver. They go into the unholy companionship of sorcerers, fornicators, murders, idolaters, the fearful, the unbelieving, the abominable, and all who make lies (Rev. 21:8; 22:15).

The lostness of humanity gives a legitimate reason for concern. Christians want people to live with Christ. They should be concerned that a person has the best life in this world. They should also be concerned that people be saved from dying without Christ. Do you honestly believe that a person without Christ knows that he is missing the chance of experiencing the wonderful life in Christ? Do you honestly believe that unbelievers are lost, tragically lost, and eternally separated from God?

Notable Examples of Concern

The Scripture records numerous examples of God's concern for lost people. When Adam and Eve rebelled against God's word, they hid themselves from the presence of God. The Lord could have left them alone. Instead, he came to earth and sought these erring human beings. God could have been apathetic and been good. He could have responded in vindicative punishment and been just. Wherever you see an erring human being, you find a gracious, loving God who wishes to recover and to restore.

The burden of Jesus' heart was lost people. There is no greater example of a concerned person than the Lord. When Jesus looked at the multitude, he saw them lost, scattered as a sheep without a shepherd, despairing, defeated, doomed, dying, damned. "Souls! Souls! Souls!" was the burden of Christ's heart.

The predominant emotion that the Lord demonstrated toward sinners was a broken heart. Sometimes the erroneous notion prevails that God seeks primarily to punish sinners. No—whenever the Lord observed sin he was grieved greatly. He grieved over adultery in a Samaritan woman, extortion in the publican, robbery in a thief. The note of compassion can be detected in Jesus' voice when he looked on the city of Jerusalem. "O Jerusalem, Jerusalem, thou that killest the prophets, and stonest them which are sent unto thee, how often would I have gathered thy children together, even as a hen gathereth her chickens under her wings, and ye would not!" (Matt. 23:37). Christ's love for the lost made him the supreme evangelist. He provided a notable example for the followers.

God's kind of compassion could be observed in some of the first Christians. Andrew is an example of one with a supreme concern for others. Andrew heard John the Baptist speak and then followed Jesus. Immediately, Andrew "first findeth his own brother Simon" (John 1:41). Without a doubt Andrew was anxious over the predicament of his brother Simon. And again, there is the experience of Philip. When Jesus said to Philip, "Follow me," then "Philip findeth Nathaniel" (John 1:43, 45).

These notable examples should stir Christians to have a soul-deep, soul-crushing, Christlike concern for lost souls. The compassion for lost souls and the effort to reach them for Christ are normal for spiritually healthy Christians. Concern for others does not have to come in sporadic spurts. Continuous compassion can come in the daily lifestyle of Christians. Whenever they come in contact with people, they can manifest a magnanimous concern for people. Compassion for lost people is not an abnormal virtue worked up once or twice each year. It is that trait which prevails perennially.

The Assurance of a Conquering Power

Some people are saying in bewilderment, "What is a Christian to do in such a world and such times as these?" Comparing the number of converts to Christianity to an exploding world population could be depressing. The growth of other alternate selections such as The Unification Church of Sun Myung Moon causes a sense of frustration. Christians need to seriously study the Bible and to learn of the assurance of a conquering power. In such a world as this the biblical injunction is "Evangelize!"

The Conquest of the Gospel

Jesus lived in a day which could have caused bewilderment and frustration. The confused multitudes of his day were asking, "What can we do? Where is the way out?" The sensualists answered, "There is no good way out. Eat, drink, and conform to the world. What's the use?" The Sadducees said, "There is no God, or else he would not have allowed things to get into the fix they are in. There is no heaven, hell, or hope hereafter. Religion is folly." The Pharisees drew themselves apart in complete isolation. The publicans said, "Let's get rich while the getting is good." The Zealots said, "Let's have a revolution. Let's make Jesus, the miracle worker, our king; and let's do something violent."

In Jesus' day Greek and Roman idols sought the allegiance of people. In the midst of a large population, the followers of Jesus were only a few. Nonetheless, Jesus was not intimidated. He had no feelings of defeat. In times when people were saying things very much as we hear them said today, Jesus said, "Repent; change your way of thinking. Repent, for the kingdom of God is at hand. You can reach out and grasp God at your very right hand, if you will. Follow me, for I am the way out. I am the way to God!" Jesus went out under this magnificent obsession to seek and to save that which was lost.

The apostles dared to preach the gospel to a wide audience. They began with the Jews, affirming that Jesus fulfilled messianic prophecy. The apostles dared to affirm the supremacy and sufficiency of Jesus Christ over pagan ideologies and philosophies. Sharing the gospel made these disciples willing to suffer perils, privations, or persecutions unto death. The apostles desired desperately that the whole world know about the life which Jesus Christ could give. "We cannot but speak the things which we have seen and heard" (Acts 4:20), said the Spirit-filled apostles when persecutors tried to silence them. By the end of the first century, the gospel of Jesus Christ experienced a glorious success. People in Palestine, Asia Minor, Macedonia, Achaia, Italy, and even Spain had heard and received the gospel. More important than geographical conquest was the conquest against ungodliness. Wherever Christ was received, individual lives were changed and communities and cities were made better.

The Adequacy of the Gospel

The message of Christ spread not because of its faddishness but because Christ answered the perplexing problems of people. The gospel was adequate for a troubled time. He allowed human beings to know God and to have a continuous fellowship with him. The Lord brought a personal development. Character was transformed from self-centeredness and self-seeking to a better self. The changed person allowed the possibility for promising relationships with other people. Christ did not erase the trials and problems of life, but he promised to be present and to strengthen his followers. Christ was never tried and found lacking. Christ met the needs of the first-century world whenever people opened their lives to him.

The apostle Paul believed in the sufficiency of the gospel amid an exploding population and a cosmopolitan setting. Somewhere between the time of A.D. 55 and 58 Paul wrote a letter to the Christians in Rome. The letter preceded his visit to Rome. This was the largest city in Paul's day. It was the melting pot for all kinds of religions and philosophies. It was saturated with materialistic sensualism. At the time of Paul's writing to the Romans, only a small group of Christians existed in the enormous city.

Paul sent the essence of the Christian message in a letter. Later, he hoped to come and share personally the good news. The theme of Paul's Roman letter can be found in Romans 1:16-17. Sandlay and Headlam in their monumental commentary on Romans speak of these verses as expressing the "theme" of the epistle. The apostle is ready to preach the gospel to those in Rome. He has been pleased with the adequacy of the gospel in other places. He has confidence that when he shares the gospel with the Romans, it will be adequate for them. The gospel has power to save. It can make people righteous.

The famous Statue of Liberty in New York City harbor stands on a high pedestal, holding aloft the torch of liberty to welcome all the oppressed who come from afar. At the base of the pedestal is a series of floodlights throwing their rays upon the statue. A part of the inscription on the base of the structure is:

> Give me your tired, your poor,
> Your huddled masses yearning to breathe free,
> The wretched refuse of your teeming shore,
> Send these, the homeless, tempest-tossed to me,
> I lift my lamp beside the golden door.
> —*Emma Lazarus*

This is a parable. The statue is like Christ holding aloft the torch of salvation to welcome all the sin-burdened souls into the harbor of God's salvation. The Lord Jesus is lifted up by an evangelistic, mission-minded church because this group of people believes that Christ is the answer for our tangled times. The assured Christian is like a light at Christ's feet, making the person of the exalted Savior visible to those who are in spiritual darkness. Those who know Christ's gospel yearn to throw out the light of their influence so that others may see the Savior clearly. They know that the world has found no adequate answer except Christ and that people may be saved by nothing less than his grace.

The Diversity of the Gospel

Every scriptural type of evangelism can be used to bring the gospel to a needy world. No one method will win all, and no scriptural method may be omitted without loss. The first-century church utilized many methods and techniques to share the gospel of Jesus Christ. They varied their preaching with synagogue proclamation, open-air preaching, and preaching in small groups. They focused upon evangelizing the familiar and those associated with the family, such as household slaves. The first-century Christians utilized personal encounter to share the gospel. They also made formal visits to present Jesus Christ. In addition to speaking to people about Christ, one further method was writing to others about the gospel. The Gospels were written testimonies to tell about Jesus Christ. Evangelists must say with the apostle Paul, "I am become all things to all men, that I may by all means save some" (1 Cor. 9:22, ASV).

Scriptural evangelism is planned, promoted, and conserved by the churches. The strategy of first-century evangelism came by means of local churches. Individual Christians are the evangelists; yet all the results of their evangelism should go into the church life for its strength and power. The church is the promotional organization for the advancement of the kingdom of God, even as the individual Christian is the promotional unit. Any evangelism which does not emphasize and magnify the local church, bring people into the church, and advance the kingdom of God through the church is lacking seriously in some of the vital essentials of scriptural evangelism.

The Victory of the Gospel

Christians are assured of victory. The divine assurance of victory is found in the promise of the presence of the Savior, "Lo, I am with you alway" (Matt. 28:20). Ultimate victory will come for the kingdom of God. "The kingdoms of this world are become the kingdoms of our Lord, and of his Christ; and he shall reign for ever and ever" (Rev. 11:15).

Tradition says that the Roman emperor Constantine, in A.D. 312 at the Battle of Milvian Bridge, saw an apparition in the sky like a luminous cross, with the words *In hoc signo vinces,* meaning "By this sign conquer." We may doubt the historicity of that event. However, we look at the Savior, who lived and died to save lost souls, and we say, "By his power we can conquer."

Suggestions for Advanced Study

1. Write to the Federal Bureau of Investigation in Washington, D. C., and ask for statistics on the prevalence of crime in the United States. Look in the latest edition of *The World Almanac* for statistics about religious affiliation. Relate these facts to the need and incentive for evangelism.

2. Study Habakkuk, chapters 1—2, seeking out verses that tell of (a) civil unrighteousness, (b) social sins, (c) economic greed, (d) moral degeneration, and (e) spiritual ills, all of which justified the prophet's prayer in 3:2. Compare the evils in Habakkuk's time with those of today.

3. Study Romans 1:18 to 3:30, seeking out verses that tell of (a) God's revelation, (b) mankind's response to God's revelation, (c) the universality of sin, and (d) the consequences of sin. Use these biblical ideas to give a need and incentive for evangelism.

4. Secure from the Home Mission Board, 1350 Spring Street, Atlanta, Georgia 30309, some literature on the evangelistic needs for America.

5. Read Alvin Toffler's book *Future Shock.* Make some projections and assessments for evangelism based on this work.

References for Further Study

Autry, C. E. *A Theology of Evangelism.* Nashville: Broadman Press, 1966.

Bader, Jesse M. *The Message and Method of New Evangelism.* New York: Round Table Press, 1937.

Blackwood, Andrew W. *Evangelism in the Home Church.* New York: Abingdon-Cokesbury, 1942.

Bryson, Harold T. *Yes, Virginia, There Is a Hell.* Nashville: Broadman Press, 1975.

Drummond, Lewis A. *The Awakening That Must Come.* Nashville: Broadman Press, 1978.

McDill, Wayne. *Evangelism in a Tangled World.* Nashville: Broadman Press, 1976.

Starkes, M. Thomas. *Confronting Popular Cults.* Nashville: Broadman Press, 1972.

3

Evangelism Is Essential in Kingdom Building and Christian Living

From that time Jesus began to preach, and to say, Repent: for the kingdom of heaven is at hand (Matt. 4:17).

Does the average church member know what it means to "make disciples"? As Christians obey Christ's imperative commission, do they know what they are asking other people to do?

A woman who had been a church member for some years was much perplexed and concerned about her spiritual life. She had accepted her church's baptism, had completed a course of doctrinal instruction, had regularly observed the ordinances, and had been told that she was a Christian. But the woman could not have any assurance of a relationship with God. One day a friend asked her if she could speak in unknown tongues. "No!" she replied. Forthwith she was told forcefully that she was in nowise a Christian. The woman went to her pastor. He told her that her spiritual needs were all cared for in her faithful performances of her church duties. However, she could find no peace. In a conference with another Christian worker, she boldly asserted that she did not dance, play cards, drink liquor, or swear. She began to recite her many virtues. Then she asked the person if that did not assure her that she was a Christian.

In this experience three different concepts of how to make disciples emerged. First, there was a ritualistic, ecclesiastical plan. This is the belief that punctilious performance of church duties and observance of ritualistic ceremonies make one a Christian. Second, there was the emotional plan. The friend of the woman believed that ecstatic, emotional upheavals leading to rapturous excesses were necessary for one to become a Christian. Third, there was the legalistic or moral plan. The woman believed that to become a Christian one had to resist

40

series of taboos and "thou shalt not" restrictions and to submit to series of rules and "thou shalts." Discipleship, to the woman, was an organized system of denying prohibition and of observing rules. Which plan best fits the command of Christ to "make disciples"? None of them, of course.

Another friend gave the frustrated woman another story altogether. From the Bible the friend showed her that she must repent of her sins. He pointed her to the Lord Jesus Christ. The friend reminded the woman that no one of the three other plans ever mentioned Jesus Christ as Savior. No one mentioned a trust in Christ's atoning blood to cleanse her from sin. No one mentioned taking Jesus Christ as the Lord and Master of her life. No one mentioned the indwelling Christ who comes at conversion to give strength, guidance, companionship, and character.

Those who seek to help others become Christians should seek to know to whom and to what they are inviting lost people. Soul-winners must try to state clearly and intelligently what it means to become a Christian, and then what it means to be a Christian. Every Christian should know that to become a Christian means to open one's life to Christ and become his disciple. Each follower of Christ should have a vivid conception of the means of entrance into the kingdom as well as the implications of being a citizen of the kingdom.

Understanding the Meaning of the Kingdom of God

"Repent: for the kingdom of heaven is at hand" (Matt. 4:17) was the first clarion call of Christ. "Except a man be born again, he cannot see the kingdom of God" (John 3:3) was the straightforward statement of our Lord. But what and where is the kingdom of heaven?

Modern men have had their own ways of interpreting the phrase "kingdom of God." Some social reformers have built on the teachings of Jesus. The term kingdom of God *(basileia tou theou)* means the kingly rule or reign of God. The kingdom of heaven is composed of all people who are loyal to God through faith in Jesus Christ as their Lord and King.

The kingdom of God is a present possibility as well as a future hope. There are several passages which claim that, in the coming of Jesus, the kingdom of God has already come (see Luke 11:14-22).

Jesus claimed in his miracles, in his parables, and in other ways that the kingdom of God was present in his ministry. Some passages in the New Testament refer to the kingdom of God as a future reality (see Luke 13:22-30). Some of the Gospel materials portray the kingdom of God as a future reality whose realization the believer is to pray for and will one day inherit when he sits in glory with Jesus. The soul-winner seeks to lead his lost friend to enter the kingdom of heaven here on earth, assuring him that he will enter the place of heaven in the hereafter.

The People of the Kingdom

1. A personal relation.—The people who are in the kingdom of God are those who have entered into right relationship with Jesus Christ. The test of whether or not one is in the kingdom is whether or not he has opened his life and his heart to the Lord Jesus Christ. When one opens his life to Christ, the Lord lives in him; and he lives under the kingly rule of God. The crucial questions for a lost person are these: "What do you think of Jesus Christ? Do you have a relationship with Jesus Christ?" The only means of entrance into the kingdom is the acceptance of Jesus Christ.

2. A permanent relation—The experience that brings one into right relationship with Jesus is a permanent one. When a sinner puts his trust in the crucified and risen Christ, the Spirit of God works a change in his heart which is eternal and everlasting. It has both a qualitative and a quantitative effect. Because becoming a member of the kingdom is a matter of allowing God into one's life, the convert does not need to strive to stay a disciple. God works within the individual, guiding, encouraging, and even disciplining him.

3. A growing relation.—Becoming a citizen of the kingdom of God can happen instantaneously. To develop into a better citizen of that kingdom requires a continual growing process throughout a lifetime. One may become a Christian in the miracle of a moment, but the making of a saint takes a lifetime. Life has many areas where Christ needs to rule more and more perfectly.

The Lord's Prayer (Matt. 6:9-13) teaches the Christian to pray for the more perfect rule of Christ in all areas of life. This prayer indicates that the way to glorify the name of our Father in heaven is to bring in the kingdom: "Thy kingdom come." God's kingdom rule is perfected in four vital areas of living. (1) the human will: "Thy will be done"; (2) the economic life: "Give us this day our daily bread"; (3) the social realm: "Forgive us our debts, as we forgive our debtors"; and (4) the relation to the contact with evil: "Lead us not into temptation, but deliver us from evil." Let the unsaved man know that if he chooses Christ, he chooses him as King. The choice implies a new allegiance. It means a break with the old life under the kingship of self or Satan. It means an allegiance to Christ and his kingdom.

The Program of the Kingdom

Christ the King has a definite program for the kingdom of God on earth. To invite one to become a Christian is to introduce him to this heavenly program and to ask him to accept his responsibility in its promotion.

1. The ideal.—The ideal of the kingdom of heaven is summed up in this way: "Thy will be done in earth, as it is in heaven" (v. 10). The kingdom was initiated in the life and ministry of Jesus Christ. Jesus sought to eliminate everything opposed to the kingdom rule. The burden of Jesus' preaching was to call people to forsake evil and to follow him. Jesus' miracles were attempts to destroy anything that was not the will of God for a person. Jesus sought to bring a rule of love and to eliminate anything contrary to the will of God.

The Lord reigns as he indwells people in his Holy Spirit. That means lives which are victorious over such enemies as sin, ignorance, poverty, and death. That means the elimination of prejudice, injustice, dishonesty, and impurity among men. That means the destruction of fear, unbelief, disobedience, and rebellion toward God. That means the absolute exaltation of Jesus Christ to the throne in the heart of every man. This is a glorious prospect for sin-cursed, defeated, distressed, despairing, and doomed men.

2. The unit.—The unit of the kingdom of heaven is an individual who is a new person in Christ. Such a person has turned from the life of self-will, self-trust, and self-assertion. He has been led into the selfless life by the one who gave up the glories of heaven to come to earth and die on a cross. God the Father has forgiven this kingdom man. God has redeemed him by the blood of his Son. God has indwelled him with his Holy Spirit. Of such the kingdom of heaven is built. Jesus' Sermon on the Mount provides the design for living in the kingdom of God. Any person who desires to repent of the self-centered life and to open his life to the King can become a member of the kingdom of heaven. Surely this is a glorious possibility to which lost people may be directed.

3. The organization.—The organization which Christ formed as the promotional agency of his kingdom is his church. When a person accepts Christ as Savior and Lord, his love for Christ leads him to enter the church. Through the church he gives his life in spreading the kingdom. No other group except the church can or will do very much to bring others into the kingdom of heaven. Without churches the task of evangelism would suffer greatly.

Primacy of the Kingdom

Jesus commanded his kingdom subjects: "Seek ye first the kingdom of God, and his righteousness" (Matt 6:33). Therefore, the one who goes to make disciples should make it clear that to enter and become a disciple in God's kingdom means to give the Lord Jesus Christ the very first place in one's life. Becoming and being a Christian are not just parts of life. They compose life itself. In truth, Christ must be "Lord of all or else he is not Lord at all." All authority is his. If one does not mean to renounce his own selfish will and gladly accept the sovereign will of his sovereign Lord, he has no right to profess being a Christian.

Presenting the Plan of the Kingdom of God

Any person who seeks to obey Christ's imperative commission needs to have an intelligent understanding of God's plan. In the epistle to the Ephesians, Paul presented an inspired exposition of God's plan for the whole universe. Throughout the Ephesian letter, Paul insisted that God is working out his great plan for mankind by calling men to Christ and forming in Christ a new, redeemed society. This redeemed society, which constitutes God's new people, is referred to in various ways in the letter—for example, God's building (2:19-22), Christ's body (1:22-23), Christ's bride (5:22-31), the church (1:22; 3:10,21), and one new man (2:14-15). The suggestion in all these figures is that God now has a people in the world who belong uniquely to him. In them he plans to effect his intention for the whole universe. The letter to the Ephesians is the most concise statement of the eternal purpose of God and the place of Christ and his people in that purpose.

Paul's statement in Acts 20:21 about the response to Christ gives the absolute requirements for a person to get in on God's eternal plan. He summed them up in the words *repentance* and *faith*. So the soul-winners must know intelligently what God intends to do and must proclaim authoritatively that in order to get in on God's plan, one must experience "repentance toward God, and faith toward our Lord Jesus Christ."

God's Word Teaches But One Plan

God's Word reveals but one plan of God. It is agreed that human beings must respond in faith to the God who redeems. "Neither is there salvation in any other: for there is none other name under heaven given among men, whereby we must be saved" (Acts 4:12). Every sinner who has ever been saved was saved through repentance toward God and faith in the Lord Jesus Christ as Savior.

1. One plan for atonement.—The idea of atonement or reconciliation in the Bible discloses how men have always been saved. Atonement is God's work of overcoming the estrangements bound up with man's sin. Just as sin involved man in an estrangement from God and from his fellowman—and from self—so atonement tells of God's work in bringing man into proper relationship with God, with himself, and with his fellowman.

God worked from the beginning of man's estrangement to atone. The appearance of God in the garden soon after Adam and Eve's rebellion was an attempt to reconcile a breached relationship. Later the sacrificial system of the tabernacle and temple worship portrayed God's plan for atonement. The Day of Atonement, described in the sixteenth chapter of Leviticus, reveals that God worked from the earliest times to reconcile man to himself. The high priest offered a goat for a sin offering. While the congregation knelt and beat upon their breasts, they confessed their sins in true repentance toward God; and they pointed to the blood on the altar. The blood in the sacrifice pointed to the gracious and merciful God who provided a means of relating to a holy God again. Therefore, the people exercised "repentance toward God, and faith toward our Lord Jesus Christ" (Acts 20:21).

2. *One common experience.*—Since God has only one plan, to provide for man's atonement, he has only one expected response. From the beginning God wanted man to open his life to him. This is called *faith* in the Bible. People during the days of the Old Testament, during the New Testament times, and in our day must respond to God in faith. "Without faith it is impossible to please him" (Heb. 11:6). The people in ancient times came into a relation with God by faith. Each one had to open his life to the Lord. They allowed God to be a part of their lives.

The writer of the Epistle of Hebrews gave an excellent summary of the one common experience of faith in Hebrews 11. The saved person was one who looked to God. The author of Hebrews gave four prominent examples of faith throughout the ages: the antediluvian faith (those leading up to Abraham), Hebrews 11:4-7; the faith of the patriarchs, Hebrews 11:8-22; the faith of Moses, Hebrews 11:23-29; and the faith of other Old Testament heroes, Hebrews 11:32-38. The one experience common to Israel was the response of faith. God has ordained that the proper experience to him is faith.

> Not all the blood of beasts
> On Jewish altars slain,
> Could give the guilty conscience peace,
> Or wash away the stain.
>
> But Christ, the heavenly Lamb,
> Takes all our sins away;
> A sacrifice of nobler name
> And richer blood than they.

God's Character Demands Repentance

Repentance is the most reasonable thing that God ever required of sinners. God's character moves him to want people to reverse their fall. Whereas man sought to find the whole meaning of his existence within himself, God demanded a better way of life for a person. The character of God demands repentance.

1. The demand of repentance.—All the great soul-winners of the ages have preached and taught the necessity of repentance toward God. The mighty men of the Old Testament times proclaimed this righteous requirement of God. John the Baptist came demanding that men should "bring forth therefore fruits meet for repentance" (Matt. 3:8). Our Lord took up the same message, saying, "Repent: for the kingdom of heaven is at hand" (Matt. 4:17). Simon Peter preached repentance on the day of Pentecost. Paul preached it at Athens, at Ephesus, and wherever else he went. Our Lord vigorously reiterated the truth: "Except ye repent, ye shall all likewise perish" (Luke 13:3,5). Surely everyone who would make disciples should know that people should repent of their sins.

2. The meaning of repentance.—Furthermore, those who seek to make disciples should know exactly what the experience of repentance means. The Greek *metanoein* translated repentance means a change of mind or a change of attitude. True repentance means more than feeling shame for sin, having a fear of sin's consequences, or quitting one's meanness. Repentance is a reversal of one's thinking which will result in an alteration of one's way of living.

Notice the substance of what Jesus said: "Change your attitude. Take your mind off yourself. Put your mind on the kingdom." The one who repents takes his mind off his selfish concerns and puts the attitude in the kingdom's concern.

Genuine repentance does not come except by the conviction of the Holy Spirit. "He will reprove the world of sin, and of righteousness, and of judgment: Of sin, because they believe not on me" (John 16:8-9). The Holy Spirit brings a person to the dislike of the emptiness and ugliness of sin. The Holy Spirit points to Jesus Christ as the only means of righteousness. Then the Spirit will seek to persuade people to renounce their self-centered lives and to affirm Jesus, the author of the self-denying kind of life.

3. The permanence of repentance.—One enters the Christian life at the point of repentance. Entering the kingdom by repentance leads to a complete and final reversal of one's direction in life. Of course, the status of reversal of life is accomplished; but the process of life being altered requires a lifetime. Some have been so foolish as to say, "If I could be saved, and saved once and for all, then I could sin all

I want to, without being lost." If one feels that way, he has never repented. The meaning of repentance is that one has changed his mind about himself. He wants to please and to serve God.

God's Son Merits Faith

Closely linked with repentance is faith. Those who repent from self-centeredness turn to trust Jesus as Savior. The object of faith is God's Son, Jesus Christ. Those who seek to help others become disciples should be alert to the privilege of pointing men to the Lamb of God. The whole matter of salvation depends upon the sinner's relation to him.

1. Saved by his death.—"Christ died for our sins" (1 Cor. 15:3). Nothing surpasses the life and ministry of Jesus for accomplishing salvation. Jesus came to earth and disclosed the eternal nature and character of God. He destroyed the powers of evil which sought to harm human beings. Jesus died in order that sinners could come into relationship with God and that they could have their sins forgiven.

Nothing else and no one outside of Jesus Christ can help human beings. Morality is of no avail. Charity does not save. Culture is a failure. Religious rules and rituals do not satisfy man's deepest need for relationship. The sinner can look to Jesus Christ in his suffering and death, and the Lord will merit his faith.

2. Saved through faith, not feelings.—Men are prone to trust in their feelings. A genuine relationship with God depends on him whom the sinner trusts rather than upon how the sinner feels.

Two passengers traveled in the same airplane. As they traveled, the plane got caught in terrible turbulence. In fear, one passenger asked the other if the airplane would crash. The other passenger laughed hilariously at the idea. Now which of the two was safer? Of course, the answer is obvious. Neither was safer than the other. Their safety did not depend upon their feelings but upon the airplane in which they had put their faith. Salvation does not depend upon so feeble a thing as human feelings. The sinner is safe indeed where his faith is fixed upon the Son of God.

Entering the Kingdom of God

To evangelize, Christians should know what it means to become a disciple. They should make it clear to the one whom they would lead to follow Christ that to become a Christian is to become a child of God. That definitely means that one must have a radical change from the old life. Jesus said that this change must be through regeneration or a new birth (John 3:3,5), through his Holy Spirit.

The Necessity of New Birth

1. Inherent need for new birth.—The nature of humanity is sinful. This means that it is filled with self-will, self-trust, and self-assertion. This kind of sinful nature cannot inherit the kingdom of God. The base metal of the human heart needs a heavenly alchemy to transform it into gold. Like the crabapple tree, the selfish human nature will continue to bear bitter fruit until a new nature is given by God.

> Where is one that, born of woman,
> Altogether can escape
> From the lower world within him,
> Moods of tiger and ape?
> —*Tennyson*

2. Partakers of the divine nature.—The philosopher William James in his book *The Varieties of Religious Experience* made an exhaustive study of the changes that are wrought in men when they believe in Jesus Christ. He studied the difference that faith in Christ wrought in people like Saul, the persecutor; Augustine, the profligate; John Bunyan, the profane; John Newton, the slave trader; and R. A. Torrey, the skeptic. He discovered that names which were black in dishonor became resplendent in glory. He saw the stench of sensuality replaced by the perfume of spirituality. He saw enslaved men turned into conquerors. Menials became kings. William James admitted that the Christian experience brings into human hearts some new attributes and new attitudes which can't be explained by psychology alone.

3. Not reformation but regeneration.—Becoming a child of God means more than experiencing a reforming. There is a world of difference between man's fitful desire reaching up for a better life and the omnipotent hand of God reaching down to loose him from his sins and to lift him into a new way of life. Reformation is effective only as long as man can maintain his good behavior. Regeneration is the work of God in a life. It is an eternal metamorphosis of the life.

A person can reform himself at times. But no person can "born himself again." To believe on the Lord Jesus Christ is the responsibility of man, but regeneration is the responsibility of God. When people respond in openness to God, the Lord "borns" them into his family. They become a member of God's family. The Scripture uses the passive voice to describe the change. Examine such passages as: "until Christ be formed in you"; "we are changed into the same image"; "begotten of God"; "be ye transformed"; and "to them gave he power to become the sons of God, even to them that believe on his name." Thus, the regeneration of the person can be traced to an initial act and a continuing act of God as the giver and sustainer of eternal life.

The New Life in God's Family

One of the figures used to describe a relationship with God is the family of God. This was a figure used both implicitly and explicitly in the Old Testament. "If my people, which are called by my name . . ." (2 Chron. 7:14). Figures of the family can be seen throughout the New Testament: "our Father, which art in heaven"; "sons of God"; "household of faith"; "father . . . children." No one should fail to appreciate the high privilege that is implied in those figures; nor should the serious responsibility therein be underestimated.

1. Privilege.—"Behold, what manner of love the Father hath bestowed upon us, that we should be called the sons of God" (1 John 3:1). John was deeply surprised as well as filled with wonder and amazement to be able to say that he was a member of God's family. No words of men or angels can describe the high privilege of being called one of God's children. Such should move every disciple to a consciousness of unworthiness and to a sense of gratitude.

2. Responsibility.—Great privilege brings great demand. To be a child of God demands a higher life and a more responsible life. There is a story about a king's son who was incorrigible. His instructors made every effort to induce him to walk worthily, as a king's son should. Finally they fell upon the plan of dressing him in royal purple. After that, whenever temptation allured him to deeds unworthy of his noble birth, the purple reminded him of his responsibility to live worthily, as one of royal blood. It is no little responsibility to be known as a child of God.

Living as Members of the Kingdom of God

As it has been said, to become a Christian is the experience of a moment. To be a Christian is the experience of a lifetime. To be a good Christian is to be open daily to the Holy Spirit. He will direct and give power for the fine art of superior, victorious daily living. Jesus, "the pioneer of Life" (Acts 3:15, Moffatt), promises to push back the narrow horizons of ordinary existence to give new qualities and new powers for life in the family of God. Jesus promises to give a superior type of character. He assures victory in battles with temptations. He is the way of life. He is the life.

Paul summarized superior Christian living as having three aspects: "We should live soberly, righteously, and godly, in this present world" (Titus 2:12). Also Paul described the Christlike life in Galatians 5:22-23: "But the fruit of the Spirit is love, joy, peace, longsuffering, gentleness, goodness, faith, meekness, temperance." These qualities are the kinds which God gives to those who open their lives to him.

The Life of Self-Control

When Paul mentioned "soberly" in Titus 2:12, he described the superior life as one of self-control. Christ in a person's life supplies the power for self-control, self-discipline, and self-direction. The three fruits—faith, meekness, and temperance—describe the self-controlled life. For the Christian, all the warring passions within the pre-Christian person have been put in control, if not put to death. The inner self was once one of turmoil, boiling in anger, bitterness, selfishness, and sensual indulgence. Now, there is the possibility for control. If a person submits to the Holy Spirit, life can be controlled. There is a possibility for a holier, higher, and happier life in Christ. The acceptance of the control of Christ means the continuous renunciation of the control of selfish desires.

Within every life are numerous impulses, appetites, passions, and drives. These are strong. Allowing these impulses to go uncontrolled could result in disastrous damage to our lives. Past history and current examples illustrate that the excesses of uncontrolled appetites and fleshly indulgences destroy lives. The Christian recognizes the lordship of Christ. To become a Christian is to say what John Bunyan's Christian

in *Pilgrim's Progress* said to Apollyon: "I have let myself to another."
The Christian can have self-control. It comes through the work of
the Holy Spirit within us. Self-control comes when the Christian submits daily to the lordship of Christ.

The Life of Enhanced Interpersonal Relationships

Living as a Christian means living according to superior social standards. To live righteously, as Paul said in Titus 2:12, means to live
uprightly toward others. The qualities which describe our relationships
with others in Galatians 5:22 are longsuffering, gentleness, and goodness. Here is the patience which bears rudeness and unkindness from
others and refuses to retaliate. The kindness of a Christian is God's
gift to go beyond the negative toleration of not wishing everybody
well. The goodness turns wishes into deeds. It means to take the initia-
tive to serve people in concrete, constructive ways.

Christ allows the possibility for a superior life of social relationships.
His standard was uniquely superior to any standard which the people
of his day had accepted. "Love thy neighbor as thyself" is the beginning
of Christ's standard. To love the unlovely requires a God-given grace.
The Holy Spirit supplies this love. To love one's enemies is not natural
but divine. To love others lavishly will constantly constrain a Christian
to deal honestly, think purely, speak kindly, and serve humbly in all
relations with other people. To cure the social ills of our day, Christians
should evangelize. Evangelism opens the possibility for a better social
order.

The Life of Godly Qualities

The godly life is a superior life because it is one in which all areas
of living—physical, social, mental, and moral—come under the lordship
of Christ. The world needs godly people in this present world. Paul
described godlike qualities with the terms love, joy, and peace.

The godly person has love. Love can be seen as the positive correction
of the natural life which expressed itself in self-gratification, perverted
worship, and sour social relationships. The ungodly person is one who
leaves God out of consideration in his life. He does not worship God.

The godly man has love directing his life beyond itself to God and to fellow human beings.

The godly person has joy. When the Christian receives forgiveness and experiences freedom from the burden of the old life, he finds abundant cause for rejoicing in the work of the Holy Spirit. The joy that results from the Holy Spirit does not need constant external stimulation, for it comes from within, from the living relationship between the person and God. If joy lags, it is only because we have neglected the relationship with God. Ungodly people do not and cannot have this abiding joy. They lack the assurance of the victorious life in the Spirit. They need God.

The godly person has peace. This signifies a good relationship that is established between a person and God. It is the deep inner realization that one has been brought into a right and beneficial relationship with God. No longer is one at enmity with his Master. The Christian can have peace even when struggles, problems, and difficulties abound. Peace does not mean the absence of vicissitudes or conflict. It is the inward security of a right relationship with God. No matter what happens, the Christian can trust the fact that God is with him. The ungodly people struggle for the absence of conflict and trouble. They cannot have peace outside of a settled relationship with their Master.

All conquering Christians draw on divine resources as they fight the battles of daily life. Washington needed God at Valley Forge. Gladstone needed God in Parliament. Victoria needed God to help her rule. Woodrow Wilson needed God in government affairs. Ministers and missionaries need God in their responsibilities. Merchants and professional people need God in their business matters. Parents need God in the home. Young people need God for their struggles and for their vocational choices. To be a Christian is to take God as the controlling factor in life.

The world desperately needs people with godly qualities. The world's biggest problems are problems caused by the uncontrolled life. Simply stated, the international problem is one of how nations can live together. The race problem is how to live in love instead of with prejudice. The family problem is a matter of unlovely living. In the final analysis, our world desperately needs the victorious life. Jesus said, "I am come that they might have life, and that they might have it more abundantly" (John 10:10). To make better people and a better world, Christians need to fulfill Christ's imperative commission to make disciples and to teach them how to live the superior life.

Suggestions for Advanced Study

1. Study the Gospel according to Matthew by giving a name for the major sections, using the theme "The King and the kingdom of heaven." Show how Matthew developed the idea of reaching out as well as teaching the disciple.

2. Study the epistle to the Ephesians. Seek to discover the plan of God for the peoples of the earth and his means of accomplishing his plan.

3. Make a study of the words sin, repentance, faith, reconciliation, atonement, salvation, conviction, and conversion in Frank Stagg's book entitled *New Testament Theology*, pp. 80–121.

4. Study either one of Landrum P. Leavell's books: *The Harvest of the Spirit* or *God's Spirit in You*. Examine the subject "the fruit of the Spirit."

References for Further Study

Hogue, C. B. *I Want My Church to Grow.* Nashville: Broadman Press, 1977.

Ladd, George Eldon. *The Gospel of the Kingdom: Scriptural Studies in the Kingdom of God.* Grand Rapids: William B. Eerdmans Publishing Company, 1959.

Leavell, Landrum P. *The Harvest of the Spirit.* Nashville: Broadman Press, 1976.

Smith, Bailey E. *Real Evangelism.* Nashville: Broadman Press, 1978.

Stagg, Frank. *New Testament Theology.* Nashville: Broadman Press, 1962.

Watson, David. *I Believe in Evangelism.* Grand Rapids: William B. Eerdmans Publishing Company, 1977.

Young, J. Terry. *The Spirit Within You.* Nashville: Broadman Press, 1977.

PART

II

Historic Illustrations of Evangelism

4
Evangelism Was Dynamic in Early Christian History

I am made all things to all men, that I might by all means save some (1 Cor. 9:22).

Evangelism was in full flower at the very beginning of the Christian movement. It was born full grown. Jesus was and is the perfect and ideal evangelist. The apostles seemed to "turn the world upside down" with their witnessing. The apostle Paul remains as the foremost evangelist for Christ in all Christian history. There were multiplied thousands of noble and notable evangelists of the gospel during the early centuries of the Christian era. They were less prominent than the apostles themselves; but they were faithful and fruitful, nevertheless.

This volume cannot give a complete history of evangelism. The evangelists mentioned in this and succeeding chapters have been selected because they are outstanding examples of certain types which prevail today.

Paul: Evangelism in Its Fullest New Testament Flower

The success of the apostle Paul in evangelism, amid untold difficulties and opposition, justifies our making his ideals and methods the example for evangelistic work in all ages to follow. One cannot study at length the evangelism of Paul without falling under the spell of his greatness. When one gets a vision of Paul's evangelistic power and his contribution to the kingdom of God, it is impossible to express that in words. He is the norm by which all evangelists for Christ may be both instructed and reassured.

Journeys

The story of Paul's evangelistic tours is told in fascinating literary style by Luke in Acts 13—28. After his cataclysmic conversion and thorough preparation for the ministry, Saul of Tarsus was set apart and sent out from Antioch in Syria.

1. Personal soul-winning.—His work on the island of Cyprus was personal soul-winning. The experience with the sorcerer Bar-jesus taught Saul that the gospel would conquer the superstitions that were blighting the Roman Empire. The conversion of Sergius Paulus showed him that Christ's gospel would appeal to Roman citizens of high mark. He changed his Jewish name Saul to his Roman name Paul and set his face toward the Roman cities of Asia Minor.

2. Capturing cities.—Paul visited and won converts in Pisidian Antioch, Iconium, Lystra, and Derbe. During this period he began talking about capturing whole cities for Christ.

3. Winning provinces.—When Paul, on his second evangelistic tour, had revisited the churches in the cities of Asia Minor, he received the "Macedonian call," a call to an evangelistic ideal; and he began to talk in terms of winning provinces for Christ. He thought continually of the progress of the gospel in four Roman provinces: Galatia, Macedonia, Achaia, and Asia.

4. Evangelizing the Roman Empire.—By the time Paul came to the end of his third evangelistic tour, the splendid sweep of his vision had taken the Roman Empire as his evangelistic opportunity. He expected to visit faraway Spain.

5. The world for Christ.—If Paul's ideal had stopped at the Roman Empire, then it would not have been universal. During his imprisonment at Rome, he began talking in world terms and planning for world conquest. His zeal to evangelize transcended all territorial, racial, national, and political limitations.

Methods

Paul's theory of complete evangelism was that he should become all things to all men, that by all means he might save some (1 Cor. 9:22). Paul used every conceivable method that was worthy. Churches today may well beware of the evangelist who believes there is only one method.

From the first to the last, and always, Paul was a perennial, persistent, and persuasive soul-winner through personal man-to-man interviews. He sought to win to Christ every type of person whom he met in his journeys. He dealt personally with such people as a Roman proconsul, a dissolute king, a fraudulent sorcerer, a demon-possessed girl, a lovely matron and her household, a jailer, a runaway slave, a Greek physician, many bright young men, ladies of high social standing, Greek philosophers, rulers of synagogues, a professor, sailors on ships, and soldiers in the army of Nero.

Again, Paul was a virile, versatile, and dynamic evangelistic preacher. Mass evangelism was one of his major methods. He preached the gospel and held forum discussions in the synagogues. He preached on the streets, on shipboard, before kings, in school buildings, in the face of a howling mob, in prison, in the Athenian market, and on Mars' Hill amid the classic temples of ancient Greece. Every type of sermonizing is found in the biblical descriptions of his preaching. His sermons were textual, topical, expository, historical, hortatory, didactic, devotional, apologetic, and philippic.

Furthermore, the apostle practiced evangelism through teaching, through home prayer meetings, through miracles, through letter writing, through collecting money, through disputation, and even through his vocation of tentmaking. Sometimes he traveled alone, and sometimes he was the leader of an evangelistic party. He was a master of the technique of visitation evangelism. He was a man of fervent and incessant prayer.

Message

Basically the evangelistic preaching of Paul was doctrinal in its message. His doctrine was built on four cornerstones: (1) the deity of Christ as the chief cornerstone, (2) the inerrant truth from God in the Scriptures, (3) the universality of the gospel for Jew and Gentile alike, and (4) the church as the divinely ordained organization for the propagation of the gospel. Paul's doctrine concerning Jesus emphasized four supremely important points: (1) the deity of Christ, (2) an atonement for sins through the cross, (3) the reality of the resurrection of Christ from the dead, and (4) the blessed hope of his victorious return to the earth in power and glory.

Building upon the structure of great doctrines, Paul appealed to men in every worthy manner. Relentlessly he condemned the gnostic heresy as he proclaimed Christ as the "fulness of the Godhead bodily"

(Col. 2:9). Zealously he fought the Judaizers in order that the gospel might be open to Gentiles as well as Jews. He appealed to men to repent of their sins and to believe on the Lord Jesus Christ. He wept with the weak; he taught the uninstructed; he encouraged the wavering; and he championed the underprivileged.

The personal application of the gospel which Paul preached with such evangelistic zeal in no way eliminated or contradicted his application of the social teachings of Christ. He exhorted his converts to recognize every virtue included or implied in the command of Christ for one to love his neighbor as himself. Paul applied the gospel to homelife, to family relations, to economic justice, to the slavery problem, to race prejudice, to Christian attitudes toward a pagan state authority, and to all other causes of personal enmity of social strife.

Conservation

This foremost Christian evangelist set the standard of evangelism for all succeeding generations by not stopping when the personal application of the gospel had won men to discipleship in Christ. Nor did he stop with applying the gospel to social conditions of that day. He sought to conserve and perpetuate the results of his soul-winning. He organized his converts into churches. He visited and revisited the churches, trained the converts, directed the ordination of ministers and deacons, and admonished his followers in doctrine and morals. He personally trained young ministers to take up the torch of evangelism when it should fall from his failing hand.

Thus, Paul did not fall a prey to the temptation to onesidedness or to a temporary emphasis, as many evangelists of later times have done. The apostle promoted a well-rounded evangelism which was geographically inclusive, doctrinally complete, personally all-embracing, socially Christian, and organizationally permanent in its structure. Today, Paul's work goes on, many centuries since he finished his earthly course, and while he is awaiting the soul-winner's crown. This Christ-mastered evangelist is perhaps more influential today than he was while he was on earth. He lives on and on, through those whom he won to Christ, through the letters he wrote, through the impression he left upon the Christian enterprise, and through the victories he won for Christ amid the Gentile world.

All movements toward progress in evangelizing the world move toward Paul's evangelistic ideal. The methods and the message of Paul must be more and more the methods and message of twentieth-century apostles if Christian evangelists are to win people in great numbers to Jesus Christ.

Paul's ideals, his message, and his methods were those of Paul's Master. He was truly an evangelist "in Christ" (2 Cor. 12:2).

Suggestions for Advanced Study

1. Make a list of the cities visited by Paul in his four evangelistic journeys, and indicate the methods of evangelistic approach he used in each city (Acts 13—28).

2. Make an analysis of Paul's evangelistic sermons mentioned in Acts 9; 13—14; 16—20; 22—26; 28. Compare the occasions, approaches, exposition of Scripture, tact, exhortation, and successful results.

Constantine: Evangelism by Government Decree

The Roman Emperor Constantine (A.D. 272-337) was the father of the unscriptural method of bringing people into church membership by government decree. He was the father of the baneful plan of uniting church and state.

In Hoc Signo Vinces

Constantine wanted to become sole emperor at any cost. He was about to fight his rival, Maxentius, at Milvian Bridge near Rome. Victory meant accomplishing his ambition; defeat meant disaster. He claimed to have seen in the sky a blazing banner with a shining cross, bearing the inscription *In hoc signo vinces,* or "By this sign conquer." He won the battle, fighting under a labarum like that which he claimed to have seen. Thereafter he favored the Christian religion and made it virtually the official state religion.

Converts by Coercion and Bribery

The emperor assumed the title of *Pontifex Maximus* of the Christian church. He ordered great portions of the army to be baptized and coerced the people to do likewise. In one year, twelve thousand men, plus a corresponding number of women and children, were baptized. In A.D. 324 he promised every convert to Christianity twenty pieces of gold and a white robe in which to be baptized. He himself did not submit to baptism until three days before he died. His manner of life hardly indicated any true Christian character.

Union of Church and State

Thus, Constantine became the founder of the European system of union of church and state. That means a sort of evangelism by national birth or governmental decree. It has prevailed until this day. Not only Roman Catholic and Greek Orthodox churches are state churches; but also the Lutheran (in some countries), the Swiss Reformed, and the Church of England are state churches. Even Presbyterianism in Scotland once maintained thoroughgoing union with the state. All these have accepted tax monetary support from the state and have bitterly persecuted other religionists by the authority of the state.

Results

A few good results came among the many, many evil consequences of Constantine's union of church and state. A number of people forsook idolatry and were brought under the influence of Christianity. Some social legislation developed in Rome, improving conditions of slavery, women, marriage, divorce, and pagan sport festivals. These could have been effected by New Testament evangelism without the attendant evils which Constantine's course produced.

The pagan organization of the Roman Empire was brought over into the church, with a pope like the emperor, with bishops like prefects, with nuns like vestal virgins, and with the pageantry of the ecclesiastical hierarchy like the pagan pageantry of the Caesars. Christianity was thoroughly secularized. Images of saints were worshiped like idols of former days. Mary and the apostles supplanted Christ in prominence. Priestly forgiveness and sacraments for salvation displaced inner spiritual repentance and faith. The church powers became the persecuting power over all dissenters. Religious liberty was lost as completely as civil liberty was lost under the dictatorships of the Caesars. New Testament doctrines such as the equality of believers were destroyed. In fact, the authority of the church powers became as absolute as that of the emperors; and the authority of the Bible was supplanted. Before Constantine, the pagan governments persecuted the Christians; after Constantine, the paganized church persecuted all who exercised freedom of conscience in dissent.

Perpetuation

This practice of gaining membership for state churches is in vogue in many nations today. State control of the churches, state support of the churches, and state citizenship constituting membership in the churches all make New Testament evangelism exceedingly difficult for free churches. May God deliver the world from compulsory membership in state churches through birth into a national citizenship. May God prosper the churches through voluntary church membership after spiritual rebirth.

Augustine: Evangelism by Writing

Augustine (A.D. 354-430), bishop of Hippo, is one of Christianity's outstanding examples of the power of using the written page as a means of evangelism.

"Even if he be not the greatest of Latin writers, he is assuredly the greatest man who ever wrote Latin," said Professor A. Souter, speaking of Augustine. "It may be doubted if ever any uninspired theologian has had and still has so large a number of admirers and disciples as the Bishop of Hippo," said Philip Schaff, the church historian. While Augustine was among the chief originators of Roman Catholic beliefs today, his writings were also more influential than those of anyone save the apostle Paul in producing the Protestant Reformation under Luther.

Many people name Augustine, Paul, Luther, and Wesley as the four most influential evangelists in Christian history.

Monica

Never was there a truly great man who had a fool for his mother. Monica, the mother of Augustine, is among the immortals in Christian motherhood's hall of fame. For thirty years she prayed that her wayward but brilliant son would become a Christian. Her influence hovered over him during his waywardness and profligacy until eventually he was constrained to say, "Thou, O God, hast created us for thyself, and our hearts are without rest, until they rest in Thee."

Augustine's father did not become a Christian until near his death.

Augustine's *Confessions*

The Confessions of Augustine ranks next to the fifty-first Psalm by David in its honest humility, its burning emotion, and its eloquent though humble confession of sin against the Searcher of hearts. From this book we learn of Augustine's early life of profligacy.

The boy Augustine would not study and was given to cheating, lying, and stealing. However, in grammar school he became charmed and enthused with Latin. Later he became an orator of rare ability, as well as a diligent student. In the university he fell into the miry clay of unchastity. He says, "I was not able to distinguish the brighter purity of love from the darkness of lust. Both were mingled together in confusion; youth in its weakness, hurried to the abyss of desire, was swallowed up in the pool of vice." While studying in Carthage, at the age of eighteen he followed the heathen practice of living unmarried with a woman, who bore him a son. Though they lived together thirteen years, he let her pass out of his life when he was converted. Although his life was respectable and legal in Roman society, his conversion to Christ quickened his conscience and raised his standard so much that he spoke of that episode with the most intense and penitent sorrow.

Conversion and Call

While teaching in Milan, Italy, his sins threw him into agonizing paroxysms of weeping and prayerful cries to God. One day in his garden while in such agony, he heard a maiden's voice from a neighboring house say repeatedly, "Tolle lege, tolle lege!" which is, "Take and read, take and read." He felt it was God telling him to read the Bible. His eye fell on Romans 13:13-14: "Let us walk honestly, as in the day; not in rioting and drunkenness, not in chambering and wantonness, not in strife and envying. But put ye on the Lord Jesus Christ, and make not provision for the flesh, to fulfill the lusts thereof." His conversion was vivid and completely transforming.

He was baptized by Bishop Ambrose on Easter, A.D. 387. He returned to Africa to begin a new kind of life. In the seaport town of Hippo the bishop urged the congregation to find a candidate for the priesthood, and Augustine was brought forward. Without hesitation the bishop then and there ordained him as a priest. The aged bishop soon asked that Augustine should succeed him. He was consecrated in A.D. 395 and became the bishop of Hippo the next year. Thus he was fixed unchangeably to spend the remainder of his life in a small seaport town. He made the town famous by his more than thirty years of residence there.

Evangelistic Power for Centuries

Among Augustine's personal qualities for becoming a great evangelist were a great mother, a vivid experience of conversion, a brilliant mind highly trained, and incessant labors for the Lord. Augustine ruled with his pulpit and his pen, but chiefly by the pen. His sermons were short, expository, and very numerous. They dealt chiefly with the psalms, and they were full of power.

The pen of Augustine projected the power of his preaching through succeeding ages. Some 360 of his sermons remain. His letters were prolific, portentous, and penetrating. He wrote dozens of books and hundreds of tracts. These writings, like those of Paul, went everywhere. They covered a wide range of doctrine. He wrote in the style of language current among the educated. He was adept at words, a coiner of phrases, and a master rhetorician.

Augustine's writings were intended to refute certain heresies of his day, but unconsciously he was writing his system of theological belief into the thinking of all Christendom. While he was formulating doctrinal belief and systematic theology for the Catholic Church for succeeding generations, he also was propounding certain beliefs which helped Martin Luther eleven centuries later to expose some of the errors in the Catholic system.

Martin Luther placed Augustine's writings next to the Bible. Dr. John A. Broadus said, "What we call Calvinism is the doctrine of Paul, developed by Augustine, and systematized by Calvin." [1]

Suggestions for Advanced Study

1. Read Augustine's *Confessions*. List in opposite columns some of the doctrines held by Augustine which were tenaciously taught by the Roman Catholic Church at the time of the Protestant Reformation, and some of Augustine's teachings which Martin Luther followed.

2. Outline some hindrances which the state church has with regard to evangelism. Discuss the idea of a free church and a state church with regard to the task of evangelism.

3. Study the first four centuries of the expansion of Christianity in Kenneth S. Latourette's work, *A History of the Expansion of Christianity*, vol. I, pp. 1-170.

References for Further Study

Allen, Roland. *St. Paul's Missionary Methods.* New York: Samuel R. Leland, Inc., 1931.

Dodd, C. H. *The Apostolic Preaching and Its Developments.* New York: Harper and Brothers Publishers, 1962.

Harnack, Adolf von. *The Missions and Expansion of Christianity in the First Three Centuries.* New York: G. P. Putnam's Sons, 1908.

Hurst, J. F. *History of the Christian Church.* Vol. 1. New York: Harper and Brothers, 1937.

Robertson, A. T. *Epochs in the Life of St. Paul.* (A. T. Robertson Library) Nashville: Broadman Press, 1974.

Scarborough, L. R. *With Christ After the Lost.* Revised and expanded by E. D. Head. Nashville: Broadman Press, 1952.

Wood, A. Skevington. *The Inextinguishable Blaze.* Fort Washington, Pennsylvania: Christian Literature Crusade, 1958.

Zwemer, Samuel M. *Evangelism Today.* New York: Revell, 1944.

Note

1. John A. Broadus, *History of Preaching*, p. 81.

5
Evangelism Blazed Intermittently During the Middle Ages

And the Light shines in the darkness, and the darkness never overpowered it (John 1:5, The Twentieth Century New Testament).

There has not been any century, even during the darkest of the Dark Ages, that has not had some outstanding heralds of the gospel. Three mighty evangelists of the Middle Ages are chosen for this chapter, illustrating specific types of evangelism.

Francis of Assisi: Evangelism by Self-sacrifice and Song

Francis of Assisi (1182-1226) may be something of a patron saint for evangelistic musicians. "Francis has shed more charm upon the Catholic Church and kept more people within her fold than all her cardinals." [1] His winsomeness in drawing people came through a combination of personal self-sacrifice and heavy-hearted spiritual music.

Call

Francis' father was a rich merchant who wanted his son to live in luxury and to revel in worldly pleasure. But Francis said he heard the voice of God speaking of him through the words of Jesus: "And as ye go, preach, saying, The kingdom of heaven is at hand. Heal the sick, cleanse the lepers, raise the dead, cast out devils: freely ye have received, freely give." That changed everything for Francis. He forsook his father's riches to depend upon alms. He vowed perpetual poverty. He forsook a world of sinful indulgence and vowed perpetual chastity. He forsook a carefree irresponsibility and vowed perpetual obedience.

Evangelistic Methods

The evangelistic methods of Francis profoundly affected Europe for many years after his death. There were two outstanding methods. First, his happy victory over base desires for material splendor deeply moved the people of his generation and succeeding years. How to be happy though poor was demonstrated by his self-denial; and this example won multitudes of converts from among the poor. Second, his method of spiritual singing to win converts proved to be a tremendous power. The sad hearts of lost men deeply yearn for happiness, which they cannot find in material possessions. They respond to victorious joy expressed in psalms and hymns and spiritual songs.

Order of Franciscans

Francis founded the order which is called by his name. The members took vows of poverty, chastity, and obedience. He and his followers traveled extensively, barefooted, clothed in coarse garments, begging and serving and preaching and singing as they went. They were sent out in teams of two, as Jesus sent the seventy. They went all over Italy, France, Spain, and North Africa. Because of their rough style of living, they appealed to the lower economic strata of society. So many joined the Order of the Franciscans that it became quite large and influential.

Francis and his followers found joy in their self-denial, which they expressed in songs and happiness everywhere. He was nicknamed the "Troubadour of God." Once, in an ecstasy of praise and prayer, he claimed to have received the marks (stigmata) of the wounds of Jesus on his own body.

Weakness

Francis established no New Testament churches to train his converts and to continue his evangelistic endeavors. Instead, the pope formally took over the direction of the order of the Franciscans in 1223. After the movement became an order under the pope, the requirements of self-sacrifice were toned down, and the spontaneity of free evangelism was taken away. The "troubadours of God" lost their inner inspiration for song.

John Tauler: Evangelism Through Mysticism and Prayer

The will of a sinful man must be approached through his emotions as well as through his intellect. No method of evangelism should ignore either the emotions or the intellect. The ideal would be a sane balance between the two. John Tauler (1300?-1361) demonstrated the mighty evangelistic power of the appeal to the emotions of men.

Mysticism

The mystics of the tenth through the fourteenth centuries saved the Christian faith from a dry-as-dust scholasticism on the one hand, and from the soul-shriveling attempt of the Roman Catholic Church to join the souls of men to God through the sacraments on the other hand. Mysticism was the belief that a man could come into union with God through a wholly passive surrender to God's influence. It was an effort at an immediate dealing of a soul with God. Mystics sought to hide themselves from the world to obtain spiritual union with the divine. This sometimes led to excesses of rapt contemplation, emotional ecstasy, cessation of the bodily and mental functions, miracle working, and fanaticism.

Someone has said: "Scholasticism was light without heart; mysticism was heart without light."

Greatest of the Mystics

The greatest of the mystics was John Tauler. Tauler was born in Strasbourg, Alsace, and was educated as a Dominican. He was a popular preacher in Strasbourg, Cologne, Basel, and elsewhere. During the Black Death scourge of 1347-1352 the faithful and devoted Tauler stayed in Strasbourg to minister to those who could not flee.

Transformation

When Tauler was a mature preacher, about fifty years of age, his "conversion" came. Perhaps it was what some people would call a "second blessing."

A layman friend of Tauler's, who belonged to a group called "Friends of God," visited him in Strasbourg and told him that he did not even know Christ. He persuaded the popular preacher that he needed a true experience of losing himself in God—a spiritual enlightenment. Tauler was deeply stirred. He went into two years of retirement, living constantly in prayer, fasting, penitence, and in search of the "higher life."

When Tauler first tried to preach again, he broke into a paroxysm of weeping, and he had to cease. Thereafter, when he preached, the people wept and groaned and fainted away in emotional demonstration. Tauler himself was devoted in prayer, always.

Influence

John Tauler became one of the most famous and influential evangelists of medieval times. He was assuredly the most effective preacher and successful evangelist of his generation. His powerful influence swept through all the areas along the Rhine River. His converts were affected with emotional excesses and trances, something like the "jerks" in American revivals around the year 1800.

The converts in Tauler's evangelistic efforts were not organized into churches. They formed prayer circles, continually seeking union with God. These influences kept prayer at the forefront in Christian groups of Germany for more than a hundred years.

Savonarola: Evangelism by Denunciation and Moral Reform

A true New Testament revival is accompanied by moral reform. Both the Old Testament prophets and the New Testament apostles challenged the sins of the people, called for repentance, and exhorted their hearers to cease to do evil as well as to learn to do well. John the Baptist, mighty evangelistic Forerunner of our Lord, cried, "Bring forth therefore fruits meet for repentance" (Matt. 3:8).

However, denunciation of sins and moral reform of sinners are not enough. John the Baptist also pointed lost men to the Lamb of God. Great reformers are not necessarily great evangelists. Girolamo Savonarola (1452-1498) was only a great reformer. He was a reformer of the Catholic Church long before the Protestant Reformation. But his reformation fell far short of Luther's because Luther's reforms were Bible-centered and doctrinal, with emphasis upon the plan of salvation; Savonarola's reformation was largely social and moral.

Savonarola was born in Ferrara, Italy, of worthy parentage. He became a Dominican monk and was transferred to the monastery in Florence in 1482. In Florence today there is a bronze cross in a central square showing where his body was burned after he had been hanged by the very people whom he evangelized and reformed.

The sins, follies, cruelties, and ungodliness in Ferrara drove him to a sad absorption in Bible interpretation and religious meditation. He found in Florence that the ungodly rulers, the Medici family, had plunged the moral standard to an all-time low degree. The corruption of the Catholic Church, especially of such popes as Sixtus IV, Innocent VIII, and Alexander VI, made him determine to strike hard at such iniquity.

Savonarola had visions and experiences of rapt ecstasy. He spent long nights in vigils. He predicted dire calamities to fall upon the people, and especially upon the church, because of their life of iniquity. He preached on texts from the Old Testament prophets. He hurled sermons like thunderbolts at the people of Florence, exposing sin and predicting judgment—such sermons as Italy had never heard before.

Florence was shaken to the foundation. The people wept and went to church. In front of the city hall they made a huge bonfire of the indecent books, pictures, trinkets, jewels, and vanities. The Medici rulers fell temporarily from their power. Savonarola, by the sheer force of his personality and preaching, became for a time the dominant dictator of Florence. The French invaded and conquered Italy, and he declared this a fulfillment of his prophecies. Florence was led to establish an ideal Christian commonwealth. Savonarola's evangelism was seeming to triumph. He grew more and more denunciatory, bold, prophetic, and apocalyptic.

Savonarola's popularity flourished only for a season. Florence wearied of her reformation. His standards were too high. Virtue lost its charm. People revolted against the priest-regulated moral regime. Morality no longer appealed to the fickle populace. Reformation without regeneration was transitory and undependable.

The Medici began to climb back into power. The pope excommunicated Savonarola. The reformer-evangelist was tried and condemned for heresy and sedition. He was hanged, and his body was burned in the street where the famous bonfire was built hardly a year before.

The evangelism of Savonarola calls out many observations: (1) He effected such good reforms as civil liberty, lower taxes, relief to the starving, and better administration of justice. (2) He soon discovered that raising his voice in denunciation of popular sins won popular approval and drew large crowds. But he learned also that such popularity was as fickle as that of the group who cried "Hosanna" at the triumphant entry of Jesus into Jerusalem, and later, in Pilate's court, cried "Crucify him." (3) His belief in himself as a prophet and his assurance of having a message straight from God won a large hearing. (4) Reformation without regeneration inevitably brings reaction. (5) Evangelism will fail if it is negative without the positive, critical without the constructive, sensational without the spiritual, condemning without Christ.

Suggestions for Advanced Study

1. Study the social, economic, domestic, and moral reforms advocated by Isaiah, Micah, Amos, and Habakkuk. Contrast their results with those of Savonarola, and give the reasons for your conclusions.

2. Secure statistics on the growth of religious groups in America such as Nazarenes, independent groups, Church of God, and others. In your opinion give the strength of their evangelistic appeal.

References for Further Study

Bailey, Ambrose M. *Evangelism in a Changing World.* New York: Round Table Press, 1936.
Hurst, John F. *History of the Christian Church.* Vols. 1 and 2. New York: Eaton and Mains, 1900.
Newman, Albert Henry. *A Manual of Church History.* Philadelphia: Judson Press, 1904.

Note

1. John F. Hurst, *History of the Christian Church* (New York: Eaton and Mains, 1900).

6

Evangelism Transformed Europe During the Protestant Reformation

Earnestly contend for the faith which was once delivered unto the saints (Jude 3)

A galaxy of evangelistic stars of the first magnitude burst on the religious sky of Europe at the time of the Protestant Reformation. The names of Luther, Zwingli, Calvin, Knox, and some of the Anabaptist leaders will always be notable in the history of Christianity. Among the preachers of that period, Luther was the outstanding German, Zwingli the outstanding Swiss, Calvin the outstanding Frenchman, and Knox the outstanding Scot. Theirs was an evangelism characterized by protest against the doctrines and practices of the entrenched Roman Catholic system.

No chapter of "evangelism by protest" would be adequate without something about the Anabaptists of Europe, who protested against those unscriptural practices which the "protestants" brought over into Protestantism from the Roman Catholic system.

Martin Luther (1483-1546)

Background of the Reformer

Martin Luther was typically German. From his peasant parents he inherited a burly German physique, a rough-and-ready manner, and a profound intellect. He was thoroughly schooled, attaining his Master's and Doctor of Theology degrees. He was thoroughly Roman Catholic, loyal to all its teachings, and saturated with all its superstitions. Once in a storm he feared for his life and cried, "Help, St. Anne! I will become a monk!" At twenty-eight years of age he entered an Augustinian monastery. He knew no other way to serve God.

Conversion from Roman Catholicism

The monastery gave Luther ample time for study. He read Augustine, studying his doctrines of divine predestination and election. He studied the doctrines of the martyr, John Huss, concerning the right of individual interpretation of the Scripture. Above all, he studied the Bible. Meanwhile, he sought earnestly to obtain salvation by the Roman Catholic ways of singing, praying, fasting, using self-inflicted punishment, observing the sacraments, and calling on all the saints. All failed to help him.

While serving as lecturer at the University of Wittenberg, he visited Rome in A.D. 1511. He sought salvation by ascending on his knees the twenty-eight steps of the Scala Santa, or Holy Stairs, said by Catholics to have come from Pilate's Hall in Jerusalem. His mind kept ringing with the text, "The just shall live by faith." The corruption of the priests deeply disgusted him. Later on, in Germany, an emissary of the pope, John Tetzel, was selling indulgences for huge sums, promising that as soon as the money clicked in the box their deceased loved ones would be freed from purgatory. Luther could stand it no longer.

In 1517 Luther nailed ninety-five theses, or religious propositions, on the cathedral door at Wittenberg. The Protestant Reformation was set in motion—one of the mightiest religious struggles in all history. The pope excommunicated the reformer. Luther publicly burned the official notice and set himself to expose the errors of the Roman Catholic Church. He married Katharine von Bora, an escaped nun.

Promoting the Reformation

The remaining thirty years of Luther's life were spent in the most vigorous evangelistic fervor, propagating his doctrine of the way of salvation in contrast with the doctrine taught by the Roman Catholic Church.

The variety of his evangelistic methods almost equaled Paul's. Luther was preeminently a preacher; and because of his earnest, soul-stirring preaching, he had many followers. He was a truly great teacher. His scholarship was of the highest order. He was a formidable debater, attacking the popes, the authority of the Roman Church, the Catholic doctrine of salvation, the meaning of mass, and the authority of church councils to condemn dissenters to death. He vigorously debated with other Protestants who differed with him. He was a prolific writer. One of his chief works was a translation of the Bible. He also made much of music, even writing some exalted Christian hymns.

Permanent Results

The permanence and subsequent growth of Luther's evangelistic work reveal the strength of evangelism built around scriptural doctrines of grace and promoted by many methods of approach. Luther's personal influence soon spread over all western Europe. The spread of his doctrines was amazing in rapidity and extent. The Lutheran denomination today is the strongest in northern Europe and one of the strongest in the United States. While this denomination perpetuates his insistence on salvation by grace through faith, it also perpetuates his belief in consubstantiation, infant baptism, and the state church in various European countries.

Ulrich Zwingli (1484-1531)

Western Switzerland is chiefly French; eastern Switzerland is predominantly German. What Martin Luther was to German Protestantism, Ulrich Zwingli was to Protestantism in eastern Switzerland.

Compared to Luther

Like Luther, Zwingli was at first an ardent Roman Catholic. Also, like Luther, before his own conversion he vigorously denounced the sale of indulgences. The study of the Bible helped Zwingli to become a Protestant, just as what happened with Luther. But, unlike Luther, Zwingli was not converted by a crisis or series of crises; his conversion came by a gradual process of emancipation from the Roman Catholic superstitions and doctrinal corruptions. Luther greatly influenced Zwingli as a preaching reformer. However, they eventually became engaged in a most bitter and unfortunate controversy about the Lord's Supper.

Type of Ministry

Zwingli's chief ministry was centered in Zurich. His statue stands there today, a Bible in one hand and a sword in the other. He died in battle, fighting for his cause.

Zwingli was a prodigious student of the Bible. This aided him in becoming one of the mightiest expository preachers of Christian history. He startled Zurich by beginning his ministry there with expository preaching through the Gospel of Matthew. He preached through the entire New Testament. His choice theme was the doctrine of free grace. He was a brilliant musician, both singing and playing well.

His Reforms

His practical reforms were numerous. The Catholic ceremonies in their order of worship disappeared one by one. Priests and nuns were married. Crucifixes were removed from churches. Mass was abolished, and Protestant observance of the church ordinances was instituted. All eastern Switzerland came under his influence. The Swiss Reformed denomination follows him chiefly.

He also made mistakes. He defended the union of state and church. He suppressed the Anabaptists, even while preaching freedom of conscience. They were widely persecuted, and some were executed.

John Calvin (1509-1564)

John Calvin was a Frenchman, born the year Henry VIII of England was crowned, and died the year Shakespeare was born. He was a frail little man, bent over from much study. He was destitute of humor and somewhat unwinsome in personality, but an aristocrat by nature. He has influenced the thinking of all Protestant Christianity, even to this day.

Born in France, he was thoroughly educated, first for the priesthood and then for the law. He mastered philosophy, theology, and the Greek New Testament. As a young man he was severely moral and pure.

Calvin's Writings

While studying at the University of Paris, he wrote an address for a friend, attacking the doctrines of theological doctors there. He maintained that forgiveness of sins and eternal life were by God's grace alone and not by good works. He was forced to flee from Paris for physical protection from the storm which the speech created. In 1534 he severed all connection with Roman Catholicism—the same year in which Ignatius Loyola, his fellow theological student in Paris, founded the order of the Jesuits.

Calvin went to Switzerland to study and write. He wrote an apology for Protestantism, called *Institutes of the Christian Religion,* a theological masterpiece of predestination, election, grace, and other doctrinal subjects. This apology shook all Protestantism. It lifted him, at twenty-six, to a place second to none among Protestants. The core of his theology was his doctrine of the absolute sovereignty of God.

Virtual Dictatorship in Geneva

After studying in several Swiss cities, making a sojourn in Italy, and venturing again into France, Calvin settled in Geneva, Switzerland, almost by accident. When he was passing through Geneva, a friend persuaded him that he was the mouthpiece of heaven for Geneva and that he dared not resist the hand of God. Geneva became his home and his kingdom until his death. For some years he was a virtual dictator.

Calvin became Geneva's chief preacher, teacher of theology, and almost absolute sovereign in civil as well as moral and spiritual affairs. It is miraculous how one man could have done so much work. The one great blot on his name is that he had Servetus, a stubborn and aggressive Antitrinitarian, arrested for heresy, and later consented to his being burned at the stake.

Far-reaching Influence of Calvinism

After Luther's death Calvin became the leading figure among Protestants. He directed the French Reformation from his pulpit and by his pen in Geneva. His theological tenets became directives in Italy, Poland, Germany, the Netherlands, England, Scotland, and the American colonies. The French Huguenots, the Scotch Covenanters, the English Puritans, and the American Pilgrim fathers were all Calvinistic in doctrine. He organized the teachings of Paul, which were rediscovered by Augustine and proclaimed by Luther, into clear theological form for all succeeding generations. Baptists and Presbyterians today are largely his theological descendants.

John Knox (1505-1572)

For years the Protestants in Scotland suffered persecution at the hands of Catholics. The martyrdom of Wishart powerfully influenced a priest, John Knox, to break completely from Rome and lead Scotland in a Protestant Reformation. Before that reformation Scotland suffered from a violent nobility, a corrupt clergy, and a people engrossed in superstition and ignorance.

Wrestling Against World Powers

Knox's struggle against the Catholics was in opposition to the queen regent, Mary of Guise, and later in opposition to her daughter, Mary Stuart, Queen of Scots. He once was made a galley slave by the French. Frequently he was banished. He spent several years in England and also was an English pastor in Geneva. There he knew Calvin and learned much from this preeminent Protestant theologian. Time and again Knox was tried. Once the queen herself appeared as a witness against him. She said she feared Knox's prayers more than all the demons.

When the queen regent sought to reinstate Catholicism and forbade Protestant preaching, Knox suddenly reappeared in Scotland at the risk of his life. A monk rushed into a council of Catholic clergy and screamed, "John Knox! John Knox is come! He slept last night in Edinburgh!" The council broke up in confusion and panic. The queen declared him an outlaw. But Knox preached on, proclaiming his convictions and encouraging the Protestants. The ruler tried tears and threats, sarcasm and flattery, anger and entreaty upon him—all to no avail.

Personality, Style, and Power

Possibly Knox was not as original, scholarly, or great as Luther, Zwingli, or Calvin. However, he was a dynamic Scotsman, with force of thought, stirring earnestness, and unwavering courage of his convictions. His eloquence ranks him among the greatest of evangelists. His eyes gleamed and his body quivered in the earnestness of his delivery. He held remarkable sway over men. One said of his fiery, forceful delivery, "He was lyk to ding the pulpit in blads." Above all, he was absolutely fearless. At his death the newly elected regent said, "There lies he who never feared the face of man."

He was not a writer. Little remains from his pen. He was a denunciatory preacher, condemning sins in the high and the low. He was a flaming evangel of terror and truth. He preached in churches large and small, in the courts of royalty, and in the homes of the humble. All of Scotland came to follow him.

Spiritual Foundations for a Nation

Scotland's transformation into greatness in later years can be attributed in a large measure to the powerful evangelistic gospel preached by John Knox. Catholicism was banished from Scotland, and Presbyterianism became the official state religion through Knox's reformation preaching. His appeal was based on the Scripture, and to this day the Scotch preachers have been expositors of the Bible. He perpetuated his doctrines by formulating confessions of faith for the churches.

The English Puritans of later years were influenced greatly by his reforms.

The Anabaptists in Various European Countries

Evangelism by reformation reached a high peak with the Anabaptists. They tried to reform the Protestant reformers by insisting on immersion for those who had been sprinkled, especially for those sprinkled in infancy. They were called "rebaptizers" or Anabaptists. This doctrine was preached by the Novatians in the third century, the Donatists in the fourth century, and many succeeding sects, such as Petrobrusians, Waldensians, Henricians, Paulicians, and others.

Switzerland

The first clearly defined group of Anabaptists broke from Zwingli when he ceased his insistence on rebaptism. Conrad Grebel is called the father of the Anabaptist movement. He led the revolt from Zwingli and was sorely persecuted. Felix Manz, a thorough Bible scholar in the original languages, gave a scholarship as well as an evangelistic zeal to the movement. He was martyred by drowning—a death thought to be particularly appropriate for rebaptizers. George Blaurock, a converted monk, baptized more than a thousand converts in four and one-half years. He was burned at the stake. Wilhelm Reublin joined a religious procession carrying a huge Bible, declaring it was the only object worthy of veneration, in contrast to relics. (Evangelism by religious parades!) When persecuted, he fled to Moravia and Germany. In Germany his most important convert was Balthasar Hubmaier.

Germany

Balthasar Hubmaier (1481-1528) was Germany's most prominent Anabaptist. He was highly educated, holding the Th.D. degree, and was a popular lecturer in Roman Catholic university centers. When he was converted to Anabaptist beliefs by Reublin in 1525, he rebaptized three hundred others on Easter. He preached, wrote many books and pamphlets, and scattered his doctrine everywhere while fleeing from persecution. He baptized no less than six thousand in one year. He was burned at the stake, and his wife was drowned in the Danube.

England

Anabaptists appeared in England early in the sixteenth century. By 1573 there were at least fifty thousand. There, too, they were sorely persecuted. Other sects holding radical and unworthy doctrines were erroneously called Anabaptists, which discredited the name.

"With respect to the relationship between Anabaptists and Baptists, it is safe to say that the latter are the spiritual descendants of some of the former." [1] It is quite safe to say that both the Anabaptists and their successors, the Baptists, have had their evangelistic zeal kindled and their soul-winning fervor kept at white heat by their convictions about scriptural truth. They evangelized; they suffered manifold kinds of persecution; and many of them died in order to proclaim the Bible as their one rule of faith and practice, to declare the necessity of separation of church and state, and to propagate their belief that scriptural baptism is for believers only. Those who have profound convictions and preach them will always win a following.

Summary of Evangelism During the Protestant Reformation

Using Luther, Zwingli, Calvin, Knox, and the outstanding Anabaptist leaders as types of the evangelism of the Reformation era, we find certain characteristics which seem to be true of all. Evangelism of any age will be blessed by such virtues.

Profound Scholars

These men were scholars, trained in the highest degree of learning. They continued to be consistent students throughout life. A full heart is no excuse for an empty head.

Princely Pulpiteers

These men were preeminently preachers, and the Reformation was a revival of mighty preaching. They were preachers of the Bible. Expository preaching was their style of sermonizing. They were preachers of doctrine. Evangelism that is based purely on exhortation, without indoctrination, is weak and frothy.

Preachers to the Common People

These men were preachers to the common people. Though highly educated, they spoke the language of the average man. Common people heard them gladly.

Men of Deep Convictions

These men had mighty convictions, as deep as their souls. Their deepest convictions centered about how men must be saved. People will always follow a man who knows what he believes and is willing to die for it. People hunger for a sure word from God about how they may be saved from sin and from sinning.

Prodigious Workers

These men were prodigious workers. Luther once bitterly excoriated a preacher as living an idle life, preaching only two or three times a week. These men often preached every day, months at a time, while carrying on many other labors. A lazy evangelist is a denial of the truth he declares. If there is a way to obtain eternal life, evangelists must not cease day or night to give the gospel to the lost.

Flawless Characters

These men were men of almost flawless personal morality, protected from the daggers of enemies by the breastplate of righteousness. They were men of deep piety, unceasing prayers, humility before God, and unbounded love for the souls of their fellowmen.

Suggestions for Advanced Study

1. Read a biography of Martin Luther and list his evangelistic methods. (Cf. Bainton, Roland H. *Here I Stand.* New York: Abingdon-Cokesbury, 1950.)

2. Make a study of the opponents of great evangelists, such as the Roman Catholic Church *vs.* Luther, the scholars of Paris *vs.* Calvin, Mary Queen of Scots *vs.* Knox, and the persecutors *vs.* the Anabaptists. How much opposition should real, New Testament evangelism encounter today? from whom?

3. Make a study of the use of expository preaching by the Reformation evangelists, and compare it with the types of sermonizing used by the great majority of evangelists today.

References for Further Study

Bainton, Roland H. *Here I Stand.* New York: Abingdon-Cokesbury, 1950.

Hurst, John F. *History of the Christian Church.* Vol. 2. New York: Eaton and Mains, 1900.

Lacy, B. R., Jr. *Revivals in the Midst of the Years.* Richmond: John Knox Press, 1943.

Latourette, K. S. *A History of the Expansion of Christianity.* Vol. 2. New York: Harper and Brothers, 1939.

Newman, Albert Henry. *A Manual of Church History.* Philadelphia: Judson Press, 1903.

Note

1. Robert G. Torbet, *A History of the Baptists,* p. 54.

7
Evangelism Saved England During the Eighteenth and Nineteenth Centuries

Look unto me, and be ye saved, all the ends of the earth (Isa. 45:22).

In the early part of the eighteenth century, western Europe, England, and the American colonies were ripe either for a visitation of the judgment of God or an outpouring of the Spirit of God in revival power. France suffered the former when the horrors of the French Revolution broke out in 1789. England was saved from such a baptism of blood by a baptism of the Holy Spirit in the evangelical revival led by John Wesley and others. Likewise, America was blessed by the Great Awakening and the Revival of 1800.

If the Night Is Cold and Dark, Build a Fire

J. Wesley Bready, in his book *England: Before and After Wesley*, describes the moral bankruptcy and spiritual degeneracy of England before the time of John Wesley and George Whitefield. Deism, a materialistic rationalism which led to stark skepticism, gripped the lives of the leaders in religion and government. The church prelates were blind guides. Business principles were dishonest and sinful. The sinful social order fostered horrible conditions for children, universal gambling, and such unchristian practices as slavery, unspeakable prison conditions, political bribery, and corruption. Court life was unchaste and indecent. Hanging was the penalty for no less than 160 different violations. Labor conditions were beastly. Ghastly drunkenness and vicious sensuality were the accepted order. H. W. V. Temperley, in the *Cambridge Modern History*, observes: "The earlier half of the eighteenth century in England was an age of materialism, a period of dim ideals and expiring hopes: before the middle of the century its character was transformed; there appeared a movement headed by a mighty leader, who brought forth water from the rocks to make a barren land live again." When the night was cold and dark, the Wesleys and Whitefield built fires of evangelism.

The Wesleys and Whitefield:
Evangelism by Spiritual New Birth
and Impassioned Preaching

When some villagers formed a human ladder and rescued five-year-old John Wesley from the second story of the burning rectory in Epworth, England, they pulled the future hope of England and the modern Methodist Church out of the window. They rescued one destined to become one of the noblest and most powerful evangelists of Christian history. Often he said he was a "brand plucked from the burning."

A Foreign Missionary Is Converted

Susannah and Samuel Wesley were parents of nineteen children, of whom John (1703-1791) was the fifteenth. Samuel Wesley was a minister of the Church of England, and his sons John and Charles never left that communion, even though they founded the Methodist Church.

In Oxford University the two brothers belonged to the "Holy Club," whose ascetic and methodical devotion to prayer, fasting, and Bible study gained for them the nickname "Methodists." John and Charles went to Georgia with General Oglethorpe as missionaries to the Indians; but their missionary work was not a success (in spite of the fact that then Wesley insisted on immersion as the only form of baptism!)

En route to Georgia, Wesley met some Germans called Moravian Brethren, who showed rare faith and poise in a dangerous storm. He was deeply impressed. They asked if he knew Christ and if the Spirit bore witness with his spirit that he was a child of God. He couldn't answer. Wesley said, "Thinking to convert the heathen Indians, I came to America; but oh, who shall convert me?" On the return voyage a fellow passenger, Peter Bohler, one of the Moravians, began his influence on Wesley. In London, Bohler and Wesley spent weeks together, after which on May 24, 1738, in Aldersgate Chapel, Wesley heard the reading of Luther's *Preface to Romans,* felt his heart strangely warmed, and was "converted unto God," according to his *Journal.*

John Wesley and George Whitefield Meet

"From the barroom to world evangelism" might have been said of George Whitefield (1714-1770). He hated the bar where he served alcoholic drinks as a boy. He read the Bible at every opportunity. However, life there taught him to live with all classes and to sympathize with the lowest in their sufferings.

After a spectacular conversion, he went to Oxford University. There he met the Wesleys and joined the Holy Club. He became the most popular preacher in England at twenty-five years of age. He drew audiences by the thousands and swayed them like leaves in the breeze. His voice rumbled like thunder and carried like the sound of a rifle. He could be heard by twenty-five thousand people if conditions were right. His oratory was like music. He was more emotional than intellectual, more spiritual than scholarly. His power to draw multitudes has rarely been equaled in Christian history. Whitefield traveled to America a number of times, where his influence in the Great Awakening was colossal throughout all the colonies.

Driven to Field Preaching

After Wesley's conversion, he preached regeneration and the necessity for a spiritual experience. Whitefield was preaching the same doctrines. The Holy Club members were not well received in the cold and stiff atmosphere of the Church of England. The clergymen did not like to be told that they needed to be born again. The Holy Club group were called agitators, rabble rousers, and too emotional. Bishop Butler said to John Wesley, "You have no business here; you are not commissioned to preach in this parish; therefore, I advise you to go hence." Wesley was refused the use of the pulpits.

George Whitefield sympathized with Wesley. The clergy barred him, also, from more and more pulpits, although multitudes awaited to hear him. He became more like a forsaken outcast than a popular evangelist. He was enraged when he was forbidden to preach even in jails. The state church authorities said he preached too much about being born again. He went from London to Bristol, one of the most hostile places in England. There he secured an abandoned race track and began preaching to a group of wild and brutal colliers who lived in degradation, drunkenness, and violence. England was shocked that anyone would preach to such crude and rough people. England was horrified that a man would preach outside church walls! Multitudes swamped his race track. Whitefield sent for John Wesley to help.

Wesley demurred. He himself was an Oxford graduate, scholarly and cultured. However, he went to Bristol, even though he thought it almost a sin for one to be converted outside a church. Whitefield's success in open-air preaching won him over. John Wesley preached the next day to an audience of over three thousand. The Wesleyan Revival was on! It lasted nearly fifty years.

In Labors More Abundant, in Journeyings Often

The travels and sufferings and soul-winning successes of these flaming evangelists were almost like the apostle Paul's. Whitefield went thirteen times from England to America. He preached eighteen thousand times in thirty-four years. Wesley said, "The world is my parish." He preached all over England, Scotland, Ireland, and the American colonies. Wesley preached on the streets, in the fields, in barns, in homes, and even in church burying grounds. In Epworth he preached to vast throngs while he stood on his own father's tomb. Always he pled with men to repent, believe, and begin to live a holy life. The labors of Wesley and Whitefield were prodigious. Wesley studied, preached, taught, wrote, collected money, erected chapels, organized "societies," instructed preachers, and helped in many moral movements for the social welfare of the underprivileged. He traveled in America on horseback many thousands of miles a year amid great hardships. His sister described him as "out of breath, seeking souls."

Faithful unto Death

A few hours before Whitefield's death, at the age of fifty-six, he stood outside his bedroom on the front steps, held a candle in his hands, and preached until the candle burned out. His text was: "For whether we be beside ourselves, it is to God; or whether we be sober, it is for your cause." A few days before Wesley died, at the age of eighty-eight, he preached on the text, "Seek ye the Lord while he may be found." Both preached soul-searching and soul-winning sermons, with constant appeal for a genuine experience of grace in the heart.

Characteristics, Comparisons, and Contrasts

George Whitefield, John Wesley, and Charles Wesley were a magnificent combination of evangelists. Whitefield was the mighty preacher. John Wesley was the indefatigable worker and genius in organizing. Charles Wesley was the composer of some of the noblest hymns in the music of Christendom. John Wesley was a mystic, while Whitefield was a spellbinder. Wesley was scholarly and poised; Whitefield was ecstatic and explosive. Both had a consuming and undying passion to win souls to Christ.

Wesley's work produced more permanent results than Whitefield's. Whitefield left no institution or organization except an orphanage in Georgia, for which he raised money through emotional appeals. However, it is said that Princeton and Dartmouth Colleges were begun through the influence of his preaching. Wesley organized his followers into "societies" for Bible study, devotion, and evangelism. At his death he was at the head of 511 preachers and 120,000 members of his societies. Even though Wesley never left the Church of England, his societies eventually became Methodist churches. It is said that in the eighteenth century no single figure influenced so many minds, no single voice touched so many hearts as Wesley's.

Doctrinally, Wesley and Whitefield did not always agree. The two theological ideas which dominated Wesley were pietism and Arminianism. He was influenced in his conversion by German Pietists and the Moravian Brethren, who revolted against dogmatic, intellectual disputes, and who turned to the principles of Christian experience and personal piety. Wesley followed James Arminius in rejecting Calvin's views on predestination, teaching that salvation is attained by man's free will to seek after God and that it is maintained only when men continue to live a holy life. Arminianism then and now is the outstanding doctrine of the Methodist movement. In contrast, Whitefield preached the doctrines of the irresistible power of God's elective grace in a sinner's heart and the final perseverance of all who once have been regenerated.

There was something virile and vital about the evangelism of Wesley and Whitefield. All the British Isles and the American colonies were moved toward God through their soul-winning power. England was saved from a counterpart of the French Revolution. Someone has said, "While the common people of France were cutting off the heads of their aristocrats, both patricians and plebeians in England were kneeling penitently at the Throne of Grace." Multitudes had been born again.

Charles Haddon Spurgeon:
Evangelism by a Pastor and His Church

Foremost among the divinely planned methods of evangelism is that of a God-called pastor and a church of regenerated, Spirit-filled church members making soul-winning their chief objective and endeavor. In the brilliant constellation of pastor-evangelists of the nineteenth century, the name of Charles Haddon Spurgeon (1834-1892) stands out as the star of the first magnitude.

Magnetic and Mighty Man

Spurgeon had a godly heritage. Both his father and grandfather were Congregational ministers. He joined the Baptists from conviction when he was seventeen and began preaching at eighteen. His larger ministry was spent in South London, a poor section of the city. There his lifelong evangelistic leadership led him to build the largest Baptist church in the world at that time. The influence of that pastor and church went out unto the uttermost parts of the earth.

Spurgeon was intelligent, witty, compassionate, sometimes exuberant, and sometimes wistful, always independent in his thinking, and honestly straightforward in his dealings. He was a winsome man, both in and out of the pulpit. His voice was as clear as a silver bell, his ways as winning as a woman's; and his compassion in calling lost men to repentance was akin to that of the Savior.

He attracted multitudes to hear him, and he saw a great church grow out of those whom he won to Christ. He remembered the names of five thousand or more of his members. His deacons met in the church building every Saturday night for over twenty years in order to pray for their pastor's soul-winning success on the following morning.

A Diligent Student

This mighty preacher was both a prodigious worker and a thorough, meticulous student. His personal library was immense and in constant use. He had a photographic, retentive mind. He never preached unprepared. His preparation of sermons was exacting and thorough. His language was clear, lucid Anglo-Saxon. Someone said: "One never found Spurgeon in chilling fog of lugubrious cant, or simpering out inane formalism. There was no threadbare dignity or parading pomposity about him."

His tremendous mental agility was ascribed mainly to his intense and incessant study of the Bible. He had a shelf in his head for every kind of knowledge, and he knew how to stow it away.

The Premier Pulpiteer

Spurgeon joined the Baptists in 1851 and became pastor at Waterbeach the next year. His powers as a boy preacher became widely known. He was called to London, to the New Park Street Chapel. The chapel was soon overflowing. They enlarged the chapel, using Exeter Hall while building; but neither the hall nor the newly built chapel could hold the masses who came. The church then built the Metropolitan Tabernacle, seating six thousand, where his labors were spent for the rest of his life. This building was demolished by a German bomb during World War II.

His sermons were textual and expository, Calvinistic in doctrine, and unfailingly evangelistic in appeal. Every sermon led to Christ. He preached to a middle class of people the gospel of joy and peace in Christ which the world cannot give. Many a prodigal son or tempted daughter, fresh from the slums and sweatshops around, heard with throbbing heart that all who had accepted Christ as Savior would not perish but have everlasting life. He always made salvation a wonderful supernatural hope, won through the agony and blood of Jesus Christ.

Spurgeon was fearless in his preaching and made no distinctions in fear or for favor of any rank or class or people. His sermons were marked by earnestness, simplicity, liveliness, humor, directness, and appeal to the higher emotions of his hearers. So direct was his preaching that a little girl once whispered out loud, "Mother, is Mr. Spurgeon speaking to me?"

Christ-centered, World Circumference

Spurgeon was called upon to preach all over England and Scotland, which he did with mighty, soul-winning power. Published week by week, his sermons sold literally by the tons. His published sermons comprise some fifty volumes. They were distributed around the world. He edited a monthly magazine, *Sword and Trowel.* He wrote many books, the most outstanding being the *Treasury of David,* an exposition of the book of Psalms in several volumes.

Like so many great evangelists, Mr. Spurgeon built a seminary for preachers, "The Pastors' College." He fostered many charities, such as the Stockwell Orphanage, almshouses, and so forth.

His staunch doctrinal convictions made him the leader of conservative theologians of his time. His sermon on "Baptismal Regeneration" led him into controversy with most of the Evangelical Party, both Anglican and Nonconformist. His stand on modern biblical criticism eventually led him to withdraw from the organized Baptist Union of Great Britain.

This Christ-centered man with dedicated talents, a brilliant and cultivated mind, straightforward character, and an unfailing yearning to win lost souls to Christ was easily the most popular pastor and the most successful pastor-evangelist of the nineteenth century. He exhorted preachers thus: "Build thy studio on Calvary, raise thine observatory to scan by faith the lofty things of nature, take a hermit's cell in the Garden of Gethsemane, and lave thy brow in the waters of Siloam."

Suggestions for Advanced Study

1. What religious convulsions in France during the seventeenth and earlier eighteenth centuries seem to explain why France had no great eighteenth-century revivals like England and America? Why did the 256 sensational preaching missions of Jacques Bridaue (1701-1767), French Jesuit evangelist, not save France from the Revolution, as the Wesleyan revivals saved England?

2. Compare the hymnology of the eighteenth century with evangelis-

tic singing today, both in theology, poetry, and appeal to the heart, the head, or the heels. (Cf. such hymns as Samuel Stennett's "Majestic Sweetness Sits Enthroned," Perronet's "All Hail the Power of Jesus' Name," Watts's "When I Survey the Wondrous Cross," Charles Wesley's "O For a Thousand Tongues to Sing" and "Jesus, Lover of My Soul," and Toplady's "Rock of Ages' Cleft for Me.")

3. Study the results of Spurgeon's evangelistic influence remaining among English Baptists today. How well have his college for ministers, his orphanage, his church, and his many volumes of sermons survived? How great is the influence of Spurgeon on American evangelism and in other English-speaking countries of the world?

References for Further Study

Bailey, Ambrose M. *Evangelism in a Changing World.* New York: Round Table Press, 1936.

Belden, A. D. *George Whitefield, the Awakener.* Nashville: Cokesbury Press, 1931.

Bready, John Wesley. *England: Before and After Wesley.* London: Harper and Brothers, 1938.

Day, Richard E. *The Shadow of the Broad Brim* (Spurgeon). Philadelphia: The Judson Press, 1934.

Miller, Basil. *John Wesley: The World His Parish.* Grand Rapids: Zondervan, 1949.

Spurgeon, C. H. *C. H. Spurgeon's Autobiography.* Ed. by David Otis Fuller. Grand Rapids: Zondervan, 1946.

8

Evangelism Has Been Dominant in American Christianity

O Lord, revive thy work in the midst of the years, in the midst of the years make it known; in wrath remember mercy (Hab. 3:2).

The fuel may differ, but fire is always the same. Men and methods and manifestations in evangelism may differ, but revival fires are the same wherever they may burn. No two revivals are alike, but Pentecostal fire is the essential in them all.

God's promises, based upon his conditions for a revival, are timeless. Today they are strikingly timely. During the depression of 1929-1933, Jesse Jones called some leading financiers to Washington to discuss problems and schemes all day. Eugene Black, then a district governor in the Federal Reserve system, sat silently through the conference. Mr. Jones called Mr. Black forward to give his analysis of the difficulty and his suggestion for possible recovery. That noble Christian man came forward slowly, faced the group, and with confidence reminded them of God's promise: "If my people, which are called by my name, shall humble themselves, and pray, and seek my face, and turn from their wicked ways; then will I hear from heaven, and will forgive their sin, and will heal their land" (2 Chron. 7:14). The solution is the same for the problems of depression or inflation, for peace or war, for rural or city life, for home or school or government. A heaven-born, sin-destroying, soul-saving, Christ-honoring, character-building revival of godliness and righteousness will solve all ills.

Intermittent revivals have blazed across American life from colonial days. America's greatest days of peace and progress have been the days during and immediately following great revivals of religion. Another great revival can come today, a revival adapted to conditions

92

in our own twentieth century, if God's people will meet God's condition for a revival.

The Great Awakening (1734-1770): Evangelism by Sane, Scriptural, Spiritual Preaching

The first great American revival is accurately called the Great Awakening. The breath of God swept over the American colonies through the medium of some of the greatest preaching done since the apostolic days. The Great Awakening fixed evangelism in the foundation of American Christianity even before the Constitution of the United States became the foundation of the American way of life.

Moral and Spiritual Degeneration

The first three decades of the eighteenth century are said to have been the darkest days of moral and spiritual decline since the Dark Ages. Germany was cursed by rationalism and unbelief. France was scourged by stark atheism and sordid sensuality. England had degenerated through belief in deism and through fossilized formalism in the churches. The American colonies had experienced no great religious revivals in a hundred years.

Early colonists came to American shores chiefly to worship God, but second-generation colonists sadly declined in morality and spirituality. Church worship was cold, rigid, and uninviting. State churches prevailed, ruled, and persecuted dissenters. The imported clergymen were often bigoted, lazy, unspiritual, and frequently immoral. Theology was of the unevangelistic, hyper-Calvinistic type. Sermons were long, impractical, and powerless. Churches were full of unregenerate members because of the "Half-way Covenant" adopted in 1662 by the churches in the Massachusetts Colony, which provided that children of good church members be admitted to full church membership without any profession of faith or personal regeneration.

Decline in religion meant disastrous decline in morals. Where atheism and infidelity prevailed, there immorality, lewdness, and drunkenness were rampant. "Witches" were being burned in New England. Purity and fidelity to the marriage vow were sneered at. Funerals were occasions for drunkenness and licentiousness. Politicians and politics grew desperately corrupt. Baptists and Quakers who dissented from the state churches were fined, flogged, imprisoned, and banished.

Giant Preachers in Those Days

Revival fires were kindled by gigantic preaching. The Great Awakening burst into full flame under the preaching of Jonathan Edwards (Congregationalist) simultaneously with the Evangelical Revival under Wesley and Whitefield (Methodists) in England. Theodore J. Frelinghuysen (Dutch Reformed), Gilbert Tennent (Presbyterian), and his brothers were mighty men in this revival. There were scores of others with lesser fame but similar flame. Baptists and Quakers had been so bitterly persecuted that they had not developed sufficient strength to manifest their real evangelistic power in leadership.

Frelinghuysen came to America from Holland in 1720 and began to fan the flames of evangelism in New Jersey, where he became a pastor. Gilbert Tennent was the son of the founder of an evangelistic spirited school of preachers in Pennsylvania called the "Log College." In gratitude to God for restoring him from a serious illness, Tennent devoted his life to evangelism. He was used of God as a mighty soulwinner before Jonathan Edwards began his revivals, and he served many years thereafter with Edwards, Whitefield, and others.

Jonathan Edwards of Northampton (1703-1758)

The great revival actually began under Jonathan Edwards in 1734, while he was pastor of the Congregational church in Northampton, Massachusetts. He was stirred to the depths of his great soul and to the remote reaches of his mighty mentality by the immorality, iniquity, and spiritual lethargy of his people. He combined the powers of his scholarly mind and his fervent heart in a series of thunderous doctrinal sermons. Northampton was shaken like an earthquake and soon was humbled into repentance and faith. When Edwards delivered his famous sermon on "Sinners in the Hands of an Angry God," the people held on to their seats as though fearful of falling into hell.

The fire and fervor of Edwards' preaching spread all over New England, and hundreds of towns experienced revivals. The spiritual awakening lasted a generation.

Dross Purged, Gold Purified

The results were remarkable and revolutionary. The Great Awakening fairly established aggressive evangelism in the American way of religious life. It is estimated that in a generation, about one-seventh of the population of New England was converted; and proportionate results were seen in the other colonies. Christianity was restored to favor. The churches which formerly were practically dead under the weight of an unregenerate membership became alive with spiritual power. Morals were purified and exalted. Missionary and educational activities were set into rapid motion. For the first time in the history of human government, religious liberty was given a fair chance to flourish. Home-life was restored to higher planes.

Baptist Leaders Emerged

With the renewed study of the Bible and with the sweeping evangelistic fervor in the colonies, toward the close of the Great Awakening, Baptists began to flourish for the first time. Two great Baptist leaders, Shubal Stearns and Daniel Marshall, were converted from other denominational beliefs and became aggressive pioneer Baptist evangelists. Stearns won thousands in North Carolina, while Marshall went to Georgia and established the Baptist cause there for the first time. Great evangelists of similar strength appeared in Virginia and throughout all the colonies southward. Even in these colonies they were frequently arrested, imprisoned, fined, and driven out for their preaching.

The Revival of 1800 (1785-1812): Evangelism by Spontaneous Spiritual Upsurge

The next great American revival was a spiritual upsurge manifested all over the land, rather than being centered in great personalities. It is called the Revival of 1800, although it began about 1785 and continued until the time of the War of 1812.

Spiritual Devastation by War

The Revival of 1800 was preceded by King George's War, the French and Indian War, and the Revolutionary War. These wars wrought spiritual havoc with the good results of the Great Awakening. They threatened to wipe Christianity entirely out of the colonies. Soldiers from Europe brought infidelity from France, Deism from England, and Illuminism from Germany. Every fundamental Christian belief was challenged and ridiculed. An age of godless immorality ensued. The manufacture of liquor in America was begun about 1783. Brandy was made from peaches, wine from grapes and grain. A drunken debauch followed. The marriage vow was disregarded, and homelife degenerated. Gambling, vice, and profanity held sway. Infidelity so gripped the schools that no college had a dozen students who would admit being Christians. The churches grew empty and impotent.

Altar Fires Rekindled

The Great Awakening had started with gigantic preaching; the Revival of 1800 started with humble people humbly praying. Some rural Baptists along the James River in Virginia began to pray for a revival. Methodists and Presbyterians joined in. The spirit spread into Georgia. It developed in Maine. Soon it came with Pentecostal power through the South, through the North, and to the frontiers across the mountains in Ohio, Kentucky, and Tennessee.

The victories ranged all the way from a great revival in Yale University under the preaching of its president, Timothy Dwight, to the emotionally violent camp meetings in frontier areas.

Permanent Influences Set in Motion

During this revival the Presbyterians were multiplied by three, the Baptists by four, and the Methodists by five. Homelife was purified. Lawlessness abated. The rank atheism gripping the schools was dealt such a body blow that it dared not raise its ugly head to seriously menace American education for a hundred years.

Some lasting influences set in motion were the establishment of the first denominational paper, the rapid increase of Christian schools, the organization of the first denominational programs for home mission work, the first organization of Sunday School work, and the birth of the foreign mission enterprise in America.

Suggestions for Advanced Study

1. Secure from a library a copy of Jonathan Edwards' sermon "Sinners in the Hands of an Angry God." Compare it with an evangelistic sermon by Spurgeon or Truett, noting theological content, illustrations, personal applications, and appeals to intellect, emotions, and will.

2. Study the history of the "Log College" of the Tennents, showing the educational background of these forerunners of the Great Awakening.

3. Make a list of some nationally known evangelists in America during the latter half of the nineteenth century, comparing their preaching power with that of Edwards, the Tennents, Frelinghuysen, Wesley, and Whitefield of the eighteenth century.

4. Look up records of some effects of the Welsh Revival on American evangelism during the early years of the twentieth century.

The Revival of 1857-1858:
Evangelism by Laymen's Prayer Meetings

Another significant revival in America was that which came in 1857-1858. The year 1858 may have been the most significant year in Christian history since the days of the apostle Paul. Doors were opened that year for millions of people to receive the gospel through missionary witness.

Gold and Ungodliness

The ten years preceding 1858 were years of unprecedented prosperity. Gold was discovered in California. Railroads stretched out like ribbons across the prairies. Bridges spanned the rivers. Industries hummed. Cities sprang up like mushrooms. Morals collapsed. Worldly pleasure was rife, while the churches were prayerless and powerless. But in October 1857 Wall Street collapsed, and a panic or depression paralyzed the financial world.

Adversity and Humility

The country in human helplessness turned to God in prayer. A businessmen's prayer meeting was started on Fulton Street in New York. Other businessmen took it up. The plan spread throughout the land. One man traveled from Omaha to New York and said that he passed through no sizable city without finding a businessmen's prayer meeting. God's people humbled themselves before him.

Prison Doors Unlocked

The prison doors in Jerusalem were unlocked when the people prayed, and Simon Peter went free. When people prayed as they did in 1858, it is no wonder that more than a million people united with churches in the United States that year. It is no wonder that spiritual doors were opened for a billion people. In 1858 Benito Juarez overthrew the tyrannical control of the Roman Church over Mexico, and all Central America was opened to the Christian missionaries. In 1858 David Livingstone began one of his far-reaching tours of Africa, giving millions in that land opportunities to hear the gospel message. In 1858 the British East India Company turned over India to the British government, and in many parts of that country the people were made accessible to Christian missionaries. In 1858 the Treaty of Tientsin was signed, opening up the port cities of China with her more than 400,000,000 people.

Evangelism Through Powerful and Unique Personalities

The virile and vital evangelism such as has prevailed throughout our national history has produced strong and unique personalities who for a time held the attention of the nation. Lack of space prevents our telling of them all. We will mention five, each one of whom had some unique characteristic in his evangelism.

Charles Grandison Finney (1792-1875): Evangelism by Protracted Meetings

Charles G. Finney was born during the year after John Wesley died, and he died when Dwight L. Moody was just emerging as America's foremost evangelist. Mr. Finney experienced a remarkable conversion from reading his Bible while he was a practicing lawyer in Adams, New York. He said he had "enlisted in the service of Christ and had a retainer to plead his cause," and began to win souls immediately.

Finney pioneered in conducting the protracted meeting, which has held so large a place among methods of evangelism until this day. He began his protracted meetings in schoolhouses and small churches, but his phenomenal success soon led him to the greatest cities in the state of New York. His sweeping revival meetings brought him invitations to Philadelphia, many New England cities, and Great Britain. Thousands were converted in his meeting in London, England. During a meeting in Rochester, New York, it was reported that 100,000 people connected themselves with churches. That was a victory which is perhaps unparalleled in the history of local revivals.

After years of arduous and spectacular success in conducting evangelistic meetings, Finney became a pastor in New York. Later he became president of Oberlin College in Ohio in order to train young ministers. His book *Lectures on Revivals* is still a standard work on evangelism.

Dr. Arthur T. Pierson, in a memorial address, mentioned many secrets of Finney's success, such as character, candor, courage, conscientiousness, and Christlike consecration. His preaching was simple, sincere, scriptural, and spiritual. He preached the law with its stern command and the gospel with its amazing grace. He opened his soul entirely to the Spirit of God. The windows of heaven opened to pour out spiritual power upon his soul-winning efforts.

Dwight Lyman Moody (1837-1899): Evangelism Combining Mass Evangelism and Personal Soul-Winning

D. L. Moody set the standard for American evangelism for a generation following the Civil War. He showed the world what God can do through a man who will let him.

Mr. Moody was converted when he was a shoe clerk. He immediately began to do personal soul-winning. He did YMCA work and mission Sunday School work in Chicago before the Civil War. Through personal soul-winning, his chief method, he won some amazing victories for Christ. During the war he won thousands to Christ, both by preaching and by personal work. He developed remarkable power in using the Bible to win souls.

After the war he became a layman evangelist, uniting with Ira D. Sankey as evangelistic song leader. It is claimed that Moody preached to as many as fifty million people before his death. His greatest city-wide campaign was in the summer of 1893 in Chicago, during the World's Columbian Exposition. Moody took about two years to prepare for this. He gathered around him about forty evangelists from America and England, besides the students in the Moody Bible Institute. He trained them in his technique. They preached to multitudes from all over the earth, using theaters, old stores, tents, churches, vacant lots, and street corners. One Sunday afternoon he rented Forepaugh's circus tent, and his preaching drew more people than went to the fairgrounds. Moody made several evangelistic tours to England, Scotland, and France.

American evangelism received from D. L. Moody the technique of the union evangelistic campaign, in which all denominations unite for a series of meetings. He was a genius in evangelistic organization, evangelistic publicity, evangelistic training for personal work, evangelistic financing, the use of evangelistic music, and plain Bible preaching directed straight at the hearts of the multitudes. Eternity alone can calculate the full length of his spiritual influence upon America. One of his admirers said that he "reduced the population of hell by a million souls."

Moody's influence is perpetuated through a school for boys and another school for girls at Northfield, Massachusetts, and the Moody Bible Institute, of Chicago, all of which he organized. His published sermons have been scattered over the entire English-speaking world.

Sam Jones (1847-1906): Evangelism by Humor

Perhaps no other American, except Lincoln and Will Rogers, is remembered for his terse, witty, pungent sayings as much as is Samuel Porter Jones, the "Mountain Evangelist." After Moody's death, Jones was the most popular evangelist in America. His quick wit, his hilarious sarcasm aimed at liquor and other evils, and his use of uncouth sayings to drive home his point all helped to draw vast crowds to hear him. Sam Jones was first a lawyer, but liquor ruined his legal career. After his conversion he fought liquor incessantly. Often he told crowds that he knew a drunkard could quit drinking—for he had done it himself a hundred times. He preached in churches, in town halls, on Chautauqua platforms, before national political meetings, in huge camp meetings, and wherever else he could find an audience. His theology was Arminian, typical of the Methodist denomination. His major emphasis was "quit your meanness," an application of the social aspects of the gospel. His meetings produced high enthusiasm and vast numbers of converts. Methodism today shows the influence of this man.

William A. ("Billy") Sunday (1862-1935): Evangelism as "Big Business"

Moody was followed by many evangelists using city-wide organizations, such as R. A. Torrey, J. Wilbur Chapman, B. Fay Mills, "Gipsy" Smith, Sr., "Gipsy" Smith, Jr., George Stuart, W. E. Biederwolf, and Mordecai F. Ham. It remained for Billy Sunday to carry the methods of the downtown, city-wide, tabernacle-type campaign to such extremes that he lived to see its popularity all but completely die.

Billy Sunday was a converted big-league baseball player. While working in the Chicago YMCA, he assisted J. Wilbur Chapman in some meetings. He was invited to hold a meeting himself, and he went with about a dozen sermons which Mr. Chapman had written out for him. It was commonly believed that thereafter he had "ghost writers" continually working up his sermons. Into these he put his own personality, slang, jokes, acrobatic stunts, and fervent appeals to people to "hit the sawdust trail."

Evangelism became big business. Sunday had a tremendous organization of workers. Homer Rodeheaver was his song leader. He had a business manager, publicity man, pianists, Bible teachers, assistant evangelists, advance agents for organization, tabernacle builders, and a personal attendant to give him massages after preaching. Subscriptions of huge sums of money were necessary to finance one of his campaigns, and large "love offerings" were taken at the end of the meetings. Sunday preached a conservative gospel, attacked both sins and sinners in high places, often kept the people in uproars of laughter, performed amazing acrobatic stunts while preaching, and sometimes appealed to the prejudices of plain people against churches, deacons, rich people, and political leaders.

During his career a million people were claimed as converts; but everyone who went forward in the droves who answered his invitations was claimed as a convert. Doubtless many thousands were truly converted, although hordes went forward merely to shake hands with the famous man. Much good was done in civic morals. His meetings did not always strengthen the local churches. He lived to see the time when he could hardly draw a crowd to fill a good-sized church auditorium. The depression beginning in 1929 made such meetings absolutely impossible. That type of city-wide union meeting was supersensational, hyperemotional, and ultra commercial. It died.

George W. Truett (1867-1944): Evangelism by Denominational Leadership

Not every century has produced even one such evangelist as Augustine, Luther, Wesley, or Spurgeon. The twentieth century, however, produced George W. Truett, a man quite comparable to these. He is modern Christianity's outstanding example of evangelism through denomination leadership.

1. Many Christlike qualities.—George W. Truett was truly a Christlike character. Like Paul, to him to live was Christ. His silver-tongued oratory was like Chrysostom. His powers of voice resembled Whitefield. He had something of the humility of Francis of Assisi. His power to stir the emotions of vast audiences was akin to Tauler. He had a pastor's heart like Spurgeon. His zeal for souls was much like Moody. For a generation he kept the undisputed leadership and held the unrestrained love of the millions of the growing Southern Baptist forces.

Dr. Truett had none of the contentiousness and censoriousness of the sixteenth-century reformers. He provoked none of the emotional excesses of the seventeenth and eighteenth-century evangelism. He had little sympathy with shallow compromise of doctrine like that of the nineteenth century. He never stooped one moment to the cheap sensationalism characteristic of some of his contemporaries.

2. "I will look unto the hills."—George W. Truett was born in the beautiful Blue Ridge Mountains of North Carolina, near the Georgia border. The rugged strength of the mountains was interwoven into his personality with the strength of his Scotch-Irish ancestry. At nineteen he was converted in a small mountain church during a revival meeting. During that meeting he exhorted many others to repent and believe. He soon began to preach. His power was immediate, electric, and overwhelming. A short time after he was graduated from Baylor University in 1897, he accepted the pastorate of the First Baptist Church, Dallas, Texas, where he remained until his death in 1944.

This man of the mountains became the most powerful preacher of the plains. His unrivaled and undisputed leadership of the Baptists in Texas spread to leadership of all Southern Baptists as president of the Southern Baptist Convention, and then of all world Baptists as president of the Baptist World Alliance. He made many trips to many foreign countries. Throngs invariably overflowed the largest auditoriums in America and Europe wherever people knew that Truett would preach. Perhaps the most notable address delivered by any preacher in America during this century was his address on "Baptists and Religious Liberty," delivered Sunday afternoon, May 16, 1920, from the steps of the Capitol in Washington, D.C. More than fifteen thousand people stood in intense summer heat for one hour and fifteen minutes and listened, spellbound.

3. Leading and molding a denomination.—Dr. Truett's leadership of the Baptists of the world began by his maintaining so evangelistic a program in his own church that it became the largest white Baptist church in the world. Although he gave much of his time to raising money for Baptist causes and to official duties in the denominational positions to which he was elected, he found time to hold revival meetings in city-wide campaigns, to preach to cowboys of West Texas, to fill extensive engagements in colleges, to hold camp meetings in his native mountains, and to travel extensively and preach continually on the mission fields of Europe and South America.

No one this side of eternity can measure the influence of this man of God in leading Southern Baptists to become the most evangelistic and the fastest-growing denominational group in the nation. He influenced Southern Baptist preachers to stick to the Bible and to preach the fundamental doctrines of grace. He influenced them to avoid alliance with any interdenominational groups which might weaken or destroy their doctrinal convictions. The throb of his heart in love for souls and the magic appeal of his remarkable voice kept Baptists devoted to him for nearly half a century.

Suggestions for Advanced Study

1. Compare the operation of the Holy Spirit upon the people in Finney's city-wide campaigns, like that in Rochester, with the Spirit's power on Moody's great Chicago campaign.

2. Make a list of some great American evangelists from the Great Awakening to today, who have gone into education either wholly or for part time during their latter days. Explain.

3. Compare the present-day plan of simultaneous evangelistic campaigns in cities, associations, or much wider areas with the campaigns of the nineteenth century.

4. Dare to predict the trend which American evangelism will take during the first half of the twenty-first century.

References for Further Study

Beardsley, Frank G. *A History of American Revivals.* Cincinnati: Standard Press, 1934.

Day, R. E. *A Man of Like Passions* (Finney). Grand Rapids: Zondervan, 1942.

_____. *Bush Aglow* (Moody). Philadelphia: Judson Press, 1936.

Lacy, B. R., Jr. *Revivals in the Midst of the Years.* Richmond, Virginia: John Knox Press, 1943.

Muncy, W. L., Jr. *History of Evangelism in the United States.* Kansas City, Central Seminary Press, 1945.

Rodeheaver, Homer. *Twenty Years with Billy Sunday.* Nashville: Cokesbury Press, 1936.

Strickland, Arthur B. *The Great American Revival.* Cincinnati: Standard Press, 1934.

Sweet, W. W. *Revivalism in America.* New York: Charles Scribners' Sons, 1944.

Winslow, Ola E. *Jonathan Edwards.* New York: The Macmillan Company, 1941.

Methods and Techniques in Accomplishing Christ's Imperative Commission

9

A Perennial Program of Evangelism for a Church

And the Lord added to the church daily such as should be saved (Acts 2:47).

Christ's churches are in the midst of his second great campaign of world evangelism. The first great campaign was during the first three centuries A.D., between Pentecost and the unhappy union of church and state under Constantine. The widespread knowledge of the Greek language was the medium of communication. Roman roads and Roman law made transportation and world contacts possible. The Jews in the Dispersion, with their worship of one God, gave the opportunity of approach to the people.

The second world campaign for Christ began in 1793 when William Carey went from England to India as a Baptist missionary. He was soon followed by Luther Rice and Adoniram Judson from America.

The former possibilities of communication through the Greek language are infinitely surpassed by the English language today. Communication by the printing press, television, radio, and communications satellite surpasses comprehension. Transportation possibilities in the first century, under Roman control, are infinitely surpassed today by the trains, boats, and jet travel. The advantages of the Jewish dispersion were nothing as compared with the present-day spread of the Christian faith throughout all nations of the world. The Bible has been translated into more than 1,600 languages and dialects, and more than 410,000,000 copies in whole or part are distributed every year.

This second campaign is over 180 years old, and not half won. Only about 23 percent of the people of the world are even nominal Christians. Because of increasing population, there are more unsaved people in the United States today than there were when the Declaration of

Independence was signed or at the close of the Civil War.

In this campaign for Christ the church is the divinely ordained organization for the promotion of the kingdom of heaven. Jesus said, "Thou art Peter, and upon this rock I will build my church; and the gates of hell shall not prevail against it. And I will give unto thee the keys of the kingdom of heaven" (Matt. 16:18-19). Jesus definitely declared that evangelism in its broadest sense—using the keys of the kingdom of heaven—is the imperative and supreme task of the church.

The test of the value of a church in the campaign for Christ is twofold: first, the number of people that it wins to Christ; and, second, the kind of life it develops in these people. Its value is measured both in quantity and in quality. It is folly and it means failure to leave out either phase of the church's work. Some have said, "I am not concerned about numbers; I am concerned about making good Christians of those that we have." That is as lopsided as to say: "I am not concerned about the quality; I am concerned about large numbers." Christ's imperative commission charges his followers not only to make disciples, but also to teach all things whatsoever he commanded.

Maintaining a Perennial Program for a Church

The task of winning men to Christ and of building Christlike character in them should not be done spasmodically. It is a perennial program of evangelism to which the head of the church commissions his people.

A Perennial Revival

Years ago the prayer of the people was that the churches would experience continuous revival. That prayer is being answered in scores of churches. The only magic about a perennial revival seems to be the matter of perennial penitence, perennial prayer, perennial planning, perennial personal work, and perennial preaching, because of a perennial passion for souls. The Holy Spirit honors such a church life.

Month-by-Month Plans

Great programs do not just happen. Great results are not accidental. A hit-and-miss plan misses more often than it hits. The burden of this chapter is to encourage all pastors and church leaders to plan ahead a full program of evangelism, with at least one great soul-winning effort each month.

If winning others to Christ is the supreme and primary duty of the church, surely at least one week of every month should be devoted to some special evangelistic effort.

By All Means

Beware of the evangelist who has found "the only way" to win people! No one way will win all. Perhaps all means will not win some. The churches, like Paul, must "become all things to all men" that by all means some may be won.

The chart on page 110 gives many suggestions for evangelistic possibilities in a perennial program. It contains suggestions for mass evangelism, for personal evangelism, and for evangelism in the home.

Planning a Church's Perennial Program

A revival meeting is like a mountain peak; a perennial program for a church is like a high plateau. The success of the perennial program of evangelism for a church will depend in a large measure, humanly speaking, upon how the pastor plans ahead for a perennial month-by-month program of evangelism in the church and upon the promotion of the plan.

There is no limit to the possibilities of a church that will adopt a long-range plan of evangelism for an entire year ahead.

Suggestions for Advanced Study

1. From the various commentaries at your command, compare the various interpretations of the terms "on this rock" and "the keys of the kingdom" found in Matthew 16:18-19. How are these terms related to evangelism?

2. Secure the yearbooks or outlined annual programs of several churches, large and small, to see the proportionate prominence of evangelism which is given in them.

3. Check the last ten annual reports of your church and draw a graph on a chart showing the high and low years of evangelism as indicated by the baptisms. Explain the variations.

EVANGELISTIC CALENDAR (Fill in from suggestions on the right	POSSIBILITIES FOR EVANGELISM MONTH BY MONTH
JANUARY	1. Religious census or survey 2. Visitation program for unsaved and unaffiliated
FEBRUARY	3. Program for reenlistment of inactive church members 4. A month's preparation for evangelistic meetings
MARCH	5. A revival meeting 6. Plans for conservation of new church members
APRIL	7. A Vacation Bible School with soul-winning plans for older pupils
MAY	8. Evangelism outside the church, either a preaching mission, radio revival, street preaching, brush arbor meeting, or the establishment of a mission
JUNE	9. Program for winning the lost already enrolled in Sunday School 10. Soul-winning plans during the Christmas season
JULY	11. Study courses in personal soul-winning
AUGUST	12. Associational evangelism cooperating with associational leader of evangelism 13. Enlargement campaign in Church Training and Sunday School
SEPTEMBER	14. Special evangelistic efforts planned, fostered, and promoted by the Brotherhood, the Woman's Missionary Union, and the Church Training
OCTOBER	15. A youth revival 16. Organization of a pastor's soul-winning group who meet the pastor once each week for prayer, reports, and assignments in soul-winning
NOVEMBER	17. Effort at home evangelism through rebuilding family altars and refilling family pews
DECEMBER	18. Distribution of evangelistic tracts

4. Write the Department of Statistics of your denomination for statistics about churches having great baptismal records in recent years. Seek to explain these successful programs.

Utilizing the Church Organizations

A necessary approach toward evangelizing the unchurched is to revitalize and utilize the various church organizations. Let us suggest some practical methods for using these organizations in evangelistic programs.

The Sunday School

The Sunday School has the best potential organization for evangelism to be found in the church life. It brings more lost people into the church's activities and under the church's influence than any other organization. Its organization and its personnel can be used in every type of program suggested in this book.

1. The monthly director's meeting and the weekly teachers' meeting can be used by soul-winning leaders for creating the spirit of winning others to Christ. Have a report from the teachers at each teachers' meeting concerning soul-winning successes.

2. Teachers who have character, courage, and constant concern can win lost pupils. All lost persons should be sought for the class. It is not always a matter for boasting that all the class members are Christians, when others should be found. Every class should have lost persons on roll and in attendance.

3. One month each year can be set aside by the pastor for giving an evangelistic talk and appeal to the children (ages 9-12) on the first Sunday, to the youth (ages 13-17) on the second Sunday, to the college and career age (ages 17-24) on the third Sunday, and to the adults on the fourth Sunday.

4. An enlargement campaign or the action program will get more of the lost people into the school.

5. Definite soul-winning efforts should be made at promotion time.

6. Winning lost parents on Baby Day is a victorious plan.

7. During the evangelistic meetings, the Sunday School classes and departments can convene each night thirty minutes before the preach-

ing hour for prayer, decision hour, and assignment of names for soul-winning.

8. Study courses in personal soul-winning are always in order.

9. Visitation for soul-winning is vitally necessary.

10. Teachers may always take their pupils or send them to the pastor for conferences about salvation.

Church Training

If the supreme objective of the Church Training is training in Christian service, surely the members should not stop short of the highest possible service, personal soul-winning. There are many things which members of this organization can do in a church's perennial program of evangelism.

1. They can win souls during the revival meeting and at all other times.

2. They can teach and attend classes in soul-winning.

3. They can conduct cottage prayer meetings, street meetings, jail services, and so forth.

4. They can go with the pastor into the associations to conduct evangelistic services in churches and mission stations.

5. They can conserve, assimilate, indoctrinate, and enlist in service all those who come into the church during the year. Orientation classes for new church members should be conducted periodically by the Church Training, and especially after every revival meeting.

The Woman's Missionary Union

Missions means soul-winning. The program of the Woman's Missionary Society and its auxiliaries is evangelism in an extensive form.

1. The spirit of missions should make the Woman's Missionary Union members concerned for souls and active in soul-winning.

2. Soul-winning should be made the first item in the personal service department.

3. The young people's organizations should be used for soul-winning.

4. Those who volunteer for mission work at home or abroad should demonstrate their fitness by winning souls at home.

5. The establishment of family altars in the homes is one of the

great and needy evangelistic fields in which the missionary society can work most efficiently.

The Brotherhood

One of the objectives of the Brotherhood is "a greater emphasis upon personal evangelism." They may reach this objective in some of the following ways.

1. They can make soul-winning a prominent topic in the meetings with prayers, reports, and assignments to the members.

2. They can encourage capable laymen to do lay preaching, going both as individuals and in groups to other churches in the association, to meetings in unchurched communities, and to meetings in the public parks or on the streets.

3. They can organize personal workers' groups to coooperate with the pastor in getting the lost to Sunday night services and leading them there to accept Christ.

4. They can volunteer to the pastor and Sunday School director to send laymen evangelists into the Sunday School departments on the proper occasions.

5. They can conduct an annual Layman's Day in the church, telling personal conversion experiences and relating experiences in soul-winning.

6. They can promote evangelistic programs over radio and television.

Inside Church Revival

A pastor of a large church enlisted his whole church in evangelism during a campaign of four weeks, including five Sundays. He found that there were at least 400 who were prospects for church membership, either by transfer of letter or by profession of faith on the rolls of the Sunday School. The youth of the church conducted a revival meeting for the first week, the women for the second week, the laymen for the third week, and the entire membership for the fourth week. All the members were utilized, and all methods of evangelism were used. At the end of the period exactly 401 persons had united with that church. The entire membership had been splendidly revived and richly blessed.

Suggestions for Advanced Study

1. Check your Sunday School to see how nearly the following figures are true: 75 percent of the children, 45 percent of the youth, 15 percent of the college and career, and 8 percent of the adults attending Sunday School are evangelistic possibilities.

2. On a mimeographed card take a poll of your church leaders to see which of the following persons was most influential in leading them to Christ: pastor? deacon? visiting evangelist? Sunday School teacher? friend? mother? father? some other relative? someone not designated here? Draw some deductions about who is doing the soul-winning in your church.

3. Outline how a miniature Sunday School session can be held during evangelistic services, Monday through Friday nights, thirty minutes before the preaching hour; and tell what can be done in this way toward finding and winning the lost.

Conducting a Revival Meeting

Since the days of Charles G. Finney, the use of mass evangelism in special seasons of revival meetings has been integral in the program of evangelical churches in America. In a vast number of churches, a majority of the members first made a profession of their faith and united with the church during a revival meeting. The technique for revival meetings is becoming more and more extensive.

It is tragic that some churches do not baptize one person during an entire year. Some churches hold revival meetings without results. Great battles are sometimes lost or won on the day before. Certain things should always be done if a church is to have a successful revival. Adequate advance preparation, day-by-day promotion after the revival begins, and then, of course, effective gospel preaching—all are essential.

Preparation

1. The church membership should be organized into committees such as publicity, visitation, religious census, entertainment, decorations, transportation, music, ushers, finances, and soul-winning.

2. The spiritual life of the church people must be deepened. Plan a dedication service for committee members and church officers to

encourage them in soul-winning. There must also be prayer in groups, in cottage prayer meetings, in church organizations, and in private devotions.

3. The possibilities for soul-winning must be determined through a census or survey.

4. Soul-winning passion must be developed through inspiration and training. Preparation programs in Sunday School departments, Church Training, Woman's Missionary Union, and Brotherhood will help in every way. Also, a study course in personal soul-winning can inspire many to witness to others for Christ.

5. A sense of expectancy must be disseminated in the church through publicity and personal visitation. Wide publicity through announcements, newspapers, radio, window cards, and posters is needed. The signing of cards by church members, promising to attend the evening services of the meeting unless providentially hindered, will help the attendance. Letters of invitation written by the pastor to all unaffiliated prospects and to many unsaved people, inviting them to the services, can be used of the Holy Spirit in reaching many. Visitation to the unsaved and unenlisted is both scriptural and successful. A careful study of the chapter on "Two-and-Two Visitation Evangelism" should be made. Its principles, put into action, usually multiply greatly the number of souls won to Christ who would not be won otherwise. This plan of soul-winning can be carried out with victorious success along with the preaching services each evening.

Promotion

1. If the church has a visiting evangelist, the pastor should spend his time during a meeting in unceasing prayer and personal work.

2. A daily report of some new feature of the meeting should be made to the papers, if there is a daily paper. The radio is often available and always valuable. In smaller cities, window cards in the stores are helpful; stickers for the car bumpers are useful; and visitation groups are most effective.

One pastor installed a private telephone in the church for two weeks, and had every member of the church called in regard to his attendance and service in the meeting.

3. It is good for the pastor and people to conduct as many extension

meetings outside the church as possible. A daily radio program is excellent. Shop and factory meetings, dignified and spiritual street services, talks in school chapels, addresses to service clubs, and other meetings, wherever possible, are helpful.

4. The pastor can find a splendid opportunity to develop soul-winners by promoting a two-and-two visitation program each evening or by meeting his soul-winners' group thirty minutes before the preaching hour for prayer, reports, and assignments.

5. A service for children on Saturday morning at the end of the week is effective preparation for Sunday.

6. The Sunday School on Sunday at the end of the first week is a glorious time for soul-winning. Many different methods can be adopted.

7. The pastor should establish a quiet place and appropriate time when the members can have private conferences with the visiting evangelist. The pastor and people can guide hard cases to the evangelist for interviews. The visiting evangelist should be protected from those who have no real need of his time.

8. As many prayer meetings as possible should be held.

Preaching

Here one should be reminded of Pentecost's plan of preparation in prayer, promotion in personal soul-winning, and then the preaching of the gospel of grace to lost souls. Preparation and promotion are necessary, but preliminary preaching by God-called men is the *sine qua non* of a far-reaching, epoch-making revival. Preachers come and go, and the popularity of evangelistic preaching may wax and wane; but great preaching will never lose its power to draw and to win. "For the preaching of the cross is to them that perish foolishness; but unto us which are saved it is the power of God. It pleased God by the foolishness of preaching to save them that believe" (1 Cor. 1:18,21).

In spite of the busy tension of present-day life, men yet will stop to hear the impassioned pleas of a burning heart, whether the preacher be a courtier like Isaiah or a rustic like Amos or Micah. Men's hearts yet may be melted by the loving appeals of a modern Hosea or by the sobbing prophecies of a present-day Jeremiah. Men today will be intrigued by the prophetic truths and spiritual visions of preachers like Daniel or Ezekiel. Men will be arrested and gripped by forthright and rugged preaching like that of John the Baptist in the wilderness or that of Paul on Athens' Acropolis. Preachers of truth are yet being heard gladly by the multiplied thousands.

Evangelistic preaching in a changing world order must face conditions realistically and meet modern life with a message adequate for the age. There are certain conditions and characteristics which must be recognized.

1. New competition.—The automobile, athletics, the movies, and television are in direct competition with preaching in the claim upon the time of the people. These competitors furnish the tang of challenge to the preacher who feels that he has in Christ the answer for the problems of a worldly, wicked, war-torn, and weary humanity. The preacher of the gospel has what none of his competitors can furnish to satisfy the hearts of men. Men want forgiveness for their sins and victory over their temptations. They strive for an incentive and a method of happy living, and they yearn for the assurance of a heavenly life beyond the grave. Victorious is the evangelist who can grip the hearts of men with his message, assuring them that all these can be found in the Lord Jesus Christ.

2. New approach.—Because of changing conditions, the approach of evangelistic preaching has radically changed from that of the decade 1920-1930. Then evangelistic preaching was ultracommercial, hyper-emotional, and supersensational. Then evangelists frequently drew crowds who had itching ears to hear vituperative attacks upon the clergy, the deacons, and other church members. Such evangelism left little deposit of strength or spirituality in the churches, but, rather, left grave problems for churches to solve. Today the evangelistic preaching that wins is of a saner sort, of a more spiritual import, and of a more scriptural content.

3. New demands.—If evangelistic preaching reaches the leaders of our present-day life, it must meet the intellectual as well as the spiritual demands of the times. True science and genuine Christianity are joining forces today against enemies common to both realms of thinking. Science has revealed hitherto unknown truths and loosed hitherto unknown powers of destruction which have driven the scientists to seek through the spiritual forces of Christianity a way of safety for civilization. From

Christianity the scientists must take the power and wisdom of the Spirit of God; from science the Christians must take the method of searching, experimenting, and adopting only known truth. Evangelists today must *know* something as well as *feel* something. God never puts a premium on an empty brain just because one has a full heart. Paul prayed that his converts should "be filled with the knowledge of his will in all wisdom and spiritual understanding" (Col. 1:9).

4. New emphasis.—Evangelistic preaching today is emphasizing more and more of the social teachings of the Master. Evangelists are seeing that if evangelism lasts, it must produce both character that is more Christlike and social righteousness that is more Christian. Someone has said, *"If evangelism ends at regeneration, it ends."* To this another replied, *"If evangelism does not begin at regeneration, it never begins."* It is not a case of *either* the personal or the social; *both* personal and social applications of the message of Jesus are vitally necessary today.

5. New doctrinal content.—Evangelistic preaching that builds abiding results must be based on doctrine as well as exhortation. The four most influential evangelistic preachers in Christian history, Paul, Augustine, Luther, and Wesley, were mighty preachers of doctrine. Their preaching was built around convictions which were heart deep and soul felt. A sin-sick soul needs a "thus saith the Lord."

The great doctrines proclaimed by our Lord Jesus Christ were based on the kingdom of God, or, as Matthew called it, the kingdom of heaven. Jesus preached mightily on such doctrines as the fatherhood of God, the reality of the Holy Spirit, sin, forgiveness, repentance, faith, regeneration, sanctification, brotherhood, assurance, heaven, and hell. Such doctrines are vital for constructive evangelistic preaching today. All doctrine without polish, illustrations, and warmhearted exhortation would be like a skeleton; all exhortation and illustration without doctrine would be like a jellyfish.

Suggestions for Advanced Study

1. Take a poll in your church to see how many people made a decision for Christ in special revival meetings and how many at other

times. Segregate children, youth, college and career, and adults to see if the percentages agree or disagree. Draw deductions about trends in mass evangelism.

2. From a set of six or more books of evangelistic sermons of recent date, check how many are topical, how many are textual, and how many are expository sermons. See what doctrines are preached, what percentage of material is given to social questions, and how much is pure exhortation.

References for Further Study

Barnette, Jasper N. *The Place of the Sunday School in Evangelism.* Nashville: Broadman Press, 1945.

Caldwell, Max L., comp. *Positive Evangelism Through the Sunday School.* Nashville: Convention Press, 1978.

Dobbins, Gaines S. *Good News to Change Lives.* Nashville: Broadman Press, 1976.

Drummond, Lewis A. *Leading Your Church in Evangelism.* Nashville: Broadman Press, 1975.

Feather, R. Othal. *Outreach Evangelism Through the Sunday School.* Nashville: Convention Press, 1972.

Lindgren, Alvin J. *Foundations for Purposeful Church Administration.* Nashville: Abingdon Press, 1965.

Shinn, Roger L. *The Educational Mission of Our Church.* Philadelphia: United Church Press, 1962.

Young, J. Terry. *The Church—Alive and Growing!* Nashville: Broadman Press, 1978.

10
Evangelism in Season and Out of Season

Preach the word; be instant in season, out of season; reprove, rebuke, exhort with all longsuffering and doctrine. But watch thou in all things, endure afflictions, do the work of an evangelist, make full proof of thy ministry (2 Tim. 4:2,5).

To fulfill Christ's imperative commission requires a continuous effort to make disciples. The participle "go" in Matthew 28:19 is subservient to "make disciples." Jesus told the disciples that wherever they went, they would make disciples. The task of making disciples requires more than a sporadic effort and more than a limited technique. There must be manifold approaches to manifold types of personalities. There must be many efforts and many approaches outside the regular Sunday services. Many people of the world will not come to the organizations and worship services of the local church. The Lord commanded the disciples, "Go ye."

Paul instructed Timothy to preach the word "in season" and "out of season." Paul wanted Timothy to take every possible opportunity to present the gospel to a lost world. There is no "open" or "closed" season for presenting the gospel. Disciples are not shooting ducks or deer. They are telling people the wonderful words of life. If the season seems "closed" because of one reason, then "open" it, using godly wisdom in making the opportunity. Making disciples does not belong to one methodology or technique. Christians can consider numerous diversified possibilities to present the gospel to the world. There is no closed season, and there are numerous methodologies to utilize for evangelism.

120

Utilizing Various Opportunities

Churches cannot do the best job in evangelism by restricting the presentation of the gospel within the four walls of the church buildings. Churches will need to utilize the four walls of the church building each week, but the people of God can seize numerous other kinds of opportunities. Outsiders can be reached by diverse methods. Churches must promote programs outside the walls of its building.

Method of the Master

Jesus utilized various methods to invite people to the kingdom of heaven. He used the weekly attendance at the synagogue or Temple. Within the order of the synagogue and the Temple worship, he evangelized. But Jesus spent much time outside the traditional settings. He spoke to groups and to individuals on mountains, by wells, and on the roadside. Jesus possessed the unique ability to reach people where they lived. Jesus encountered people in their life setting and related the kingdom of God to their deepest needs for living.

A Variety of Approaches

Taking a cue from the Master's methods, Christians have used daring, innovative, and expansive approaches in presenting the gospel. Numerous strategies and approaches have been effective in reaching people for Jesus Christ. Throughout human history God has used numerous media to deliver his message. The Lord used plagues, rainbows, manna, and other means to get his message across. In the Old Testament an inspired statement is recorded as coming from the mouth of an ass (Num. 22:28). In Amos he roared like a lion; in Daniel he wrote with human fingers. Dreams played key roles in both Testaments by conveying the divine message. The letter to the Hebrews describes "diverse manners," many media, through which God spoke to humanity. Christians can use varied approaches to go to the world with the gospel.

1. Media.—Christians can use the media of radio and television to present the gospel of Christ to those outside the church. Millions of people have heard the gospel by these twentieth-century inventions.

The gospel is able to penetrate the lives of people who would not be attracted to a worship service in a church building. With satellite communication, program packaging, home video, and dozens of other television innovations, the gospel can be presented effectively with this medium. Few people in the world are without some type of radio. Within a few hours people all over the world can hear the news of a revolution in the Middle East.

2. *Printed materials.*—Another way the Christian can get outside the walls of the church building with the gospel is with reading material. The printed page offers a means of confronting the world with the gospel. Some people will read when they will not attend a crusade or a worship service to hear a gospel sermon. Books, tracts, Bibles, New Testaments, portions of Scripture, magazines, and other reading material have been used to present the gospel. Thousands of people have entered the kingdom in the twentieth century through such tracts as "How to Have a Full and Meaningful Life," "Four Spiritual Laws," "Steps to Peace with God," and numerous others. In the last fifty years books such as Billy Graham's *Peace with God,* C. S. Lewis' *Mere Christianity,* and Charles Colson's *Born Again* have been read by people searching for answers to the meaning of life. The American Bible Society and other organizations have circulated the Scriptures. People of many languages have been given a copy of the Bible. Many have accepted Christ by reading the Word of God.

3. *Mass evangelism.*—Throughout history, mass evangelism has been an effective means of getting the gospel outside the walls of the church building. John Wesley, George Whitefield, Charles G. Finney, Dwight L. Moody, R. A. Torrey, Billy Sunday, and Billy Graham represent some great personalities associated with mass evangelism. Churches have cooperated to promote city-wide crusades. This method of evangelism arrests the attention of a large area. People will come to such a service when they will not attend a church service.

Churches should attempt to conduct a crusade in an open-air stadium or in an enclosed coliseum. Several churches could work together to conduct a crusade. Mass evangelism opens the door to more personal forms of evangelism and to an individual penetration of Bible teaching. During mass crusades, believers and churches are often more flexible and willing to use other forms of evangelism.

Churches can adopt the model of Jesus by proclaiming the words of the kingdom and by performing deeds of mercy for the kingdom. Jesus' ministry was one of preaching the gospel, but it was a caring ministry—a tender and loving identification with the impoverished, the bruised, the captives, the blind, the broken victims.

Churches should send people to the hospitals, jails, convalescent homes, orphanages, and other social service institutions. Many will be presented the gospel when Christians offer a cup of cold water in the name of Jesus Christ. There are so many people hungering and thirsting and waiting to be found.

4. *Special Bible studies.*—Christians can promote Bible study outside the program of the church. The youth on high school and college campuses will respond to informal group Bible studies. Some churches sponsor Bible studies for businessmen in hotels or in conference rooms at business places. Ladies' groups sometimes meet in homes for neighborhood Bible studies. Families could cluster in a group for a study of God's Word. Whenever a sane and capable Bible teacher opens the treasures of Scripture, people will be exposed to the truths of the gospel.

The apostle Paul sought every possible means to present Christ. To reach the Jew, he became as a Jew. To those living under the strict legalism of the law, he identified, though he did not come under the law. In order to reach those outside the law, he became as one outside the law. Paul said, "I am made all things to all men, that I might by all means save some. And this I do for the gospel's sake, that I might be a partaker thereof with you" (1 Cor. 9:22-23). Disciples of the twentieth century cannot expect to make as many disciples by remaining in narrow structures. We, too, must become all things to all men to save some.

Practicing Evangelism on Special Occasions

Quite often Christians put the task of evangelism in a category all of its own. They have the mistaken notion that there is evangelism, and then there are the other endeavors of the church. Making disciples should be practiced in season and out of season. There are times throughout the year when the spirit of the occasion could be an evangelistic opportunity.

Special Days and Seasons

The passing of time has an interesting influence upon people. Various days and seasons could provide openings to think about the gospel.

1. New year.—New Year's Day is especially fitted for appeals to the lost to begin the new life in Christ. This is a time when many think of new beginnings and of resolutions. Christians should present Christ as the meaning, purpose, and power for the right kind of life.

2. Christian home evangelism.—In the springtime and early summer, attention is focused on family living. Mother's Day, Father's Day, and numerous weddings offer an opportunity to explain how Christ can change family living. Individuals who seek to be better mates in their marriages could find help in Christ. Parents and children could strengthen their mutual relationships by a relationship to the Lord.

Christian Home Emphasis is a glorious time for emphasizing family religion, for establishing family worship, and for encouraging the occupancy of family pews. A printed card (see p. 125) could be distributed to all families of the church. A magnificent month of emphasis upon religion in the family could be worked out from it.

3. Easter.—The world seeks an answer for life and for death. The celebration of the resurrection of Jesus Christ affords an opportunity to give a reason for living and a hope for dying.

4. Christmas.—Surely the Christmas season is an advantageous time for winning others to Christ. December is a good time to emphasize the real meaning of Christmas. Attractive words such as peace, joy, and goodwill, could attract an unhappy and troubled world. The Christian gospel speaks of a relationship which brings peace and the ability to have goodwill toward others. The church should utilize the Christmas season to the fullest for evangelistic efforts.

5. National holidays.—The evangelistic church can use Labor Day, Thanksgiving, Independence Day, and Memorial Day. For example, one church held a conference on "Death and Destiny" and gave the Christian perspective on death on the weekend before Memorial Day. Independence Day affords an excellent opportunity to present the Christian ethic regarding citizenship.

Family Religion Month

Realizing our holy responsibilities and heavenly opportunities as parents in maintaining a Christian home, we happily and prayerfully purpose to endeavor to carry out the items checked below:

_____1. We will do our human best, under the Holy Spirit, to lead to Christ the following members of our family who are of conversion age but not Christians:

Name _____ Age _____

Name _____ Age _____

Name _____ Age _____

_____2. We will maintain a family devotion, having daily Bible reading and prayer in our family circle.

_____3. We will invite the pastor to dedicate our new home to God.

_____4. We will invite the pastor to our home for a service in which we wish to dedicate ourselves to the task of rearing our baby in the fear and nurture and admonition of the Lord.

_____5. We will endeavor to attend the special "Family Day" service announced by the pastor, sitting together as a family in our accustomed pew.

_____6. We will make the worship service of the church henceforth a "preferred item" in the budget of our time.

Signature:

Father _____

Mother _____

Unusual Experiences

Various crisis experiences which people share could afford evangelistic opportunities. Sane evangelism does not disturb them more than they are already disturbed, but it shares the gospel as a vital means of helping.

1. Funerals.—Unsaved people are often led to Christ at the time of funerals, when their hearts are tender. A funeral sermon should not necessarily have an evangelistic appeal, but the Word from the Bible will have some relationship to the news about Christ. The personal ministry or visit in the home after the funeral could present evangelistic possibilities.

2. Marriages.—Marriages offer a good time for ministry. Before the pastor performs a wedding, he could share the Christian gospel and how a home could be much happier when both members are Christians.

3. Sickness.—Visits to lost people during a time of sickness open the minds of the lost to the kind words of a friendly visitor. A pastor, a Christian physician, a Christian nurse, and church visitors have unusual soul-winning opportunities during or after a sickroom visit.

4. Other crises.—Numerous crises come to the lives of people: the loss of a job, the birth of a child, the handicap of a child, the rebellion of a son or daughter, the move to a new location, the breakup of a home, a financial loss, or numerous other crises. Caring for people during these types of crises can open the door for presentation of the gospel.

Living As Christ's Disciples in Daily Living

The task of making disciples is never out of season. Evangelism must be understood and evaluated in the context of the Great Commission. Most Christians interpret a twofold commission from Christ's words. They see that Jesus said to evangelize and to disciple (which means to baptize converts and teach them). This assumes a chronological sequence with evangelism first followed by discipling. Christ intended those words as a solid single command rather than a dualistic one. His primary object in the command is "make disciples." The one verb, "make disciples" *(matheteusate),* is the imperative, while the others are verb forms which help the task of making disciples. See Karl Barth, *Church Dogmatics,* vol. 4, p. 860.

The task of evangelism does not belong to a select few within the church. It is the joyful responsibility of every believer. Every Christian is a disciple. If the church could make every believer aware that he is a witness each day, the task of evangelism would be a twenty-four-hour per day activity of every Christian. Nothing would multiply the

total of evangelism any more than every Christian living every day
the life-style of Christ and sharing Christ with others as a natural
part of living.

Implied Evangelism

One of the most difficult tasks for church leaders is to get every
believer to recognize that he is a witness. A Christian, simply defined,
is one who has decided personally to follow Jesus. He or she is considered
a disciple. Consequently, the matter of being a witness is implied in
the act of becoming a disciple. Somewhere in the development of
the church, the mistaken notion arose that the church has only a
select number of "witnesses." The task of evangelizing has been rele-
gated in this thinking to the professional church leaders and to a few
"super Christians" in the church. One does not have to read far in
the New Testament to see that every person who decided to follow
Jesus became a witness. Actually a witness is one who has had an
experience. When people encountered the historical Jesus, they became
a witness of the experience. A Samaritan woman shared her experience
with Christ to the entire community. Lepers, paralytics, and demon-
possessed people went joyfully to declare what Christ had done. When
Jesus healed the demon-possessed man who lived in the tombs, the
Lord said, "Go home to thy friends, and tell them how great things
the Lord hath done for thee, and hath had compassion on thee" (Mark
9:19-20). That was a quick study course on evangelism. The healed
man "departed, and began to proclaim in Decapolis how great things
Jesus had done for him." (Cf. Mark 5:1-20.) The man became a witness
as soon as something happened to him.

The moment that any person becomes a Christian is the time he
also becomes a witness. If a church has a membership of five hundred
believers, they have five hundred people who are witnesses of Christ's
saving power. The responsibility of a local church is to penetrate the
community with these Christian witnesses. The local church is a living
body of interacting parts through which the kingdom of God reaches
out each day. Every member is a personal evangelist who touches the
lives of others with the good news about Jesus Christ. God wants his
disciples to take seriously the task of "going into all the world." God
wants individuals to share the good news they have experienced and

to follow the New Testament example of continuous, constant, dynamic evangelism.

Applied Evangelism

Disciples, not mere "decisions," are the aims of the Great Commission. If discipleship is the aim, the soul-winner will present Jesus as Savior and proclaim him as Lord. "Therefore let all the house of Israel know assuredly, that God hath made that same Jesus, whom ye have crucified, both Lord and Christ" (Acts 2:36). The earliest confession of first-century converts was the expression *Kyrios Jesus Christos*—"Jesus is Lord."

The Great Commission calls men and women to acknowledge Christ's total command over their lives and their relations to others. Jesus Christ never offered a potential disciple "cheap grace." The cost of becoming and of living Christ's life-style was stated graphically by the Lord. "Whosoever will come after me, let him deny himself, and take up his cross, and follow me" (Mark 8:34). Jesus intended a follower of his to follow him both in active private and in public discipleship. Evangelism calls for an applied evangelism in the private life. It calls for a repentance that implies withdrawal from the world. The convert should study the Scriptures constantly and pray faithfully.

When the convert takes the "journey inward," the Lord demands the "journey outward." Studying the Bible and conversing with God forces one to be sent into the world to apply the teachings of Christ to every area of living. Following Christ means commitment to the purposes of the Lord in history. It means that the convert's personal life-style ought to point unambiguously to Jesus. An evangelistic invitation to become a disciple involves a call to join in the living Lord in the work of his kingdom. It will call attention to human needs beyond the convert's private concerns. In every area of living—work, play, family, friends—the principles of Christ will be applied.

Multiplied Evangelism

The genuine objective of the Great Commission is discipleship. Jesus sought to develop quality in his followers, but he also sought quantity. Therefore, evangelism that produces disciples of quality will multiply as each disciple becomes a partner in the evangelistic enterprise. In this way the gospel will reach into all nations by the process of multiplication rather than addition.

Let us observe the multiplication process of making disciples. Suppose a convert could win one person to Christ each year. But also suppose this soul-winner were to nurture and train his convert to the point where his son in the faith was capable of leading someone else to Christ and training that person to nurture and to train the convert. Evidently Paul thought of multiplication evangelism. "And the things that thou hast heard of me among many witnesses, the same commit thou to faithful men, who shall be able to teach others also" (2 Tim. 2:2).

At the end of the first year the second soul-winner will have doubled his ministry, at the end of the second year quadrupled it, and at the end of the third year multiplied himself eight times. Of course this is based on the idea that each disciple must win and train one person per year. Such a process appears excruciatingly slow, with only seven converts in three years. By the nineteenth year, though, more than ten million converts could be won by this principle if followed diligently.

The Great Commission was never intended to be fulfilled by a few select soul-winners. Not many are gifted evangelists like Billy Graham or R. G. Lee. Every child of God is a disciple. The church should accept the challenge of developing and deploying laypersons to evangelize. The Great Commission aims at discipleship. This discipleship seeks to live Christ's kind of life. It commits itself to the task of going into the world and multiplying the number of those who would follow Jesus.

Suggestions for Advanced Study

1. In one sentence each, explain something of the meaning of the following terms: educational evangelism, clinical evangelism, youth evangelism, mass evangelism, media evangelism, social evangelism, family evangelism, and target group evangelism.

2. Work out a plan for organized, definite action by a church to reclaim church members who are indifferent, continually absent from services, failing to support the church finances, and receiving no blessing whatsoever from the church.

3. Organize a Life-Style Evangelism Group. Order the materials from the Home Mission Board, 1350 Spring Street, N.W., Atlanta, Georgia, 30309.

4. Plan and conduct a Lay Renewal Weekend for the adults and youth in your church. This is a focus on deep, full, complete commitment of self to Christ. Materials may be ordered from the Home Mission Board, 1350 Spring Street, N.W., Atlanta, Georgia, 30309.

References for Further Study

Blackwood, Andrew W. *Planning a Year's Pulpit Work.* Grand Rapids: Baker Book House, 1975.

Fackre, Gabriel. *Word in Deed: Theological Themes in Evangelism.* Grand Rapids: William B. Eerdmans Publishing Company, 1975.

Haney, David. *Journey into Life.* Memphis: Brotherhood Commission of Southern Baptist Convention, 1974.

Hogue, C. B. *Love Leaves No Choice: Life-Style Evangelism.* Waco, Texas: Word Books, 1976.

Marcum, Elvis. *Outreach: God's Miracle Business.* Nashville: Broadman Press, 1975.

McGavran, Donald. *Understanding Church Growth.* Grand Rapids, Michigan: 1970.

Pierce, J. Winston. *Planning Your Preaching.* Nashville: Broadman Press, paperback 1979.

Price, Nelson L. *I've Got to Play on Their Court.* Nashville: Broadman Press, 1975.

Sweazey, George. *The Church As Evangelist.* New York: Harper & Row, 1978.

Trotman, Dawson. *Born to Reproduce.* Colorado Springs: Nav Press, 1975.

11

Two-and-Two Visitation Evangelism

After these things the Lord appointed other seventy also, and sent them two and two before his face into every city and place, whither he himself would come (Luke 10:1).

No evangelism is complete until the evangelized become evangelists. It is God's positive plan for all Christians to become soul-winners. He plants the desire to win others in the newly converted heart as the primal passion of Christian love. The loss of this first love is one of the tragedies of Christian churches today.

The evangelistic program so blessed of God at Pentecost was three-fold: (1) The church members prayed and the Holy Spirit came upon them; (2) they went throughout all Jerusalem bearing witness for Jesus; (3) Peter preached the greatest sermon of his life. Three thousand souls were won to Christ. Possibly no more people would have been there to hear Peter preach than come now to the usual sermon by a prominent man, if people had not been witnessing throughout Jerusalem. We cannot improve upon these three points; nor can we change their order without weakening the program. When pastors are successful in training and inspiring the rank and file of the church members to follow prayer with personal work, the unsaved people will come to the preaching services and be saved. Pastors as a rule are good salesmen; but they must also become sales managers. Pastors are good soul-winners; but they must train church members in soul-winning if the evangelistic task is done today.

The nearer pastors and others imitate Christ in soul-winning, the more successful all will be. The primary method of Christ was person-to-person evangelism. He was never too busy to seek out a lost soul, sit down with him, and talk to him about his relation to God. Less

131

than 5 percent of the people who become Christians do so without personal influence from others. Hardly more than that become Christians solely under the influence of preaching. Personal influence or the personal interview coupled with gospel preaching is the most effective way. Christ taught his disciples how to win souls when he sent out the seventy, two by two, to do personal witnessing before he came to preach.

We cannot improve on Christ's method of sending out soul-winners in teams of two. This method is both more enjoyable and more effective. Teammates share responsibility, inspire confidence, supplement each other's appeal, and make stronger impressions upon the lost. They are far more difficult to turn away or to discourage than when one individual goes alone to win people to Christ.

Technique of Christ

Jesus left on earth a group of trained, experienced, and joyous soul-winners. His technique in training them is found in Luke 10:1-17. This should be followed in detail.

He sent out "seventy others," the rank and file of his Christian followers, other than the twelve apostles (v. 1).

He showed them the plenteous harvest and the paucity of laborers. The difficulty in soul-winning today is not with the lost people; it is in getting Christian people to try (v. 2).

He sent them on spiritual business which would require no purse or wallet. He told them not to wear shoes as if on a social visit. They wore sandals for swift movement, on urgent business (v. 4).

He told them to salute no man socially, but to go directly on the soul-winning mission (v. 4).

He sent them into homes for soul-winning (v. 5). Lost people are easier to win to Christ in their own homes than anywhere else on earth, except in the church sanctuary.

He gave them a tactful thing to say on entering a home (v. 5).

He gave them the message of the Kingdom as the sole topic for discussion (v. 9). He knew how apt a lost person can be in diverting the conversation into irrelevant sidelines.

He warned them about difficulties (vv. 10-11).

He differentiated between the responsibility of the soul-winner and the unsaved man (vv. 12-15). The soul-winner is not responsible for success or failure; he is responsible for presenting Jesus Christ as tactfully, winsomely, and earnestly as possible. It is the responsibility of the hearer as to whether he accepts or rejects Christ.

He identified himself with soul-winners in their success or failure to win others (v. 16). If Jesus can bear to be rejected, surely Christians can.

Those whom Jesus sent out returned with the joy of victory (v. 17).

Just so, the rank and file of church members may return today, rejoicing in soul-winning victory, if they follow Christ's instructions and methods in soul-winning. Every visiting evangelist should leave in the wake of his campaign some new, happy-hearted, victorious soul-winners who have been trained and inspired and guided under his leadership.

Preparation Plans

Victorious campaigns do not happen accidently any more than ships drift into harbor. There are certain specific details of preparation which must accompany earnest periods of prayer, if victory is to come.

Find the People

Jesus did not send the seventy indiscriminately "from house to house" (Luke 10:7). He was too efficient for that waste of time. Evidently he sent them directly to individuals with specific instructions. One of the first tasks is to find the lost whom the soul-winners are to see. There are various means of doing this.

1. *The Sunday School rolls.*—Those who are in Sunday School are probably the most likely to turn to Christ. The names of those on the Sunday School roll should be checked against the church roll so the unsaved and the unaffiliated can be found and listed.

2. *A survey.*—A pastor can pass out mimeographed sheets with blanks for the name, age, address, and other information about every lost person or unaffiliated church member whom the people in the congregation of Sunday School know.

3. *A religious census.*—No type of search for the unsaved is as important or as comprehensive as taking a religious census. This should be

done at least six weeks before the visitation program begins. The information gathered should be carefully tabulated.

Prepare "Assignment for Visitation" Cards

The name of everyone to be visited should be inscribed immediately on an Assignment for Visitation card, giving the address, approximate age, and every bit of helpful information possible. This should be done well before the actual visitation begins.

ASSIGNMENT FOR VISITATION

Name _____

Address _____ Age _____

Nonchurch member _____ Member elsewhere _____

Place of membership _____

Sunday School member _____

Other information _____

Visited by _____

Date _____

　　(Please make report on other side)

Enlist the Workers

About three weeks before a visitation evangelism campaign, the pastor should begin to enlist the workers. Their names should be signed on Visitation Agreement cards.

Approximately 70 to 75 percent of the workers should be men. The entire group would be composed of mature men, mature women, and young adults. They should be selected for their Christian character, consecration, poise, personality, and ability to deal tactfully with people. Insurance men, salesmen, merchants, professional men, receptionists, teachers, nurses, and the like make good soul-winners if they have the spiritual qualifications.

VISITATION AGREEMENT

I am willing to join a fellow Christian to form a team
for soul-winning and evangelistic visitation.
I will endeavor to attend the instruction classes to be
given under the direction of the pastor and our visiting
evangelist.

Name _____

Address_____

Date _____

These workers should be personally selected. It is dangerous to call
for volunteers, for sometimes the most unfortunate personalities will
volunteer. Jesus selected his apostles; he did not call for volunteers.
Again, the leaders in the Sunday School, Church Training, Woman's
Missionary Union, and Brotherhood are a group already selected who
can be and should be utilized in a program of evangelism.

For the average campaign, one visitor should be found for about
every seven or eight persons to be visited. For example, if there are
four hundred names on Assignment for Visitation cards, there should
be not less than fifty visitors, making twenty-five teams. Thus each
team would have sixteen persons to visit in a week's program.

Prepare Assignment Envelopes

Envelopes prepared for two and two visitation should be filled with
assignments for visitation, one envelope for each team for each evening
(see preceding sample of report mimeographed on envelope). Three
to five names and addresses should be in each envelope. A team can
see two or sometimes three individuals within an hour. The extra cards
should be included for use in case of wrong addresses, misinformation,
and those absent from home. The addresses in any envelope should
be in the same section of the community. Some envelopes should be
prepared for men visitors, with names of men or couples. Others should
be prepared especially for women visitors. Young adults should go to
see people their own age or younger.

Each envelope should contain a half-dozen decision cards, to be

STREETS

_____

_____

_____

_____

_____

Men _____

Women _____

Boys _____

Girls _____

VISITORS

Name _____

Name _____

Date of visitation _____

Please return this envelope and all cards tomorrow evening, whether you made the calls or not.

Kindly write complete reports on all cards, whether not at home or visited.

Please attend each instruction meeting for prayer and evangelism.

REPORT

1. No. individuals interviewed _____

2. No. decisions to accept Christ _____

3. No. decisions to transfer letter _____

used in seeking to bring the unsaved to a decision for Christ. These cards have blanks whereon one may indicate the decision to accept Christ, the decision to unite with the church on profession of faith, or the decision to transfer church membership to the church where he can serve best.

Plan a Supper Meeting

The best time for two-and-two soul-winning visitation in the homes is usually a short while after the evening meal. More people are at home then than at any other hour of the day; and they are also more at leisure then. Therefore, plans should be made for an early supper meeting for the soul-winners who are going out.

Those who sign the Visitation Agreement cards are asked to cooperate in a schedule something like the following:

DECISION CARD

1._____ I put my faith in Jesus Christ as my Savior, and I purpose to try to obey him as my Lord in Christian living.

2._____ I desire to unite with the _____ Church on profession of faith and plan to present myself for membership on (date) ____

3._____ I wish to transfer my membership to _____ Church. For letter write to_____
at_____

Further details _____

Name_____

Address _____

Date _____

Sunday

3:00 to 4:00 P.M. A full hour of instruction in the technique of visitation soul-winning (no visitation is planned for Sunday afternoon)

Monday through Thursday

5:45 P.M. Supper at the church.

6:10 to 6:30 P.M. Testimonies about soul-winning successes or problems. Added instruction about soul-winning.

6:30 to 8:00 P.M. Visitation by teams of two each, as assigned by the pastor.

8:00 P.M. Preaching service in the church.

Suggestions for Advanced Study

1. Compare the instructions Jesus gave when he sent out the seventy with the instructions he gave the twelve (Matt. 10:1-42; Luke 10:1-

12). Did Jesus make a difference between the "clergy" and the "laity" in the duties of soul-winning?

2. Study Acts 2, giving Scripture for the following points of technique: (a) assembling of a congregation, (b) seeking spiritual power, (c) personal witnessing, (d) evangelistic preaching, (e) invitation and exhortation, (f) baptism, and (g) instruction of new converts.

3. Outline Peter's evangelistic sermon in Acts 2, giving the subject of the sermon, points in his thought material, Scripture proofs of his points, application to the lives of his people, and the call to faith and open confession.

Promotion of the Visitation

Usually the group of teams can visit practically all the people whose names they have if they visit one hour to an hour and thirty minutes for about four nights.

The soul-winners should choose their own teammates. Men should go with men and women with women. Naturally, a husband and wife can work together. In no case should mixed couples of the younger people go together.

The pastor will give each team an envelope containing three to five names and addresses of lost people or unaffiliated church members. Each team is requested to visit two or three people each night. Each team is asked to make a report of each visit, written on the card. The envelope with all cards is to be returned to the leader on the following night at supper. An entirely new envelope with new assignments is given each night.

The visitors are requested to report on the outside of the envelope the number of people interviewed, the number of lost people who made a confession of their faith in Christ, and the number of unaffiliated church members who promised to transfer their church letters.

At the supper, night after night, the reports of the work done on the previous day should be put on the blackboard.

Instructions for Soul-Winners

The first problem in soul-winning is the soul-winner. Soul-winners are made, not born. They must be inspired, instructed, and directed. A Christian is not any more likely to become a successful soul-winner purely through exhortation from the pulpit than one would become a great pianist merely through being exhorted to play well. The soul-winner should be carefully instructed, specifically directed, and continually encouraged to keep on trying to win someone.

Instruction on Gaining an Interview

The leader in two-and-two visitation evangelism should tell the teams how to pray together in the automobile before they start into the home where they have been assigned.

At the door the team should say: "We are visitors from our church. May we come in?"

Inside the door the visitors should ask for the one whose name they have on the Assignment for Visitation card.

It relieves any awkwardness or tension when the visitors compliment something or make some pleasant remark between the door and the living room. Take interest in the children, some flowers, a lovely picture, or an evidence of a hobby.

Never sit down until the individual you are seeking is in the living room. By all means maneuver to sit next to him. For example, it is poor salesmanship to let a Christian woman sit between the soul-winners and her unsaved husband. She might answer all the questions for him.

Begin talking about the thing you came there to do. Never let the conversation get into other channels if you can avoid it. The subject of the lost man's salvation should be under discussion within three minutes after sitting down.

If the television is going, say, "We will be here only a few minutes, and we want to talk about an important matter. You would not mind turning off the television for a few minutes, would you?" If there is a talkative person in the room, let one of the team try to keep that person quiet by nodding but not answering, directing attention to the other soul-winner while he talks to the lost man. If too much outside company is there, use your own judgment about the wisdom of opening up the conversation with the lost man. One might say, "We will come later." However, often soul-winners have been able to lead to Christ any friends or guests who might be in the home—people whom they had not expected to see.

Methods of Dealing with an Individual

"What shall I say?" is the most pressing problem to most soul-winners. A tactful approach has been suggested by Dr. Guy Black, a prominent pioneer in the technique of modern two-and-two visitation evangelism. He suggests these four assumptions in the soul-winner's approach.

1. Assume that the person is a Christian and has been a church member, unless the situation is positively known to be otherwise. It is far more tactful to say, "I suspect that sometime in your life you have been converted to Christ and have been affiliated with a church, haven't you?" than to say, "I wonder why you have never become a Christian," or even, "Are you a Christian?" The former approach assumes the best about a person; the latter approach is like a slap in the face. The assumption creates no resistance. It will encourage him to tell his background and past experience.

2. If the person has never been a church member, the soul-winner can assume that he has had a religious background, a Christian home, a praying mother, or some experience in Sunday School. It is tactful to say, "I feel sure that you came from a Christian home, that your parents were Christians, and that perhaps you have been to Sunday School. Is that not true?

3. If the person has had no Christian background, the personal worker can assume that he knows about Christ and would like to be a Christian.

4. If he does not know about Jesus and the life which Jesus makes possible for those who believe on him, the soul-winner can assume that he believes in God.

Promotion of the Interview

Let him talk. A good physician makes the patient tell everything possible before writing a prescription. Get all his background. Notice his attitude carefully. Build up a friendly atmosphere. Strive never to ask a question which is liable to bring forth "No" as an answer. Ask easy questions which will get him to say "Yes," "Yes," "Yes," until finally he may say "Yes" for Christ.

Christ is your talking point. Keep the conversation on him. The poorest thing on earth to say is, "Why don't you join the church?"

Christ has a better reputation than your church. Christ, not the church, is the Savior. Christ is our best, our only talking point in soul-winning. Church membership is scriptural only after one has believed on the Lord Jesus Christ and is already a child of God.

Don't argue. Successful soul-winning is not a debate; it is witnessing. Men are not won by logic or mental gymnastics or superiority in argument. They are won by clear, winning words of love for Christ and love for those whom we would win. A personal worker may win the argument, but he may lose his man. Soul-winners are not prosecuting attorneys; they are witnesses for Christ.

Most excuses offered by the lost do not have to be answered. Ignore them by saying, "In spite of that, you still want to be a child of God, to be like Christ, and to be saved, don't you?" Sometimes there is an honest doubter. Be considerate of him. But bypass flimsy and silly excuses.

Put your personality into the interview. Tell your own experience. If Jesus has done anything good for you, tell it.

Securing a Decision

You are aiming to get a decision. Do your utmost to get it before leaving. Create atmosphere. Devote two-thirds of the interview in presenting Jesus, and then press for a decision.

Use the Decision Card as an aid to reach the lost man's will. Do not produce it until you think he should be ready to make his decision for Christ. Have the card and pencil ready. Read, or let him read aloud, the decision you wish him to make. Ask him if he will not then and there make that decision fully and finally.

If he says yes, ask him if he would not like to go on record by putting his name and address at the bottom of the card, so this splendid decision can be reported to the pastor. Gently but persistently urge a decision, using the right motives. Expect results. Look for a decision. Ask for a decision. Pray for a decision. Try every worthy means to get a decision.

Make appeals to the lost man's will on these three bases: Appeal first to his conscience to repent of sin and trust Jesus Christ to save. Bring your lost friend face to face with Christ. The other two appeals, both of which support the appeal for Christ, are the appeal for a Christian home and the appeal for service. Christian living and church membership enable one to serve God, to influence others, and to perform the highest duties of Christian citizenship.

Some "Don'ts" in a Program of "Do"

1. Don't get discouraged. You will win someone.
2. Don't talk about extraneous matters. Keep the lost man face to face with Christ. Introduce your lost friend to Jesus, the best friend you have.
3. Don't ever argue or show irritation.
4. Don't have two conversations going on at once. That is worse than static over the radio.
5. Don't monopolize the conversation. Let the unsaved man tell his problems and experiences, and even his false hopes.
6. Don't get too many no's. Get yes, yes, for everything possible until you get the person to say yes for Christ.
7. Don't think you have to answer all excuses. Bring the conversation back to Christ. One can say, "Yes, there may be hypocrites in the church; but in spite of that, you want to become a true child of God, don't you?"
8. Don't stay too long. If the case is hopeless, tell him you have to go and talk with someone else who will be more interested. But remember that Jesus said to tell him that he has been right at the open door into the kingdom of God (Luke 10:11).
9. Don't be content to invite people to the revival, and then write on the Assignment for Visitation a note saying, "Good place for the pastor to call; good prospect." Do your human best to win that person to Christ.
10. Don't be sidetracked into a social visit. Press for a decision to belive on Christ and confess him.
11. Don't fail to pray both before you enter the house and with the person who signs a Decision Card.

Suggestions for Advanced Study

1. From the Scripture tell how Jesus began soul-winning interviews with points of contact with Nicodemus, the Samaritan woman at the

well, the lawyer, some of the twelve apostles, the rich young ruler, and Zacchaeus.

2. Show how Jesus warded off the attempts of the Samaritan woman to start an argument (a) on social differences, (b) on religious differences, and (c) on racial issues, while he was winning her to the kingdom of God (John 4).

3. Secure literature from your denominational headquarters on the approved plan for visitation evangelism.

4. Make a list of a dozen basic appeals to accept Christ to be used with lost people, such as salvation from sin, abundant life, Christian fellowship, and so forth.

References for Further Study

Dobbins, Gaines S. *A Ministering Church.* Nashville: Broadman Press, 1960.

Drakeford, John. *The Awesome Power of the Listening Ear.* Waco, Texas: Word Books, 1967.

Havlik, John F. *People-Centered Evangelism.* Nashville: Broadman Press, 1971.

Scarborough, L. R. Revised and expanded by E. D. Head. *With Christ After the Lost.* Nashville: Broadman Press, 1952.

Sisemore, John T. *The Ministry of Visitation.* Nashville: Convention Press, 1954.

Tournier, Paul. *The Meaning of Persons.* New York: Harper and Row, Publishers, 1957.

12
Planning and Promoting
a Local Church Revival

O Lord, I have heard thy speech, and was afraid: O Lord, revive
thy work in the midst of the years, in the midst of the years make
known; in wrath remember mercy (Hab. 3:2).

Wilt thou not revive us again: that thy people may rejoice in thee?
(Ps. 85:6).

Historically, Baptists in the United States have grown out of a revival-
istic caldron. When the term *revival* is defined and understood, there
is no way for Christ's followers to have outgrown a need for this spiritual
experience. According to *Cruden's Concordance*, the word translated
revive in the Old Testament appears seven times; the word *revived*
appears seven times, while the word *reviving* appears one time. In
some of these instances the reference is to physical reviving, while in
others it is to a spiritual experience.

Webster's Seventh New Collegiate Dictionary gives the definition
for the word *revive* as follows: "to return to consciousness or life: to
become active or flourishing again." The word *revival* is defined in
this way: "an act or instance of reviving: the state of being revived."
The third definition of revival alludes to our specific subject: "a period
of renewed religious interest."

In actual experience, Christian churches today have moved from
the definition of the word *revival* to a synthesis with evangelism. While
it is true that genuine revival will inevitably produce evangelism, some
kinds of evangelism are not produced in revival.

There are ways in which revival can be likened to sanctification.
The validity of this analogy is based on seeing sanctification in three
tenses: past, present, and future. Like revival, it is neither once and

144

for all nor static, but it is a work of God that continues among his people when his conditions are met.

Some churches across America no longer schedule revivals. Among these can be found growing evangelistic churches as well as dry, atrophied congregations. The pastors of growing churches who do not schedule revivals generally state that a series of services with an outside preacher and singer diverts the church from its soul-winning mission and that revival is the order of the day in the regular Sunday services.

It is true that a week of revival should require a church to set aside most of its routine activities. In this way priority is given to the special services, but even this should emphasize, not eliminate, such functions as the Wednesday night or Sunday School meetings and the continuing outreach visitation.

Most pastors will agree that the period of revival services is the most demanding and difficult week in a pastor's annual personal schedule. In the personal experience of the writer, after almost three decades as a pastor of local churches, there was seldom a week of revival which was not interrupted by the death of one or more prominent church members, hurricanes, tornadoes, torrential rains, accidents involving the church family, or some community scandal which diluted the concentration of God's people on spiritual matters. In one scheduled week of revival, the visiting preacher and singer "rode out" a hurricane on the Mississippi Gulf Coast in a local hotel.

For the alert and perceptive pastor, this should not be a matter of great disappointment or defeat. It merely makes clearer the fact that the adversary, Satan, will direct his fiercest attacks toward the people of God who get serious about spiritual renewal and growth. A congregation should be reminded that Satan will see to it that revival never comes without an awesome struggle.

Other sources of stress on a pastor during revival time include concern for the response of the people to the evangelist, the attendance or lack of it, the reaction to the time of invitation, and the giving to defray the expenses of the revival and the love gift for the visitors. When all these pressures are added to the regular responsibilities of the pastor, some conclude that revivals are not worth the effort. Nevertheless, in spite of all the personal sacrifice that is demanded, there is little that can compare with the joy which comes in the knowledge that God has moved in a direct and often measurable way and has done a mighty work in the hearts of his people and his church.

The physical and emotional demands exacted from the pastor, staff, and numerous church leaders are not too high a price to pay to receive and experience a new infusion of the love and power of God in human life. This kind of undeniable, unforgettable revelation of God's response to human need will not be seen in every scheduled week of revival. However, it will always come when God's people "humble themselves, and pray, and seek my face, and turn from their wicked ways" (2 Chron. 7:14).

In spite of all excuses given for not scheduling revivals, most growing, evangelistic churches still schedule them. In a recent year in the Southern Baptist Convention alone, there were over forty thousand such events conducted. It certainly can be shown that growing churches that do have seasons of revival have warmhearted evangelistic services week after week.

Perhaps the bottom line on the matter of revivals is this: Before giving up on revivals, try one!

Route to Revival

The well-known evangelist of another generation, Dr. Charles G. Finney, spoke truth when he said, "It is useless to expect a revival simply by asking for it, without bothering to fulfill the laws which govern spiritual blessings." There seems to be a divinely ordained route which must be followed as we seek the blessings of God in spiritual renewal. True revival involves prayer, confession of sin and repentance from sin, and becoming involved in a closer walk with Jesus Christ on a personal, daily basis.

Organize

1. Enlist the singer and preacher.—The pastor is the key, and he should have the prerogative of personally choosing these leaders. By all means, the pastor should know them personally, and he should possess a knowledge of their work. These should be persons who are above reproach morally and whose commitment to Jesus Christ is never in question. It is wise to avoid singers and preachers who seem more interested in golf than God. These are sometimes referred to as "hotel evangelists," and they spend their time in personal pursuits and are uninvolved in the efforts at the church. If the visitors do not get involved in the life of the congregation and its members, it is doubtful that any lasting contribution will be made.

Don't be afraid to enlist the help of a vocational evangelist. It is true that some are charlatans, but this is also true of some pastors, musicians, and persons in every known field of endeavor.

It is often effective for a pastor and church staff to conduct a "do it yourself" revival. Many times congregations will respond more readily to the leadership of their own pastor than anyone else. After all, he should be more familiar with the spiritual needs of his flock than any other person on earth.

2. Establish the time.—It is impossible to find clear dates on a community calendar in our generation. One can only choose a time with the least major conflicts and a season of the year when the people will respond the best to such an emphasis. Make certain that there is no conflict with the local church program, enabling the people to give single-minded attention to this one emphasis.

3. Engender enthusiasm.—Church members can immediately discern a lack of enthusiasm or halfheartedness on the part of the pastor. When there is warmth and fire in the pulpit, those elements inevitably spread. If the pastor cannot and does not genuinely commend the visiting preacher and singer to his people, it is hardly possible that they will respond to that leadership. The people must be led to claim God's promises and to expect God to give the victory.

4. Elements involved.—The assignment of responsibility is indispensable to involving people in such an effort. Keep in mind that the involvement of the largest number of persons possible is not for bragging purposes, but to place them under the influence of the preaching and singing and to make it easy for them to respond to the leadership of God's Spirit. It is easier to do God's will in the company of other committed Christians than it is when surrounded by pagans.

Among the committees that might be needed are prayer, attendance, hospitality, ushers, music, counselors, and possibly others. In small churches one person might suffice for each area, while larger churches would need committees.

Visualize

In John 15:8 we read: "Herein is my Father glorified, that ye bear much fruit; so shall ye be my disciples."

This one statement from the lips of our Lord should be sufficient to make every believer dissatisfied with the status quo. Under the preaching and pastoral leadership of the spiritual undershepherd, a congregation of believers must be led to see humanity's deepest need. The two truths that stand in relation to humanity are: (1) You will never meet a human being who is not in desperate need of what God offers in Jesus Christ; (2) you will never meet a human being whom God does not love and want saved.

One of the grave dangers facing every church is the possibility of behaving like the fictional character who "got on his horse and rode off in all directions." Determination must be made regarding the areas where growth is needed. For instance, the same kind of preparation would not be made for an evangelistic crusade that would be made for a stewardship revival. Goals must be established.

Goals must be *meaningful*. It is worthwhile to desire that the church be painted, but this requires mere action. Long-range planning, involving a number of years, is essential to achievement of meaningful goals. Perhaps these should include Sunday School enrollment and attendance, baptisms, worship service attendance, tithing, and other elements that are inseparably connected with spiritual growth.

The Sunday School Board of the Southern Baptist Convention presently has a plan for Sunday School growth called "The Growth Spiral." This is an excellent means of establishing meaningful goals for reaching people with the study of God's Word.

Goals must be *manageable*. God is in the miracle business; yet it is possible for men to set impractical goals that will discourage.

Goals must be *measurable*. Some persons would question the value of placing numerical goals on spiritual attainments. It is no less valid to set a measurable goal for baptisms and Sunday School average attendance than to establish measurable dollar goals for budget, foreign and home mission offerings, or the contract price for a building project. Perhaps it depends on the motive that prompts the establishment of the goals. If these are set for the glory of God, not for the elevation of man's ego, then they should be set.

Goals must be *motivating*. To challenge the best in individuals and a congregation, goals must require something greater than business as usual.

Most humans are born with a competitive spirit. Properly channeled, this characteristic can be used with great benefit for the kingdom. Never forget that we are in daily competition with Satan and have been admonished to "resist the devil."

Jesus said that the Father was glorified when we bear "much fruit." This is not a short crop, or a piddling pile, but should be a huge and overwhelming bumper harvest.

Agonize

A concerned Christian must never forget that he is involved in serious business. The witness we bear to our salvation through Jesus Christ has a direct bearing upon the eternal destiny of human beings.

Heaven and hell hang in the balance. All of our questions about these are not answered in the pages of the Word. However, we know enough to be positive that heaven is desirable and hell is to be avoided. The horror of hell is so extreme that Jesus warned us that it would be better to go through life without hands, feet, and eyes than to retain such offending members and go to hell (Matt. 18:8-9). It is impossible to describe the excruciating agony of the condemned, just as the peace and joy of heaven defy description.

Paul reminded us of the glory of the redeemed: "But as it is written, Eye hath not seen, nor ear heard, neither have entered into the heart of man, the things which God hath prepared for them that love him" (1 Cor. 2:9).

In every way open to the Christian, the challenge to pray must be issued. The possibilities are numerous.

Cottage prayer meetings, or gatherings in the homes of church members for prayer, have proven to be of great value. In large cities these can be organized on a neighborhood basis, while in smaller churches perhaps the homes of deacons can be opened for such gatherings. Someone should be in charge of such prayer meetings, normally the host or hostess. Specific prayer requests must be shared and seasons of prayer observed.

There should never be a worship service when prayer is not offered specifically for revival. The urgency of such petitions sets the tone for the revival. Testimonies regarding personal salvation experiences are effective in leading up to the special services. In smaller churches sometimes sentence prayers effectively involve the congregation in this aspect of spiritual preparation. In larger churches, the most deeply spiritual persons of the congregation, both men and women, can be enlisted to lead in public prayer for revival.

Around-the-clock prayer meetings are effective in revival preparation. This involves assigning certain time segments to specific individuals for a twenty-four-hour chain of prayer. It is usually best to have the persons involved come to a specific place for prayer throughout the night. This can be a room at the church or perhaps the chapel.

Centuries ago a great teacher's student came to him desiring wisdom. The famous teacher and philosopher led the student to water and suddenly plunged his head underneath the surface. He held the student in that position until his lungs almost burst. When he released him, gasping and confused, the great teacher asked, "Do you want wisdom?" Then he immediately added, "When your mind longs for wisdom the way your lungs just longed for air, you shall have it."

When our hearts yearn for revival, not out of custom or tradition but from a Christlike compassion for the lost and for spiritual growth, God is ready and abundantly able to hear our prayer and supply our need.

Evangelize

This involves *personal work.* It is unlikely that lost persons will seek out the churches in large numbers. Like the lost sheep, they must be sought in a one-to-one presentation of the gospel of Jesus Christ. The days of the special services are not for relaxation and "enjoying the preaching." They are the days for drawing the net and securing commitments. Many, and perhaps most, of those who make public decisions in the services will have already made personal decisions in their homes or other places.

To evangelize in a local church revival requires *preaching.* We do well to take our cue from the New Testament. The proclamation of Simon Peter on the day of Pentecost was a specific identification of

Jesus, the Christ. It was doctrinal in context and was uniquely blessed by the Holy Spirit.

There is a difference between revival preaching and the regular Sunday morning edification of the saints. The revival message must have an unusual sense of urgency, emphasizing such things as the brevity of life, the lostness of man without Christ, and the sufficiency of God's grace.

To evangelize involves *pleading*. This is the pull of one heart upon another, like that of Paul when he wrote, "The love of Christ constraineth us" (2 Cor. 5:14).

The lost person can spot a phony a long way off. Yet a person without Christ also discerns the ring of sincerity in a concerned Christian. If our pleading is in the Spirit of Christ, and not a mere membership drive to count up noses and nickels, they will hear and heed.

Utilize

The importance of follow-up after revival cannot be overstated. This is the key to continuing revival, and, again, the leadership of the pastor is the hinge upon which it must turn.

The preaching ministry of the pastor is a gauge to the depth of the experience, for genuine revival brings new conviction concerning the authority and inspiration of God's revealed Word. If the ministry of the word from the pulpit does not take on new vitality, revival will be short-lived or may even prove to have been a mirage.

If revival flows normally into Christian growth and development, a common notion must be banished. This is the widely held idea that after a demanding and exciting time of experiencing new blessings from God, the church needs to take some days or weeks off to "get back to normal." The days and weeks following revival are the worst times of the year for a pastor or staff member to leave town!

To maintain the spirit of revival requires that the fruits of revival be utilized or put to use. If persons have been saved, or if saved persons have made a new dedication to the Lord Jesus, it is imperative that each one be led into continued spiritual development through Bible study, prayer, witnessing, and tithing.

One method of achieving this is to assign every new member of the church to the Sunday School class or department for his or her age group. This makes certain Sunday School units directly responsible for meeting the new member and welcoming that one to Bible study and fellowship. Spiritual growth is realized in learning and doing the will of God. As the Bible is our primary source of written information concerning Jesus Christ, it is not possible to become like him without studying the Word to know how he lived.

The assignment of "babes in Christ" to extant Bible study units will often revitalize those groups. It is easy for such groups to grow stale and complacent. As is true in a home, the coming of a new baby makes dramatic new demands. Priorities are changed; schedules are revised; and the home finds its focus in meeting the needs of the baby. Everything is changed, and the hearts of the family members expand to include love for a new brother, sister, or child.

A sure cure for the humdrum weekly meeting of Sunday School classes and departments is the inclusion of a steady stream of new Christians. This prevents the group from becoming introverted or atrophied.

It is likewise important to provide new Christians with a sense of worth by giving them an opportunity to fill a place of responsibility. This can be an invitation to serve as an usher, to sing in the choir, or to serve on a committee. A new member enlisted in one of these or other ways will quickly develop a sense of belonging. Revival will not be real until the saved are launched in a program of growth in Christlikeness.

Another vital aspect of the utilization of new Christians is the development of Christian stewardship in regard to material possessions. Jesus Christ clearly commended tithing in Matthew 23:23, so it becomes obligatory, not optional, for a Christian. One has not begun to be obedient until the tithe is returned faithfully to the storehouse. Little else can give a new Christian a feeling of worth like the knowledge that he or she has assumed a worthy part of the financial commitment of the church. Other members may give more dollars, but every tither shares equally on a percentage basis. Real revival will be marked by a surge in the income of a local church and a heightened sense of joy that inevitably accompanies faithfulness.

The importance of calling a person by name cannot be overstated. It is unthinkable that a member of the family would be unrecognized by brothers and sisters. Every effort must be made to identify every new member by name, along with the "oldtimers." Some churches have new members wear name tags for several weeks, which is especially helpful in large congregations. In other churches efforts are made during the invitation time to identify a person by name, family, occupation, and things of the kind.

In one church, a new member's class was held on Sunday evening, prior to the worship service. New members were expected to attend these sessions for four consecutive Sunday nights. In the initial meeting each person was asked to state the circumstances of his or her conversion. Relating where one was, how Jesus Christ was received, where and when the public profession of faith was made, and what human had the most to do with bringing one to Christ all constitute a personal testimony. The greatest contribution a Christian can make to the kingdom and to a local church is to share one's testimony with lost people on a regular basis. If new Christians are led to become soul-winners, perennial revival will be the result.

Criticize

If local church revivals are to be a source of individual and corporate Christian growth, it is absolutely mandatory for church leaders to offer constructive criticism of the planning, promotion, and procedure of a revival experience. The best time for a candid evaluation is within a month following the conclusion of the event. By then it can be discerned whether or not the impact is continuing or, indeed, if anything helpful in the life of the church has actually occurred.

This criticism must be an inside job, done by the church leaders. Sometimes this will be the pastor and certain other leaders such as in Sunday School, Church Training, Woman's Missionary Union, Brotherhood directors, and other organizations. In larger churches it would involve the entire church staff, plus the church council or pastor's cabinet.

Questions such as these must be asked: "Did the people attend faithfully? If not, why not? Was the preaching what was needed at this time in the life of the church? Were the people properly informed by the publicity? Was the time period relatively clear of major conflicts? Was the prayer preparation effective and adequate? Did the people respond positively to the preacher and singer? How did the pastor and staff perform before, during, and after the effort, graded on a scale of one to ten?"

If there is no honesty and candor in admitting weaknesses and failures, there is no way for revivals to contribute to spiritual or numerical development. If an earnest effort is made to improve performance, revivals can prove to be indispensable components in a viable church program.

Suggestions for Advanced Study

1. Order the booklet "Revival Preparation Planbook" from the Evangelism Department of the Home Mission Board, 1350 Spring Street, N.W., Atlanta, Georgia 30309. Adapt as closely as possible the suggestions for a local church revival.

2. Order the packet of materials "Lighting esday evenings before the week of revival as a time of preparation.

3. Write a pastor-evangelist or a full-time evangelist for suggestions in how to get ready for a week of revival.

References for Further Study

Bryan, Dawson G. *A Workable Plan of Evangelism.* New York: Abingdon-Cokesbury Press, 1945.

Bryson, Harold T. *Prayer Meeting Resources: Lighting Revival Fires.* Nashville: Convention Press, 1975.

Evans, W. Glyn. *Profiles of Revival Leaders.* Nashville: Broadman Press, 1976.

Fish, Roy J. *Giving a Good Invitation.* Nashville: Broadman Press, 1974.

Sangster, W. E. *Let Me Commend.* London: The Epworth Press, 1961.

Wirt, Sherwood Eliot, ed. *Evangelism the Next Ten Years.* Waco: Word Books, 1978.

13
Training Laypersons for Evangelism

And the things that thou hast heard of me among many witnesses, the same commit thou to faithful men, who shall be able to teach others also (2 Tim. 2:2).

Jesus demonstrated a profound concern to reach the multitudes during his three-year earthly ministry. The Gospel writers recorded his great and grave concern for the crowds. He sought to help the multitudes by healing them. "And at even, when the sun did set, they brought unto him all that were diseased, and them that were possessed with devils. And all the city was gathered together at the door. And he healed many that were sick of divers diseases, and cast out many devils" (Mark 1:32-34). The Lord fed five thousand people, using the occasion as an opportunity to feed the hungry multitude and to teach them about the true bread of life. The target group for Jesus' teaching, preaching, and healing was the thousands and thousands of people. "As he landed he saw a great throng, and he had compassion on them, because they were like sheep without a shepherd; and he began to teach them many things" (Mark 6:34, RSV).

How did Jesus seek to reach the multitudes? By reading the Gospels, we can detect a variety of ways. He reached the multitudes by teaching, preaching, and ministering to large groups. The Gospel writers record groups of four thousand and of five thousand. Also, Jesus sought to reach the masses by contact on an individual basis. Reading the four Gospels closely causes one to detect the primary method which Jesus used to reach the multitudes. He called twelve men who would be his disciples, and then he trained them and sent them to reach the multitudes. Let us never forget the humanity of Jesus. He limited himself by the restrictions of time and space. There was no way he

155

could reach the multitudes without help.

The selections and endowment of the twelve represent attempts by Jesus to reach the multitudes. "And he ordained twelve, that they should be with him, and that he might send them forth to preach, And to have power to heal sicknesses, and to cast out devils" (Mark 3:14-15). After a time of intimate fellowship with these men and some training, Jesus would utilize these men to do his work. The Lord spent much time with these men. He taught them the principles of the kingdom of heaven. When Jesus deemed the task wise, he sent these men by twos on a tour of the villages. He gave them the authority to do his work. When the apostles returned, the Lord supervised their work. "On their return the apostles told him what they had done. And he took them and withdrew apart to a city called Bethsaida" (Luke 9:10, RSV). They reported the joys of helping people as well as the disappointments of negative responses.

The twelve apostles evidently reached other disciples. Some time after the tour of the twelve, Jesus sent seventy disciples out on a tour of the villages. Where did he get seventy? The gospels do not say specifically, but it would be logical to think that the seventy came in large part from the twelve who went out to make disciples. The Lord and the twelve spent time in training the seventy for the mission. Training was not restricted to passive teaching. It would lead to active involvement. The seventy disciples went out two by two to enlist disciples for Jesus. The seventy returned and reported both the great joys and the unexplicable rejections they encountered.

The Lord has not changed his great concern to reach the entire world. His parting word in the Great Commission included going into all nations. The church should seek to imitate the methods of the Master. It can use large gatherings. It can emphasize a one-on-one experience. It can also utilize the training of laypersons to reach the multitudes. The church should reach the multitudes. The church should utilize laypersons for the evangelization of the world. It should endeavor to build a program which will recruit and train men and women and boys and girls to fulfill Christ's commission of making disciples. This does not need to be a sporadic type of program. It would be the kind of mobilization and recruitment which would ensure an ongoing evangelism year after year in the local church.

Principles of Training Lay Evangelists

Before one can train and utilize laypersons, some biblical principles need to be understood and applied. These concepts could differ drastically with some ideas expressed in some churches today.

Recognition

Oddly enough, the first principle in training laypersons for evangelism is to recognize every Christian as a witness. Jesus commissioned his followers, not just the twelve apostles, to make disciples in all of the nations. Jesus recognized every follower as a witness. The seventy did not occupy an official position as "apostles." Instead, they were disciples, followers of Jesus, who went to share the word of the Lord.

The first-century churches recognized every disciple as a witness. Numerous examples could be cited of this recognition, but let us examine one. During the persecution of Saul of Tarsus, the Christians scattered. "They were all scattered abroad throughout the regions of Judaea and Samaria, *except the apostles*"(Acts 8:1, author's italics). "Therefore they that were scattered abroad went every where preaching the word" (Acts 8:4). "They" does not refer to apostles. The word translated "preaching the word" is the Greek word *euangelizo,* which means "evangelizing." This means that the disciples went everywhere evangelizing. Without a doubt the apostles did their share, but the inspired writer wanted to emphasize that everyone evangelized. The task of making disciples was not restricted to the apostles.

The whole Roman world was introduced to the Lord not by a few professional soul-winners but by all the people of God. Everyone was evangelizing. The church recognized everyone as an evangelizer.

Perhaps the greatest heresy to beset the church was dividing the church into professional and amateur evangelizers. Somewhere in Christian history the idea has taken firm root that the church has a staff and a few super Christians to evangelize the world. The mentality of "Let the pastor or some of the deacons lead others to Christ" or "I am just a layperson!" pervades the contemporary church.

New life is coming into many churches by the recognition that every Christian is a witness. More and more laypersons realize that they are witnesses, and they desire to know how to be more effective evangelizers.

Enlistment

Recognizing the status of every Christian as a witness is not enough. An attempt should be made to enlist a group of people who would be willing to be used and to be trained for the task of evangelism. Perhaps the greatest responsibility for enlistment rests upon the pastor. In the fourth chapter of Ephesians we see that God has given to the church "some, apostles; and some, prophets; and some, evangelists; and some, pastors and teachers; For the perfecting of the saints, for the work of the ministry, for the edifying of the body of Christ" (Eph. 4:11-12). This is the King James translation. Perhaps the Greek prepositions in these verses could best be rendered "for," "unto," "unto." This would mean that God has given pastors to the church "for the equipping unto the work of the ministry, unto the upbuilding of the body of Christ." With this concept the pastor would seek to enlist and to equip workers rather than considering himself as the solo evangelizer.

Of course, the ideal is to enlist and to equip everyone. Perhaps with the dualistic heresy abounding so greatly, the best place to begin would be with small groups. The pastor could enlist the deacons. He could train them to be soul-winners. Then the pastor could encourage the deacons to enlist their wives; then the deacons could enlist one other layperson and train him. The pastor could enlist Sunday School teachers. A group could be enlisted at the discretion of the pastor or on a volunteer basis. The Lord selected twelve and started. The point is to *enlist!*

Training

Involving laypersons as soul-winners obviously does not come by mere recognition and enlistment. The people must be trained for the task of making disciples. Jesus spent much time in training his followers.

Where does one begin in training a layperson? The proper place for lay training comes within the structure of the local church program. Nothing can replace the study of God's Word in the Sunday School. Excellent instructions could be received in the Church Training and other church programs.

Aside from the regular routine of the local church program, laypersons need to be trained in the following ways: class instruction, personal work, and on-the-job training. Some type of continuous class instruction needs to be given those who plan to be involved in soul-winning. These classes could run consecutively on Sunday through Friday, or they could be held once a week. During the class instruction, lectures could be given as well as practice of what the disciples learn within the group.

Personal work must comprise a part of the lay training. The disciples will need to engage in prayer and Bible study on an individual basis. They will also need to master the lessons of the class sessions.

Nothing surpasses the phase of instruction called "on-the-job training." Jesus used this type of instruction. When he sent out the twelve as well as the seventy, the disciples learned from each other. One could send a trainee with a trained individual. As the trained person endeavors to lead someone to Christ, the trainee could listen and learn.

When people are trained, the group should be ready for more definite evangelistic outreach. The pastor will have developed a deeper spiritual relationship with his congregation. The people can take the responsibility that rightly belongs to them in fulfilling Christ's commission.

Involvement

Let us review these principles of training laypersons for evangelism. First, recognize that every Christian is a witness. Second, enlist a group to be trained. Third, train the group by class instruction, personal work, and on-the-job training. The fourth principle is extremely important—involve the layperson in soul-winning. Numerous church members have some type of diploma for a soul-winning class, but they have never shared with a lost person. Jesus enlisted and trained, but there came a time when he sent them to the villages. They became involved.

Nothing will involve the layperson more than the assignment of a prospect. This is an objective. He can go to this person and present the gospel. Of course, the person will have apprehension and hesitancy, but the layperson must become involved in the actual task of sharing the gospel.

Another way to involve the layperson in soul-winning is to tell him to be alert to any opportunity. Within the traffic of life, opportunities will arise so that the committed disciples can present the gospel. Of the two methods of involvement—assignment and traffic—the method of assignment will have the great motivation.

To develop a soul-winning church, one must consider these principles: recognize all Christians are witnesses; enlist a small group for soul-winning; train the recruits; and involve them in actual presentation of the gospel.

Practical Illustrations of Lay Training

Various training programs have emerged to train laypersons in the task of evangelism. Most of the groups have utilized in some measure the above basic principles. A review of a few illustrations of lay training might be helpful.

The Lay Evangelism School

Several years ago Southern Baptists of the Home Mission Board developed a program of lay training called "The WIN School" (WIN stands for "Witness Involvement Now"). The name was changed to Lay Evangelism School, but the basic emphasis of training and involving laypersons in soul-winning is the same. The Lay Evangelism School seeks to involve a group in a concentrated effort of learning the basics of "how to witness." Various educational techniques are combined with the small-group process and the on-the-job training concept.

The Lay Evangelism School consists of a three-month preparation period, one week of intense training, and a three-month time of continuing training. A church should not attempt a Lay Evangelism School unless the full schedule of preparation, training, and follow-up can be given priority. The three-month preparation involves the following matters: spiritual preparation, promotion and registration, locating lost people, materials, arrangements, and witness assignments. The church staff and lay leadership must be involved in the preparatory stages.

The one week of intense training consists of nine hours of classroom time and three hours of on-the-job training. The sessions need to be conducted Monday through Friday nights. Each night's session is divided into three parts. First, a trained Lay Evangelism School teacher leads each night on the subjects of The New Life, The Cleansed and Controlled Life, The Witnessing Life, The Courageous Life, and The

Growing Life. A second phase of each night will be small-group activities in which communication, motivation, and relational skills are considered. The third phase of each night's session will include personal testimonies, making a presentation of the gospel, and developing strategies for sharing the gospel.

During the week of intense training, three witnessing visits will be made by teams of three. The teams visit lost people on Thursday night, Saturday, and Sunday. A sharing time is conducted after this Thursday night witnessing visit.

The three months of continued training is scheduled for twelve weekly sessions of two hours each. It is designed, of course, for those who participated in the week of intense training. For twelve weeks the teams of three continue to visit lost people. They report on their activities each week in their meeting. These sessions consist of times of prayer and sharing from the visits. The members learn within the group. In addition, the Lay Evangelism School leader makes home study assignments.

Southern Baptists have reaped two major dividends of the Lay Evangelism School. First, people are being won to Christ. Second, in the process of people being won to Christ, a large number of laypersons receive training and involvement. Southern Baptists of the Home Mission Board have also developed a similar training to the Lay Evangelism School in WOW (Win Our World). The latter is an attempt to develop the youth in fulfilling Christ's imperative commission for making disciples.

To engage in a Lay Evangelism School, a church needs to secure *Lay Evangelism Church Manual* from the Home Mission Board, 1350 Spring Street, N.W., Atlanta, Georgia 30309. To conduct a WOW Emphasis, a church needs to order *WOW Preparation Guide* from the same address.

Andrew Club

Dr. Roland Q. Leavell, a successful pastor, denominational leader in evangelism, and educator, utilized Andrew Clubs. Wherever Andrew is mentioned in the Scriptures, he is working with others. The first impulse of his heart, after he found Jesus, was to find his brother Simon Peter. "And he brought him to Jesus" (John 1:42). Again, on the outskirts of the crowd, Andrew performed the matchless service of introducing a boy with five loaves and two fish to put all his resources in the hands of the Savior. On another occasion, when some Greeks said, "We would see Jesus" (John 12:21), it was Andrew who leaped over the bounds of race prejudice and told the Master about them.

All Christians cannot preach a mighty sermon as Peter did at Pentecost, but all Christians can be soul-winners as Andrew was. It was normal Christianity in action when Andrew "first findeth his own brother Simon . . . and he brought him to Jesus" (1 John 1:41-42). Church members need to be brought up to the healthy state of being normal, consistent soul-winners for Christ.

1. Purpose.—An Andrew Club has but one purpose, that of helping Christians to win the lost to Christ. Jesus recognized the value of fellowship and mutual encouragement in personal soul-winning. He sent out his personal workers two by two. Andrew Clubs promote fellowship and provide encouragement in soul-winning. They provide opportunities for Christians to pray together, to exchange experiences, and to share mutual joys of winning others to Christ.

2. Personnel.—The first secret of building a soul-winning church is to have a soul-winning pastor. The pastor should be interested in every Andrew Club. The ideal personnel for Andrew Clubs would be from the leaders of the Sunday School, Church Training, Brotherhood, and Woman's Missionary Union. A group of soul-minded Sunday School teachers make an ideal Andrew Club for soul-winning. They are a picked group, trained, and in service. The Andrew Club will remind them constantly that their promotion, teaching, visitation, and other Sunday School activities must be tuned to winning others to Christ. A Church Training Andrew Club recognizes that only by winning others to Christ do they reach the highest form of Christian service. An Andrew Club within the Woman's Missionary Union and within the Brotherhood will keep the missionary spirit throbbing in the hearts of the members. Likewise, the pastor can keep his deacons alert with a deacon's Andrew Club. Often an Andrew Club can be organized among new converts and new church members who have affiliated by transfer from other churches.

The purpose of having these inner groups within the personnel of various church organizations is to keep them from making the organization an end within itself and to help them use the organization as a means to the ultimate end of soul-winning. Members of an Andrew Club are a picked group, not volunteers. As Jesus prayed earnestly and then selected the twelve, so should a pastor pray earnestly and select the nucleus of an Andrew Club.

The average Andrew Club has from six to twenty members. Small churches can have one or more clubs. Larger churches should have many soul-winning groups working constantly.

3. *Program.*—The program of an Andrew Club should be planned to conform to the work of the organization out of which it is formed and to conform to the church activity as a whole. Yet it should be planned to do one and only one thing: that of promoting and soul-winning.

The Andrew Club could meet at any time agreeable to the group. Thirty minutes every Sunday morning before Sunday School time is an excellent hour for a general Sunday School group to meet. Church Training groups could meet before these sessions. Some groups meet before or after the mid-week prayer service. One group of deacons met for lunch once each week in a downtown hotel. The meetings should not be long, but they should be frequent. Primary attention should be given directly to the matter of assigning the members to go to see specific lost people.

Every meeting should be compassionately prayerful. Members of an Andrew Club should keep prayer lists. These could be read or referred to in each meeting.

Members of the Andrew Clubs should have a New Testament and some gospel tracts. Nothing would be more helpful than to mark significant verses to be used in soul-winning.

Andrew Club members need to be faithful in worship services. Members should bring unsaved people to these services, sit with them, pray for them, and introduce them to the pastor and other church members.

Evangelism Explosion

James D. Kennedy's *Evangelism Explosion* has been an effective and popular training program in evangelism for laypersons in the local church. James Kennedy conceived of an evangelism program for utilizing laypersons in 1962. Beginning with a membership of less than fifty in the Coral Ridge Presbyterian Church in Fort Lauderdale, Florida, Kennedy recruited several people from the congregation to learn and practice evangelism with the pastor. He started with four. At the end of the training program, these individuals enlisted more, and so on, until the congregation had hundreds of people practicing evangelism consistently and methodically.

New workers are recruited by a personal visit. A trained participant in the program explains it briefly and then invites the prospective soul-winner to a center, where a greater explanation of the goals and principles of the program is shared. Testimonies from participants are given. Potential workers are asked to commit themselves for the entire four and one-half months training program or else not start at all.

Kennedy's program of Evangelism Explosion offers three basic types of training in evangelism. First, there is class instruction on the day the recruits come to the church for visitation and before they go out into the community. A brief lecture on the week's topic begins the session, and assignments are given for the following week. Then class members are divided into pairs to practice what they learned the previous week. Second, homework is given that focuses on portions of Scripture to be memorized and used in the course of "witnessing" during visitation. These are recited and checked each week in class. Kennedy's book *Evangelism Explosion* gives details of the methods. Third, there is on-the-job training. Each trainee goes out with a trained worker and listens as this person endeavors to lead someone to Christ. Giving a simple personal presentation of the gospel characterizes the Kennedy program.

Kennedy designed an involvement with an evangelistic visitation with two three-hour periods each week. One is in the morning, one in the evening. After each visitation, the teams report back to a larger group. Follow-up procedures include several return visits with an attempt to get the new convert into a small Bible study group of several mature Christians and four or five newer Christians.

Some time after the convert's training in studying the Bible, prayer, and the Christian life, he or she is encouraged to come into the evangelism program to learn how to share his or her faith with others. The evangelism explosion method strongly emphasizes "spiritual multiplication."

Christ's imperative commission must not be restricted to a few disciples. The task of making disciples requires all disciples. The church should be making a serious attempt to involve more in the task of evangelism.

Suggestions for Advanced Study

1. Read Robert Coleman's book *The Master Plan of Evangelism*. Relate the methodology of Jesus to your plan of evangelism for your church.

2. Conduct a Lay Evangelism School. Order the *Lay Evangelism Church Manual* from the Home Mission Board, 1350 Spring Street, N.W., Atlanta, Georgia 30309. Plan to execute each step without alteration or without elimination.

3. Plan a WOW Emphasis for the youth of your church. Order *WOW Preparation Guide* from the Home Mission Board, 1350 Spring Street, N.W., Atlanta, Georgia 30309.

4. Read James D. Kennedy's *Evangelism Explosion*. Rev. Ed. Using this program, plan a program for training laypersons for evangelism.

References for Further Study

Benjamin, Paul. *The Equipping Ministry.* Cincinnati: Standard Publishing, 1978.

Coleman, Robert. *The Master Plan of Evangelism.* Old Tappan, New Jersey: Fleming H. Revell Company, 1963.

Fish, Roy J., and Conant, J. E. *Every Member Evangelism for Today.* New York: Harper and Row, 1976.

Haney, David. *The Idea of the Laity.* Grand Rapids: Zondervan Publishing House, 1973.

Havlik, John F. *The Evangelistic Church.* Nashville: Convention Press, 1976.

Kennedy, James D. *Evangelism Explosion.* Rev. Ed. Wheaton, Illinois: Tyndale House Publishers, 1977.

Worrell, George E., *Resources for Renewal.* Nashville: Broadman Press, 1975.

14

Conserving the Results of Evangelism

From that time many of his disciples went back, and walked no more with him (John 6:66).

The Lord commissioned his church to make disciples. This includes bringing the lost person to an initial experience with Christ. Making disciples also involves growing people in Christ and sending people out for Christ. Gaining a convert is only the beginning of the total responsibility of the local church. Each convert needs personal care and guidance to experience normal spiritual growth. He must be taught how to live a Christian life. The convert needs instruction in how to pray, study the Bible, share his faith, and discover his own unique Christian ministry.

Christ's imperative commission involves consecration. Evangelism can never be defined or practiced as enlistment. It is the making of disciples, the maturing of converts. One of evangelism's most serious problems is the large number who join the church and eventually drop out of active church life and service. According to recent reports, 40 percent of those who join a church each year will be lost from the program and from the influence of the church within ten years. Why is conservation a serious problem? Is evangelism to blame? Isn't it largely because churches have simply interpreted Jesus' imperative commission as an enrollment campaign instead of as the task of making disciples? As fishers of men, have we not carelessly put our fish in a sack with a hole in the bottom? Have we not left our new-born babes in Christ outside for a while to see if they will live before bringing them into the house as active members of the family?

Children do not grow automatically. An infant's physical growth depends upon care, nourishment, and training after the moment of birth. Likewise, a new Christian requires proper care and instruction. Evangelism of the Great Commission attempts to provide helps that will be conducive to spiritual maturation. "As newborn babes, desire the sincere milk of the word, that ye may grow thereby" (1 Pet. 2:2). The New Testament portrays a Christian as a person who has experienced a new birth and thereby has the potential for spiritual growth. The progression toward maturity begins with conversion and continues throughout a person's life. Let us study some of the tried and successful methods of conserving the results of evangelism by enlisting and training and using the converts who are won to Christ.

Continue the Contact

In most cases converts are won to Christ by a Christian's taking a personal interest in a lost individual. The Great Commission says to make disciples "as you go." The going involves an identification and relationship with another person. It communicates the fact that a person cares for another's precious soul. The helpful human element in the conversion experience is a concerned Christian who takes a personal interest.

If the contact helps to win the person, the convert can be conserved by continual contact. The new convert needs someone to be his special friend, someone to spend time with him. Jesus' first concern for the newly chosen disciples was that they be "with him." "And he goeth up into a mountain, and calleth unto him whom he would: and they came unto him. And he ordained twelve, that they should be with him, and that he might send them forth to preach" (Mark 3:13-14). Jesus knew that committed disciples would gain much from personal association. Let us examine some possible ways the church can continue the contact with the new Christian.

Contact by the Pastor

The pastor is as responsible for enlisting and developing new members as he is for winning new converts. "Feed my sheep" was the Savior's command. "Teaching them to observe all things" was in Christ's imperative commission.

1. A pastoral visit.—The alert pastor will do well to visit every new member within two to four weeks after one joins the church. The sooner it comes, the better. Infant mortality among spiritual babes in the church can be reduced greatly by a little personal care from the pastor. Few pastors have so many annual baptisms that they cannot visit every new convert. Nothing will replace the concern of a pastor for a new Christian.

2. *A letter of welcome.*—Every new member will appreciate a letter of welcome as well as a visit from the pastor. It is helpful also to send a certificate of baptism to the convert. One might enclose a copy of the church covenant, and literature about the church may be sent.

3. *A gift book.*—The church should furnish the pastor with a gift book for each new member. We suggest: *Finding God's Best* by John Hunter; *After the Spirit Comes* by Jack Taylor; *The Key to Triumphant Living* by Jack Taylor; *Thinking About God* by Fisher Humphreys; or *Mere Christianity* by C. S. Lewis.

4. *Occasional recognition.*—The pastor could utilize several ways to recognize new members who have recently come into the church. The new members could sit with the pastor during the time of the Lord's Supper. An annual recognition service may be helpful. An occasional reception in the church parlors or pastorium given in their honor could be exceedingly helpful.

5. *Pastoral encouragement.*—The pastor could work with each individual convert and encourage him to take up six habits of life:

> Yielding to the Holy Spirit each day
> Reading God's Word daily
> Praying daily
> Faithful attendance at worship services
> Tithing income into the Lord's work
> Talking to someone about his soul at least once each week

Contact by a Deacon

The New Testament responsibility for a deacon is to minister. Perhaps the first selection of deacons was in Jerusalem, when there arose a murmuring of the Grecian widows against the Hebrews (see Acts 6:1-7). Six men were selected to minister to the needs of the congregation so that the apostles could minister more effectively with the word of God.

1. Deacon family ministry.—The church could adopt and use a type of program known as the Deacon Family Ministry. This is a plan in which a deacon has from ten to fifteen family units and seeks to minister to the variety of needs of the families. Deacons would be assigned members as they join the church. The deacon would visit the new convert two to four weeks after his joining the church. The visit would maintain the contact and deepen the relationship.

2. Informal deacon contact.—Deacons can be used to minister to new converts by informal contacts. Even if a church does not have the Deacon Family Ministry, the members could utilize deacons to maintain informal contacts with new converts for at least a year or two. This would mean that the deacon would make a visit to the convert, invite the convert into his home, or check with the convert periodically by telephone.

Contact by a Sunday School Teacher

Sunday School teachers could be valuable resources for conserving the results of enlisting disciples. The Sunday School teacher must show a genuine interest. He must personally get to know and love the person. He needs to pray daily that, as a teacher, he will experience a growing love and understanding for his pupils. He must never let the contact become a matter of duty. In many cases the teacher probably was a valuable instrument in the person's conversion. The Bible teacher can continue the contact.

1. A personal visit.—The Sunday School teacher could make a visit to the new convert. The purpose of the visit would be to celebrate the victory and to share Bible study materials used in the class. The teacher could share ways the student could study the Sunday School lessons and make them more meaningful.

2. A time for recognition.—The Sunday School teacher could take a few minutes in the class to recognize the decision of a class member. An occasional social could be planned in honor of the new convert.

Contact by a Sponsor

Another helpful means of continuing the contact with the convert is the idea of a sponsor. This is someone selected to spend time with the new Christian. This friend or sponsor needs to associate with the new convert, to answer his questions, to guide his prayer and Bible study habits, and to lead him into the larger fellowship of the local church. The sponsor would concentrate his ministry on a select few.

1. Selection of a sponsor.—The most important matter about a sponsor is choosing the right person. Pastors should follow Jesus' example of praying before he selected the twelve. If a person serves as a sponsor of a new convert, he needs to demonstrate a genuine love for Christ, faithfulness, a gift for sponsoring, and a teachableness.

2. Training of a sponsor.—The best way to train a sponsor is to follow a one-on-one procedure. The pastor should select a potential sponsor and work through discipleship materials just as the sponsor would do later with a new convert. Materials could be selected on the Lord, the Christian life, the Holy Spirit, the church, the Christian witness, and the Bible and prayer. The pastor could train one to train another. Then the one trained could be a trainer. This could be a multiplying process of helping the new Christian.

3. Assignment of the sponsor.—Within forty-eight hours of a commitment, some type of personal contact needs to be made. Every day of delay lessens the effectiveness of conserving the results of enlistment. It is necessary to assign a sponsor no longer than two to seven days after the decision. Care should be taken to match the convert and sponsor with respect to gender, age, background, and address.

Teach Them to Observe

Anyone who has made a decision for Christ should be carefully instructed in Christian living. Jesus spent much of his time with the disciples, teaching them both by precept and example how to live his kind of life. A prominent part of the Great Commission is "teaching them to observe all things whatsoever I have commanded you." Let us notice some practical insights of when and what we need to teach the new disciples of Jesus.

The Time for Instruction

Many churches have a series of orientation meetings for instructions of all new members. Time is important for the new Christian. About two to seven days after the initial decision to accept Christ, some formal instruction should be started. Failing to begin immediately with teaching will heighten the possibility of the person becoming a church "dropout." Of course, one cannot lose the relationship; but the joyous fellowship of the Christian life can be impaired.

1. *The Church Training class.*—The most likely time for teaching the new Christian is during the Church Training time. This class could be led by the pastor or by a gifted layperson. The meetings would be on a eight- to fifteen-week basis in which the new Christian would have special instruction. After completing the course, the convert could move into another phase of Church Training. Most churches have utilized the Church Training class to train new members and to continue the in-depth discipling of every Christian. No one ever graduates from the school of Christian training; therefore, the matter of conserving the enlistment into Christ continues for a lifetime. The Church Training class can also be used as a time to train converts for a place of leadership in the church.

2. *The home Bible class.*—Some churches utilize the home Bible study as a means of training the young convert. In some cases, parents can be instructed to train their children who have made a profession of faith. Unfortunately, this will not be effective when one or both parents do not give diligence to this pursuit. However, if parents will teach their children, this will be an excellent time and system to help conserve evangelism.

Another method would be to place material in the hands of the young convert and allow him to study privately. At a designated time, the convert could report progress to a designated person. One of the real problems of individual study is the lack of continual motivation from another person and the absence of guidance from a leader.

The Curriculum of Training

What does the new disciple need to learn? Numerous subjects could be discussed.

1. *The life in Christ.*—The believer needs to first acknowledge that becoming a disciple means joining his life with Christ's. Believing has not been a matter of studying or working to gain acceptance from God. Becoming a Christian has been the act of inviting Jesus Christ into one's life. This makes the salvation experience a personal relationship with the Lord.

Some word needs to be given regarding the assurance of this wonderful relationship. Sometimes after the initial conversion, the new Christian will face moments of doubt. In most cases, he examines his present feelings with the tremendous excitement he felt when he first became a Christian. The believer must not trust in feelings at this point. "For we walk by faith, not by sight" (2 Cor. 5:7). The Christian can know and be certain of a right relationship with God. Though there are many inadequacies, deficiencies, and areas for growth, the Christian can have assurance. "These things have I written unto you that believe on the name of the Son of God; that ye may know that ye have eternal life, and that ye may believe on the name of the Son of God" (1 John 5:13; see also 1 John 2:3-5; 3:14; 4:13; John 3:36). The Christian must be taught that upon the basis of faith God has accepted him, and he must stand upon the promise, integrity, and ability of God (see John 10:27-29; Rom. 8:35-39).

2. *The Spirit-filled life.*—After the disciple has learned about the beginning of the Christian life, he can learn the continuation. When a person trusts Christ, the Holy Spirit comes to live in him. He lives in the believer's body each day of his life. Therefore, living the Christian life does not mean trying to live as God wants him to. It means trusting Christ and allowing him to live in and through the believer. Nothing will help the believer any more than to know about and to yield to the Holy Spirit.

In addition to the Spirit's residency in the convert's life, the Holy Spirit fills the yielding believer with the ability to do God's will in service and witnessing. Believers need to learn that the Spirit can live in them, but they need to yield to his power. God wants every Christian to be Spirit-filled. The infilling of the Spirit gives power to work, to live, and to witness. A vital part of the new convert's instruction is to teach how to live the Spirit-filled life. Being filled with the Spirit means to acknowledge the gift of God's Holy Spirit, to confess sin, and to submit self to the control of the Spirit. The instructor could teach the believer to pray this prayer each morning: "Lord, I cannot make this day without your power. I confess that I have sinned (name your sins). I yield today to the power of thy Holy Spirit. I ask this for Jesus' sake. Amen."

3. *The life in the church.*—The New Testament knows no evangelistic enlistment without participation and involvement in the church.

Jesus Christ established the church while he was here on earth to unite disciples as a spiritual family of God. The new convert needs instruction on the church. He needs to learn that the church is a fellowship of baptized believers joining themselves together for worship and study in order to obey the commands of Christ. It is God's colony of heaven placed on earth to show a world of darkness the grace and glory of God's eternal salvation.

No curriculum of follow-up evangelism should be without the practical instructions of the believer's responsibilities to the fellowship of believers. What should be shared with the convert about duties?

Attend the church.—"Let us hold fast the profession of our faith without wavering; (for he is faithful that promised;) And let us consider one another to provoke unto love and to good works: Not forsaking the assembling of ourselves together, as the manner of some is; but exhorting one another: and so much the more, as ye see the day approaching" (Heb. 10:23-25).

Support the church.—"Every man according as he purposeth in his heart, so let him give; not grudgingly, or of necessity: for God loveth a cheerful giver" (2 Cor. 9:7). "Now concerning the collection for the saints, as I have given order to the churches of Galatia, even so do ye. Upon the first day of the week let every one of you lay by him in store, as God hath prospered him, that there be no gatherings when I come" (1 Cor. 16:1-2).

Serve the church.—"As every man hath received the gift, even so minister the same one to another, as good stewards of the manifold grace of God. If any man speak, let him speak as the oracles of God; if any man minister, let him do it as of the ability which God giveth: that God in all things may be glorified through Jesus Christ, to whom be praise and dominion for ever and ever. Amen" (1 Pet. 4:10-11).

Work to maintain the fellowship of the church.—"For your fellowship in the gospel from the first day until now; Being confident of this very thing, that he which hath begun a good work in you will perform it until the day of Jesus Christ: Even as it is meet for me to think this of you all, because I have you in my heart; inasmuch as both in my bonds, and in the defence and confirmation of the gospel, ye all are partakers of my grace" (Phil. 1:5-7).

Respect the leaders and other members.—"And we beseech you, brethren, to know them which labour among you, and are over you in the Lord, and admonish you; And to esteem them very highly in love for their work's sake. And be at peace among yourselves" (1 Thess. 5:12-13). "Bear ye one another's burdens, and so fulfill the law of Christ" (Gal. 6:2).

4. The life of prayer and Bible study.—Christ wanted the disciples to observe the command to pray and to know God's word. He spent time in teaching the disciples how to pray. The curriculum could teach the disciples some practical pointers on prayer. One helpful method would be instructions in intelligent and orderly conversation with God. If one studies the Lord's Prayer (Matt. 6:9-13), one can detect something of an order about it. The instructor of young converts could develop a pattern of prayer by using the following word design: Adoration, Gratitude, Confession, Intercession, Commitment.

Adoration.—Teach the convert to begin conversations with God with great respect and admiration. Tell the convert to look to some psalms of praise for help (see Ps. 150).

Gratitude.—Teach the convert to express gratitude to God for salvation, family, friends, health, job, church, and numerous other blessings. This is to teach people to say "Thank you" to God.

Confession.—When one comes into the presence of God, he is convicted of sin. The convert needs to confess every known sin.

Intercession.—In this part of the conversation with God the convert is taught to make requests to God—friends, unsaved people, the sick, missionaries, his needs.

Commitment.—Prayer should involve a time of making vows to God. The disciple needs to make specific commitments to the Lord.

These five words—adoration, gratitude, confession, intercession, and commitment—give the convert some direction in prayer.

In addition to prayer, the convert needs to be taught the Bible. Studying the Scripture introduces us to Christ personally. The convert could be taught the Scriptures in the Sunday School. It is a detailed weekly study of the Scripture. Studying the Scripture under a gifted teacher each Lord's Day will add an immeasurable depth to any disciple's life.

An instructor of the young convert could introduce the new convert to private Bible reading and study. There are a number of plans available for daily Bible readings. One helpful method is to read a chapter a day from the Old Testament and a chapter a day from the New Testament.

Another helpful method in teaching the convert how to use the Bible is to encourage memorization of Scripture. The King James Version is a good translation to use in memorization. Learning Scripture by memory helps a person meditate upon God's word anytime, anywhere. It also affords the convert with a resource against temptation and for witnessing. The Navigators of Colorado Springs, Colorado, offer the *Topical Memory System.* It is a 108-verse correspondence course.

5. *The life of sharing with others.*—The convert needs a curriculum which concludes with training for witnessing. We will discuss personal witnessing in part IV of this book. Also, suggestions for training laypersons were discussed in part III, chapter 13.

The instructor for new converts could conclude the new-member orientation with a time of mutual sharing of testimonies with each other. One method would be to write the testimony and to share it with the class. Another method would be to pick a partner and share Christ with one another.

The young convert could be taught the Roman Road or the essentials of the tract "How to Have a Full and Meaningful Life." Dr. Joe Cothen, a successful Baptist pastor and teacher, utilizes a unique method of teaching a Christian to share Christ with a lost person. He provides copies of *Good News by a Man Named John* from the American Bible Society for the converts. He then leads them in how to share Christ with John. In the Gospel of John booklet, he has a series of written notes:

1. On the first page he has, "Turn to page 23." On page 23 is Step 1: "Everyone Has a Sin Problem." John 8:21-24 is blocked in red ink. Then he has written "Turn to page 7."

2. On page 7 is Step 2: "But God Loves You." John 3:16-18 is marked, and a note on the page reads, "Turn to page 8."

3. On page 8 is Step 3: "Consider the Choices." John 3:6 is marked with a note, "Turn to page 18."

4. On page 18 is Step 4: "The Way to God." John 6:59-65 is marked, and a note reads "Turn to page 16."

5. On page 16 is Step 5: "What You Should Do." John 6:27-29,34-35 is marked. Then a note reads, "Turn to page 30."

6. On page 30 is Step 6: "What Christ Does for You." John 10:20-28 is marked, and a note is given: "Turn to page 36."

7. On page 36 is Step 7: "Decide Now." The passages of John 12:35-36 and 12:48 are marked.

This method or one similar to it should be used to involve the convert in sharing his faith. No curriculum of follow-up is completely without teaching involvement, the sharing of faith with another.

Involvement in Christ's Work

Each convert becomes a disciple of Christ. This makes him responsible to the Lord. Jesus never had an active and inactive state for disciples. Each disciple should be involved in the ministry of Christ. Pastors, church leaders, and a few selected laypersons are not the only ones to be involved in Christ's service. Every disciple is involved in the ministry of Christ. Let's notice some specific involvements for the new Christian.

Join the Church

Joining a church involves more than a religious performance. It means confessing publicly one's relationship to the Lord Jesus Christ. It involves much more than having one's name placed on a church membership roll. It means being involved in the worship and service of Christ's church.

1. Baptism.—The convert's experience of baptism can be vivid. Instead of a routine appendage to a service, it can be made into a memorial act of obedience and commitment. Christ's imperative commission included baptism. Without a doubt, the Lord wanted the act of baptism to be meaningful. God witnesses to the church in baptism, and the church offers its witness to the world by the same rite. Sanday and Headlam in their commentary on Romans 6:4 expressed the significance of baptism:

> When we descended into the baptismal water, that meant that we died with Christ—to sin. When the water closed over our heads, that meant that we lay buried with Him, in proof that our death to sin, like his death, was real. But this carries with it the third

step in the process. As Christ was raised from among the dead by a majestic exercise of Divine Power, so we also must from henceforth conduct ourselves as men in whom has been implanted a new principle of life.[1]

One needs to remember that the ordinance of baptism is the first official act of involvement in the church. One is not a member of a local church until the act of baptism has been performed. The act itself teaches that believers are involved with Christ.

2. *Lord's Supper.*—The convert's first experience of the Lord's Supper should be a meaningful one. Of course, the subsequent ones need to be meaningful also. New converts could be recognized in their first participation. The Lord's Supper is a time when every disciple is reminded of his intimate involvement with Christ and his work.

Participate in Church Functions

Paul declared the church to be the body of Christ with Christ as its head. This means that each believer looks to Christ to establish the work. This work may be thought of as its function. In seeking to clarify the work of the church, a special study group of Southern Baptists defined five functions of a church: worship, witness, education, ministry, and application. Each disciple should be involved in these functions.

1. *Worship.*—Worship is a person's response to God's revelation of himself. It results in the deepening of faith and a strengthening for service. Worship on the Lord's Day should be central to the Christian life. Participating in worship is a direct touch which people have with God.

Corporate worship can help the new disciple to be aware of God. "For where two or three are gathered together in my name, there am I in the midst of them" (Matt. 18:20). In worship the believer becomes involved in adoration and praise, in confession of sin, in thanksgiving, and in life commitment.

2. *Education.*—The church has the responsibility of guiding persons toward Christian maturity. This includes teaching and training. The church has Sunday School, Church Training, Woman's Missionary Union, and Brotherhood to teach members. If converts become involved in these organizations, and if the organizations remain true to their specific functions of teaching Christ's Word, then the member

can be involved in meaningful Christian education.

3. Witness.—The church must lead each member to witness with power of his own encounter with Christ. A growing faith in Christ lives out and speaks out. A church succeeds when members are involved daily in Christ's life-style and are busily engaged in telling others about the Christ.

4. Ministry.—Disciples can meet human needs in the spirit of Christ. The words *minister* and *serve* come from the same Greek root. This means that each Christian is a servant or minister. The church exists to meet the needs of people. "We then that are strong ought to bear the infirmities of the weak, and not to please ourselves" (Rom. 15:1). Becoming involved in helping others in the name of Christ will enhance the believer's feeling of fulfillment.

5. Application.—Participation in church life means far more than going to Sunday School, Church Training, and worship service. It means the practical application of Christian principles in all the issues of everyday life. A Christian disciple is one who believes and behaves. Each disciple is to respond in openness to Christ and to apply the principles of Christ.

Use Spiritual Gifts for Christ's Church

When Christ enters into a believer's life, he gives each convert a practical function to perform. Paul compared the church to the body of Christ. "For as the body is one, and hath many members, and all the members of that one body, being many, are one body: so also is Christ" (1 Cor.12:12). God gives every convert one or more "gifts of the Spirit" so that we may use them for his glory. "But the manifestation of the Spirit is given to every man to profit withal" (1 Cor. 12:7). The God who made the human body has designed the body of Christ. "Now there are diversities of gifts, but the same Spirit. And there are differences of administrations, but the same Lord" (1 Cor. 12:4-5). The spiritual gifts are much more than our natural talents. Let us summarize briefly the matter of spiritual gifts.

1. Examine the spiritual gifts.—A helpful exercise would be to study the concept of spiritual gifts in Romans 12:6-8; 1 Corinthians 12:4-30; Ephesians 4:11-12. The gifts have been classified in many ways. We shall attempt to make our own classification. First, there are the speaking gifts—apostleship, prophecy, evangelism, shepherding, teaching, exhorting, words of wisdom, words of knowledge, tongues, and interpretation. Second, there are the ministering gifts—hospitality, giving, ruling, showing mercy, faith, discernment, miracles, and healing. Third, there are the demonstrative gifts—miracles, healing, tongues, and interpretations.

2. *Discover your spiritual gift or gifts.*—After one has studied the spiritual gifts from the biblical perspective, he should seek to discover his gift or gifts. Let's look at several suggestions. First, affirm that God's Holy Spirit dwells within you. Let God show you the gift or gifts he wants you to have. Second, examine your excitement for Christian service. Lingering inward impulses and abilities could likely originate from the promptings of the Holy Spirit. Third, identify crucial areas of need in your church. Fourth, evaluate the results of your efforts to serve. Fifth, follow the guidance of the Holy Spirit as he leads you to obey the Lord. Sixth, be alert to the responses of other Christians.

Conserve the results! Think about maintaining the contact, teaching them to observe, and involving them in service. These methods will help recover the drastic drop of discipleship. To accomplish these suggestions in a creative manner will be to attempt to complete Christ's imperative commission.

Suggestions for Advanced Study

1. Mention all the methods for conservation of the results of evangelism which you find mentioned or implied in the following references: Acts 15:36; 16:1-5; 18:22-23; 1 Corinthians 4:1; 2 Corinthians 12:18-21.

2. Arrange these elements of Paul's enlistment system in order of importance; as you see them: visiting, teaching, writing his epistles, organizing churches, ordaining ministers and deacons, and admonishing backsliders. Tell why you placed the first one in the first place and the last one in the last place.

3. Work out a program of new member orientation for your church. Include the principles of contact, training, and involvement. Order

Survival Kit for New Christians from the Church Training Department of the Baptist Sunday School Board, 127 Ninth Avenue, North, Nashville, Tennessee 37234.

References for Further Study

Brooks, H. Hal. *Follow-up Evangelism.* Nashville: Broadman Press, 1972.

Foshee, Howard B. *The Ministry of the Deacon.* Nashville: Convention Press, 1968.

Kuhne, Gary W. *The Dynamics of Discipleship Training: Being and Producing Spiritual Leaders.* Grand Rapids: Zondervan Publishing House, 1978.

Lumpkin, William L. *Meditations on Christian Baptism.* Nashville: Broadman Press, 1976.

McEachern, Alton H. *Here at Thy Table, Lord: Enriching the Observance of the Lord's Supper.* Nashville: Broadman Press, 1977.

Moore, Wayland B. *New Testament Follow-up.* Grand Rapids: William B. Eerdmans Company, 1975.

Neighbour, Jr., Ralph W. *This Gift is Mine.* Nashville: Broadman Press, 1974.

Schaller, Lyle E. *Assimilating New Members.* Nashville: Abingdon Press, 1978.

Waldrup, Earl. *New Church Member Orientation Manual.* Nashville: Convention Press, 1973.

Note

1. William Sanday and Arthur C. Headlam, *Romans,* The International Critical Commentary (New York: Charles Scribner's Sons, 1910), p. 154.

15

The Soul-Winner's Self-Discipline

For God hath not given us the spirit of fear; but of power, and of love, and of a sound mind. Be not thou therefore ashamed of the testimony of our Lord (2 Tim. 1:7-8).

The authors of this book have sought to acquaint you with various facets of Christ's commission. Studies have been made into the imperative need for evangelism, the historic illustration of evangelism, and methods and techniques of evangelism. Now we shall discuss the important part of making disciples by personal evangelism. Before reading the remainder of the book, please stop and ask yourself the following three questions: First, am I really anxious to try to win others to Christ? Second, am I studying this book in order to try to learn better how to win souls? Third, if I learn some principles of soul-winning, am I actually going to use them in trying to win someone to the Savior? The most difficult part of soul-winning will have been overcome if the reader can answer these questions affirmatively.

Personal evangelism is as necessary as pulpit evangelism. God does not make pulpit evangelists out of many Christians, but he can make personal evangelists of all Christians. Indeed, if the pulpit evangelist is not also a personal evangelist, he is merely a pretender evangelist and possibly an impostor evangelist. If personal evangelism should cease for two generations, the number of disciples would be reduced substantially.

God specializes on the individual; and so every Christian should take an interest in the individual. Once someone wrote a United States senator in behalf of a wronged person. The senator replied that he was so busy with the affairs of the nation that he could not take time for individuals. The person responded to the senator, "When last heard of, our Maker had not reached this attitude." In the parables of Luke 15, Jesus did not speak of a lost flock, but of a lost sheep; not of a lost fortune, but of a lost coin; not of a lost race or nation, but of a lost boy. Jesus reserved his best for individuals. Jesus summarized the law to an unnamed scribe, and to a proud ruler he gave his great discourse on the new birth. He paused while dying for the world to take time to speak salvation to a lost thief being crucified at his side.

Personal soul-winners do not happen automatically. Christians do not become personal evangelists by birth, by accident, or by assuming a church position. Soul-winners are inspired by the Holy Spirit. They are trained in the church. They gain experience by self-discipline within their own wills, directing them in personal efforts to win souls. Christ paid the price of taking a personal interest in the needs of human beings. Christians must pay the price of purpose, consecration, and self-discipline in order to win souls. One must engage in rigid self-discipline to become a soul-winner.

Earnestly Developing Concern for People

A Christian must be deeply concerned for people, else he or she will never attempt to share Christ with a person. Every Christian meets and talks with unsaved persons. More opportunities are lost than won to share Christ with others. In most cases the average Christian does not have sharing Christ on his mind. Christians become worldly-minded, self-minded, or pleasure-minded rather than people-minded. The effective soul-winner is one whose mind is on the souls of people so sincerely that he recognizes the opportunities and grasps them when they are presented.

Inward Compassion

Every fruit-bearing tree is two trees. There would be no fruit-bearing above the ground if there were not an unseen tree underneath, with taproot and tentacles, quietly drawing moisture and minerals from the ground to give substance to the fruit. Just so, there is an inward reason for outward fruit. Compassion for other people begins within an individual. God gave his Son as the gift of concern and sympathy for people. God in his Holy Spirit must give the gift of compassion for others.

One cannot develop genuine, godly concern for others without the Holy Spirit. Also, merely looking at the pitiful plight of people does not constitute genuine compassion. No one can lead another to a genuine concern for others apart from the compassion the Lord gave.

Perpetual Passion

As one walks with Christ daily, he hears afresh the assuring words, "For the Son of man came to seek and to save that which was lost" (Luke 19:10, ASV). Living with Christ makes one thrill over how Jesus led a Samaritan woman out of her shattered romances into purity of heart and into the joy of soul-winning. Fellowship with the Savior makes one long to imitate him as he searched the soul of the rich young ruler, as he earnestly taught Nicodemus the Pharisee by night, and as he sobbed over the lost souls and the impending doom of his beloved Jerusalem.

People! People! People! To save people was the perennial passion of the Master's gracious heart. He saw people lost from the way, lost from God, lost from the highest possibilities in life, lost for time, and lost for eternity. The lostness of people was the terrifying, poignant, limitless, bottomless reality which haunted the heart of the Savior.

One who seeks to imitate the Master cannot fail to love lost people if Christ's imperative commission is to be accomplished in our day and generation. Seeking to share Christ with others cannot be a sporadic matter. It must be a perpetual, daily concern of the Christian.

There are no great soul-winners who are not diligent in fervent, intercessory prayer. The apostle Paul said, "Brethren, my heart's desire and prayer to God for Israel is that they might be saved" (Rom. 10:1). No wonder Paul made disciples and planted churches throughout the Roman Empire! Augustine, after his conversion, became a man of penitential and importunate prayer. Prayer was the chief characteristic of John Tauler's evangelism. Martin Luther once said he was so busy that he was compelled to stop for prayer at least three times a day. John Wesley is said to have hungered for souls, to have agonized in prayer for souls, and to have been out of breath pursuing souls. Henry Martyn's prayer was, "Let me burn out for Christ and for souls." John Knox prayed, "Give me Scotland, or I die." Soul-winners must have something of the fervor of intercessory prayer.

J. I. Packer wrote that "Where we are not consciously relying on God, there we shall inevitably be found relying on ourselves. And the spirit of self-reliance is a blight on evangelism." [1] One of the crucial lessons to learn in evangelism is that Christians are engaged in a powerful warfare. We are battling unseen satanic forces. Dealing with these unseen powers without prayer is folly. People will be born into the kingdom of God when we humbly acknowledge our weakness and call upon God for his strength.

Great revivals require prayer. Periods of great spiritual renewal come with fervent, importunate prayer from Christians. Prayer in rural churches caused the beginning of the Great Awakening of 1800 in America. Men's prayer groups were the real power of the revival of 1858. Fresh winds blow wherever people bind themselves in prayer, acknowledging their dependence upon God. Every Christian should be able to say to every lost person he knows: "God forbid that I should sin against the Lord in ceasing to pray for you" (1 Sam. 12:23).

Practical, Persistent Disciplines

Failing to win a person to Christ is not a sin, but not attempting to share Christ is. Consistent effort at winning souls is the product of self-discipline. There are many practical disciplines to motivate and to keep a person at the task of sharing Christ with others.

A prayer list not only reminds one of his task of winning others, but it also proves to be a channel through which God's Spirit pours his blessings. One should pray daily for those on his prayer list, weep over the lost who are indifferent, and have the prayer list in his or her Bible when they turn to read and claim the promises of God (Ps. 126:6; Isa. 55:11; Acts 1:8; Luke 11:9-13).

A definite program of visitation for soul-winning should be maintained. A weekday night, Sunday evening, or some specified time can be given priority for visiting the lost. Receiving an assignment from a prospect list of the local church has proven to be an excellent discipline for exercising concern for people.

Choosing partners in soul-winning could be genuinely helpful. If one contracts with another person to visit jointly and share the gospel with another, the motivation then seems to be stronger. The Lord recognized the wisdom and strength of a partnership. Partnership also lends itself to teaching in that one learns from the personality and the technique of the other. Furthermore, there is a sense of companionship in the task of sharing the gospel.

One needs to be persistent in sharing the gospel of Jesus Christ with another person. In a few cases a person will receive Jesus Christ on an initial visit. But in most cases, an identification and relationship needs to be established. To secure a decision for Christ will often take numerous visits and many presentations. The active soul-winner has many prospects all the time, some at various stages of the process, and is collecting other prospects all the while. The practical discipline of soul-winning involves a persistent contact with people.

Realistically Facing Personal Problems

Making disciples by personal evangelism is not an automatic task. It requires rigid self-discipline and the Spirit-filled approach to sharing Christ. Various personal problems either prohibit or hinder one from becoming a diligent, personal soul-winner. To become a more effective soul-winner, one must seek to discover various personal problems which hinder him and request God's resources to overcome them.

Fear

After a long life of soul-winning endeavor, the apostle Paul was in prison, awaiting Nero's executioner. He was writing his best advice, his gravest warning, and his most alluring encouragement to his young friend Timothy. He warned him against the young Christian's most dreadful enemy, fear. "For God gave us not a spirit of fearfulness; but of power and love and discipline" (2 Tim. 1:7, ASV).

Every soul-winner must courageously face and fight fear. Fear is a dreadful foe, living down in the inner consciousness, which reaches up with a cold and crushing hand laying hold upon the noblest impulses and the most sacred purposes of the will. Fear is a stifling, stultifying, scourging experience for soul-winners. God is not the author of fear; the devil is. Satan has found fear effective in preventing Christians from starting or continuing the task of making disciples.

People have various forms of fear which hinder personal evangelism. They are afraid that they might offend others and receive some sort of ridicule. Some are afraid that they might invade the personal privacy of another individual. Still others fear incompetency in answering questions from the possible convert. More people manifest a fear, though, because of the prospect of rejection. No one wants to be rejected or regarded as an oddity; therefore, they consider that the safest method is to keep silent.

All soul-winners will fail to win some whom they approach. Jesus failed to win some. He did not win the rich young ruler. He did not win many religious leaders. He failed to win many in his hometown of Nazareth. In spite of these failures, he won others. Jesus kept on seeking the lost. His ministry was filled with victory and defeat. Every consistent Christian who seeks to share the gospel with others will experience the joy of victory and the agony of rejection.

The personal evangelist must fight the fear of failure. How can we defeat the debilitating enemy of fear? First, listen to the command of God in his Word. Repeatedly in the Bible appear the words of God; "Fear not!" "Fear not, Abram: I am thy shield, and thy exceeding great reward" (Gen. 15:1), said God to the patriarch. "Fear thou not; for I am with thee" (Isa. 41:10), said God to Israel in captivity. "Fear not," said the angels to Joseph, to Mary, to the shepherds, and to the women at the open tomb. "It is I; be not afraid" (Matt. 14:27), said Christ to the disciples in the night. "Fear not" (Acts 27:24), said Christ to Paul in a storm. "Fear not; I am the first and the last" (Rev. 1:17), said Christ to John in persecution. Look in a concordance and see how often the exhortation to "fear not" is given.

Second, fear can be conquered by observing actual contact with people. If most people are approached in a natural and sensitive manner, they will react with interest and courtesy. God has prepared others in a variety of ways, and people wait and long for a word from the Lord. Many of our fears will vanish if we realize that God will often lead us to those who long to respond. The best antidote to fear is a love that leads us to forget our own fears and to focus on the needs of others.

Incompentency

"I simply do not know how to win others" and "I do not know how to answer their questions" are the oft-heard statements of Christians. Let no one confuse ignorance about knowing how with his fearfulness or unwillingness to attempt it. Many Christians do feel incompetent to share the gospel with another because they have never been trained. The obvious answer to this personal problem is "Learn how." The best way to overcome this type of deficiency is to learn a system of presentation and to attempt the system. No one can learn to play golf, drive a car, paint pictures, write poems, play a piano, or do any other good thing without beginning it.

When Thomas A. Edison was trying to produce the phonograph, he had great difficulty in perfecting the sound. He said, "I would speak into the machine the word 'specia,' and the hateful thing would answer back 'pecia.' I worked on that difficulty eighteen hours a day for seven months, until I finally conquered it." Why should Christians not be willing to lose some sleep and use some perseverance like that in trying to learn to win others to Christ?

"Anybody but me, Lord" is what too many Christians say when God calls them to a soul-winning task. "There are so many who can do it better than I can" is the devil's suggestion. When God called Gideon to a task, he feared his inability because of his poor family. Jeremiah feared he could not do God's bidding. Moses feared his lack of ability; but when he let God be the judge of that ability, he found himself the possessor of tremendous power. Fear of their inability made the ten spies lead Israel into nearly forty years of useless wandering before conquering Canaan. Any Christian's abilities, linked by faith to God's promised power, ensures certain success. David's boyish ability with the sling was used of God to destroy Goliath, the terror of the whole army. God made powerful the human abilities of Shamgar with the oxgoad, Samson with the jawbone of an ass, Dorcas with the needle, Gideon with the pitchers, Jael with the tent pin, a widow with two mites, and a lad with five loaves and two fish.

Inconsistency

All too frequently the convert's difficulty about personal soul-winning arises out of inward feeling about his or her Christian life. Without a doubt, inconsistency in morals which one is not trying to correct will hurt and hinder one's effort. However, no Christian will win souls if he waits for perfection in his own life. Few piano recitals would ever be given if every pianist waited until perfection in music had been attained. There were mistakes and imperfections in the lives of Peter, Paul, James, John, and the others, even while they were trying and succeeding in making disciples. They grew in grace while they were growing in the art of winning others to the Savior.

God does not wait until a disciple is perfect to use him. A disciple is a continuous learner who submits to the lordship of Christ. Throughout the pilgrimage the Christian has something to share of what God is doing in his or her life. Sharing Christ with another person doesn't mean that you are perfect. It means that you are growing into the likeness of Christ through the Holy Spirit's power, and you desire for others to join in this exciting pilgrimage.

Tact

The problem of lack of tact could hinder personal soul-winning. Tact is exceedingly essential. All the common sense and kindness and good judgment one has should be brought into play in one's evangelism. All the possible knowledge about the personality and turn of mind of the unsaved should be gained. Yet a sincere love for Christ and a sincere love for the lost man will be the best safeguards against tactlessness. Honest mistakes are scarcely seen by the unsaved if there is unmistakable evidence of this genuine love. "[Love] . . . is not easily provoked" (1 Cor. 13:4-5).

Failure to exercise tact in sharing the gospel could drive others away. The gospel of Christ does not drive people away, but the approach of people with the gospel repels many. The life and teachings of Jesus drove some away, so they followed him no more. The soul-winner's responsibility is to share God's gospel with others in as true and as attractive a manner as possible. The soul-winner can study the approach of the Lord. He established a common interest and allowed the prospective convert to share freely. Observe the Lord with the Samaritan woman at the well. Instead of condemnation, he used a tactful approach with her by conversing about water and its relationship to spiritual thirst. He courteously allowed her to give her opinion and to share with him. If one's approach with people hinders, then some self-discipline and godly wisdom needs to be sought in order to be tactful and courteous with others.

Doubt

Doubt poses a personal problem which must be solved before one can be an effective soul-winner. Christians can fall into the idea of thinking that the gospel may not change a person's life. Seeing and hearing of so many alternatives could cause one to question the validity of the gospel for the whole world. The Buddhist, the Hindu, and other religions present their way of life.

The Christian must not lose confidence in the gospel. The apostle Paul had a great confidence in the gospel of Jesus Christ. He had seen the gospel work. He had experienced the gospel, and the gospel was validated by its power in the lives of people. "So, as much as in me is, I am ready to preach the gospel to you that are at Rome also. For I am not ashamed of the gospel of Christ: for it is the power of God unto salvation to every one that believeth; to the Jew first, and also to the Greek" (Rom. 1:15-16). Even though there were many other religions in Paul's day, he never compromised or lost confidence in the glorious gospel of Christ.

Triumphantly Overcoming Personal Problems

No personal problem needs to prohibit a Christian from fulfilling Christ's imperative commission. God is willing to help anyone overcome a problem. "God is faithful, who will not suffer you to be tempted above that ye are able, but will with the temptation also make a way to escape, that ye may be able to bear it" (1 Cor. 10:13). God can help us face and fight any problem which hinders us from becoming soul-winners.

Love for People

In seeking an antidote for a personal problem, we find the best one in a godly love for people. "There is no fear in love; but perfect love casteth out fear" (1 John 4:18). Looking at the desperate plight of many people and exercising God's kind of love will be the best panacea for personal problems.

If one dearly loves Christ and devotedly loves some lost person, he will find a way to speak to the lost person about Christ. The greatest soul-winners in the world are those who love greatly. A large love casts out any personal problem.

Trust in the Lord

Another great antidote for a personal problem hindering evangelism is to trust the Lord. The soul-winner can search for God's promises and trust this word from God. Such a promise is found in Psalm 126:6: "He that goeth forth and weepeth, bearing precious seed, shall doubtless come again with rejoicing, bringing his sheaves with him." If one has hesitancy about going to a home or office to talk to a lost person about salvation, let him claim God's "doubtless" and by faith go on to realize the fulfillment of this promise. Let the soul-winner take seriously the words of Jesus, "Follow me, and I will make you fishers of men" (Matt. 4:19).

Persistent Prayer

Whatever the hindrance to personal evangelism, an excellent therapeutic process is prayer. One can face and fight any problem with prayer. When problems persist, the soul-winner can breathe a prayer for courage and faith and love. If the soul-winner has fear, he can ask God for courage. If the evangelist needs wisdom, he can ask God. Prayer for the unsaved fills the heart of a Christian with unselfish love for others.

Case Studies

A study of actual incidents in soul-winning will equip the person who desires to share Christ with another person. Studying the scriptural incidents of personal evangelism reveals positively that every type of Christian can be a soul-winner. The Ethiopian treasurer was won by a deacon. Timothy was won by his mother and grandmother. Ruth was won by her mother-in-law. Naaman was won by a servant girl. Simon Peter was won by his brother. Cornelius the Gentile was won by Peter the Jew. Luke the physician was probably won by Paul the patient. Children were brought to Christ by their mothers. The Philippian jailer was won by his prisoners. Onesimus was won by his fellow prisoner.

Actual Involvement

Actually sharing Christ with another is one of the finest antidotes for personal hesitancy. One incident of sharing Christ with another overcomes fear and gives confidence. One victory brings such a profound sense of real and abiding joy that the Christian will forever long to lead others in the same way. Personal problems will grow strangely dim in the light of this glorious victory. Continuing in trying to win others will help overcome personal hindrances from returning after they have once been driven away by a soul-winning experience.

Openness to the Holy Spirit

"Without me ye can do nothing" (John 15:5). A Christian cannot win another soul to Christ by mental wrestling, by a tug-of-war of mind with the mind, or by matching argument and logic against logic. Soul-winning does not require a display of magic oratory or an impassioned appeal in which the superior personality and mentality overcomes and the inferior succumbs. Soul-winning is an experience in which a loving heart is used by the Holy Spirit as an instrument to win another to accept God's love. Often a sincere sob or a loving look can be used by the Spirit far more effectively than hours of argument or persuasion. The sooner the soul-winner realizes this, the easier it will be to forget personal problems.

When a Christian opens his or her life to the infilling Spirit of God, he or she will experience a transformation in spirit similar to that of Simon Peter. The Holy Spirit transformed him from a cringing, fearful, cowardly denier of the Lord into the courageous and colorful evangelist.

Willingly Paying the Price for Soul-Winning

Personal evangelism is quite costly. Look closely into the life and ministry of Jesus Christ. To meet with people and talk about their needs drained him of energy and took much of his time. Making disciples cost Jesus long nights, hard days, heartbreaks, persecution, misunderstandings, misrepresentations, rebuffs, and exhaustion. Jesus was willing to pay the price of soul-winning so that other people might have an opportunity to open their life to him.

Christian Character

One price which the soul-winner must pay is that of growing in Christian character. The life-style of a Christian must resemble Christ. At the funeral of a soul-winner in Albany, Georgia, a Jewish rabbi said: "I know the Christian religion is a good religion because I knew Lamar Sims." Behind every victory for Christ there must be the example of a consecrated Christian character which testifies to what Christ has done and will do for a sinner. Inconsistent Christian living may have the form of godliness, but it denies the power thereof.

What won H. M. Stanley? In 1871 Stanley was sent to the *New York Herald* to find David Livingstone, who was lost in Africa. Stanley found him and spent several months with him. He could not understand Livingstone's habits, patience, sympathy, and love for the natives. Stanley said: "When I saw that unwearied patience, that unflagging zeal, that eager love spending itself for those unenlightened sons of Africa, I became a Christian at his side, although he never spoke to me directly about it." Unshaken loyalty, unfaltering love, and untiring patience are the elements of character which always impress a watching world.

Priority Planning

Giving diligence to soul-winning requires priority planning. This means to plan soul-winning visits. It could mean to set some type of goal. Some have found that setting some realistic goal has helped motivate and maintain efforts at soul-winning. Maybe you could set a goal to share Christ with one person per week. Diligent work would be required for you to pay the price to make this one soul-winning visit. One visit a week would amount to fifty-two visits each year. Making the visit would mean making it have top priority. It could mean the neglect of other activities.

Prevailing Prayer

Personal, persistent, passionate, importunate, prevailing prayer costs dearly! Yet its spiritual victories are worth far more than its costs. Sidney Lanier's beautiful "A Ballad of Trees and the Master" describes the price which Jesus paid in Gethsemane to become the Savior of souls.

One of the most pathetic scenes in the experiences of the disciples of Jesus was the spectacle of the father of the afflicted boy who was sorely disappointed because some of the disciples could not cast out the demon. He had a right to expect it, and the disciples should have been able to do it. Shamed because of their failure, the disciples asked Jesus why they were unable to cast out the evil spirit. The Master gave the answer, which is the secret of so much present-day helplessness in winning others: "This kind can come out by nothing, save by prayer" (Mark 9:29, ASV). The successful soul-winner must pay the price of prevailing prayer.

Consistent Church Life

Every phase of the work of a local New Testament church points to some phase of making disciples. The worship service should have making disciples in mind. The primary purpose of teaching the word of God in the Sunday School is to reach people, teach them, and develop those won to Christ. The Church Training should always train Christians for the highest type of Christian service. The Brotherhood and the Woman's Missionary Union have local and world evangelization as their ultimate objective. Every local church must fulfill Christ's imperative commission, else it ceases to obey the Lord's command.

Every soul-winner should pay the price of faithful attendance, prayers, support, and service in the church. The church services help to warm the heart for Christ and lost souls. The church instructs the mind in the word of God and in the spiritual needs of the world. At church the blessing of fellowship with other soul-winners is found. At church one finds people who seek to obey Christ's great commission. Great soul-winners have been faithful servants in the church.

The purpose of this book will be missed entirely if the reader does not consecrate himself both definitely and permanently to the matchless ministry of winning others to the love and service of Jesus our Lord. Wondrous experiences lie ahead for those who consecrate themselves to personal evangelism.

Suggestions for Advanced Study

1. From studying the Bible, and from reading biographies of Finney, Moody, Wesley, Truett, and others, give some illustrations how (a)

to increase one's prayer life, (b) to strengthen one's faith about soul-winning, and (c) to ensure the power of the Holy Spirit upon one's testimony for Christ to the lost.

2. Discuss the price Paul paid for being a soul-winner. What does the Christian have to suffer today instead of imprisonments, whippings, wild beasts, and banishment? Has the "offense of the cross" ceased? (Cf. 2 Cor. 11:23 ff.)

3. What person was most vital in influence leading to the conversion of the following great Christians: Saul of Tarsus, Augustine of Hippo, Francis of Assisi, John Tauler, Martin Luther, John Wesley, Charles Haddon Spurgeon, D. L. Moody, Billy Sunday, and George W. Truett?

4. Read two cases in Ken Chafin's book *The Reluctant Witness.* What lessons did you learn which will be helpful to you? Read two cases in the book edited by John Ishee, *Is Christ for John Smith?* What lessons did you learn from these cases which would help your personal work?

References for Further Study

Chafin, Kenneth L. *The Reluctant Witness.* Nashville: Broadman Press, 1974.

Finney, Charles G. *Revival Lectures.* New York: Fleming H. Revell (reprint), 1868.

Ford, Leighton. *Good News Is for Sharing.* Elgin, Illinois: David C. Cook Publishing Company, 1977.

Havlik, John. *People-Centered Evangelism.* Nashville: Broadman Press, 1971.

Ishee, John, ed. *Is Christ for John Smith?* Nashville: Broadman Press, 1968.

Little, Paul. *How to Give Away Your Faith.* Downers Grove, Illinois: Inter-Varsity Press, 1966.

Neighbour, Jr., Ralph. *The Touch of the Spirit.* Nashville: Broadman Press, 1972.

Note

1. J. I. Packer, *Evangelism and the Sovereignty of God,* (Downers Grove, Illinois: Inter-Varsity Press), p. 180.

16
The Soul-Winner's Presentation

Sirs, what must I do to be saved? And they said, Believe on the
Lord Jesus, and thou shalt be saved (Acts 16: 30-31).

Do you honestly believe that men are lost? Do you believe that
what Peter said to the rulers at Jerusalem—"Neither is there salvation
in any other: for there is none other name under heaven given among
men, whereby we must be saved" (Acts 4:12)—is true today?

It is said that one thing which inspired General William Booth to
start the Salvation Army was hearing an infidel haranguing a crowd
in a London park, denouncing Christians for their poor demonstrations
of their professions of belief. That infidel said, in substance: "If I
were a Christian and believed what Christians profess to believe—
that is, that there is a heaven to which men may be saved, and that
there is a hell to which all nonbelievers most certainly will be damned—
if I believed that, I would not stop day or night to warn men away
from hell and win men to heaven." The world expects Christians to
believe in the Lord Jesus Christ and to know how to present him
both plainly and positively.

Getting the gospel across to another person does not require one
to be a competent theologian. Paul began winning souls in Damascus
immediately after his conversion. He shared what he knew to be true—
that Jesus Christ, the Son of God, could make a difference in a person's
life. Paul learned more and more about God's will and God's way as
he grew in his Christian experience, yet he was a soul-winner all the
while. Christians would almost never begin trying to win others if
they waited until they felt that they knew enough to share Christ. It
is not as necessary for a saved person to impress the unsaved man
with his knowledge of the Bible as it is to convince him that he believes

197

absolutely in what he is offering as the only way to be saved. Soul-winners need to have every possible method of presenting the gospel of Christ. They should also learn any skill which would enhance their ability to present the gospel systematically and clearly.

Opening a Personal Interview

"How can I begin a personal interview with someone?" This is usually the first and often the greatest problem to one who would like to win someone to Christ. It is an exceedingly important question. The soul-winner must seek to identify and to build relationships with lost people. An extended discussion of this has been given in chapter 11, some points of which should be reviewed.

A Tactful Beginning

The soul-winner should have a heart like a lion but a hand like a woman. He must have the courage of convictions, but also he must have the courtesy of his convictions. Some Christians have been washed from their sins but not ironed. In no place are courtesy and compassion more compelling than in a tactful beginning. Tact is nothing more than consecrated culture and common sense.

1. Knowing the individual.—The successful fisherman knows the fish, their habitats, and their habits. He knows the bait they like and the bait they will not bite. He knows the way to hook them and the way to handle them after they are hooked. "Fishers of men" should seek to follow these principles.

2. Making conditions advantageous.—When it is possible, the soul-winner or the team of soul-winners should be alone with the one to be sought for Christ. A blaring television, a crying infant, or someone who insists on interrupting the conversation can ruin almost any soul-winning endeavor. However, there are times when one must speak under distracting circumstances or lose the opportunity forever.

3. Assuming the best.—Perhaps the most tactless approach possible is to assume the worst about an unsaved man and begin talking with an implied accusation. "Why don't you join the church?" is among the worst of all approaches. There is an implied attack in the question "Are you a Christian?" unless it is asked in an exceptionally kind and friendly way. Doubtless the reason so many people retort about the hypocrites in the churches is that they are seeking to defend themselves against the soul-winner's attack.

Let us emphasize the better assumptions which should be implied in the soul-winner's approach. First, the soul-winner should assume that the man to whom he speaks is perhaps already a Christian. "You are a Christian, aren't you?" is infinitely more tactful than "Are you a Christian?" or "Why aren't you a Christian?" Ask the man if, deep in his heart, he does not feel that sometime in his past life he has put his trusting faith in Jesus Christ. That always elicits his appreciation, goodwill, and confidence. Usually he will begin telling some experience, worthy or unworthy, which he believes to be a way of salvation for him. This enables the soul-winner to explain mistakes, clear up doubts, and point to Jesus.

If the man being approached says he has never had an experience which he thought was conversion, the next assumption should be that he has had a Christian background. Assume that his parents were Christians, that he once went to Sunday School, or that he knows something about the biblical way of salvation through early Christian training. That will bring out his story, which the soul-winner must have to deal with the person intelligently.

The third assumption is that he knows about Christ and would like to live daily like Christ. In extreme cases one may use the fourth assumption—that is, that the person believes there is no God.

4. Using a point of contact.—Educators well know the principle of beginning a lesson or lecture with a point of contact—that is, beginning with some subject well known to the hearer and going from the known to the unknown. Jesus had no cut-and-dried approach to a sinner, but began dealing with the uniqueness of each person. He began with each one in the realm of that one's own personal experience, taking into consideration his heritage, his history, and the attitude of his heart. To the lawyer he began with the law; to the woman at the well he began with water; to the nobleman he began with the necessity for a nobler birth.

5. Avoiding argument.—Jesus carefully avoided argument, always showed his sympathy, and consistently revealed his love, all the while searching to find the difficulty in the way of the one with whom he was dealing. It is a poor victory to win an argument and lose your prospect. Love never fails.

6. *Giving one's testimony of conversion.*—If you know good things about Jesus, be sure to tell others about him. A personal testimony of what Christ has done for you is worth a hundred theories about how to be saved. Paul's testimony quieted the mob, made a king tremble, and gave a gripping appeal to his sermons and to his epistles. Many great evangelists such as D. L. Moody, Charles G. Finney, Gipsy Smith, and Billy Sunday used their own personal experiences of conversion with mighty soul-winning power. It is experience, not philosophy or logic, which grips the hearts of men. There was no way to contradict the words of the man born blind when he said, "One thing I know, that, whereas I was blind, now I see" (John 9:25). This is exactly what Jesus meant when he said, "Ye shall be my witnesses" (Acts 1:8, ASV). A sincere personal testimony will always help a soul-winner in opening up an interview with a lost person.

Poise and Positiveness

There is no need for a soul-winner to assume a strange attitude, use a subdued and funerallike voice, or take on any supersanctimonious air when talking to another about his salvation. A friendly, forthright naturalness of conversation, touched with love and concern, will be both winsome and winning.

The soul-winner should speak with the unfaltering positiveness of sincere conviction about the sinner's need and the Savior's ability to save. Jesus said that every person needs salvation: "Except ye repent, ye shall all likewise perish" (Luke 13:5). Jesus believed that the load of sin which all unbelievers were carrying was heavier than those back-breaking loads which he saw men carrying along the streets of Jerusalem. The supreme need of everyone is to repent of sin and come to God through faith in God's Son. His words indicate no wavering, hedging, or hesitation, such as the oft-quoted words of some timid soul who said, "Except ye repent (so to speak), and believe (as it were), ye shall be damned (in a measure)." The soul-winner should present Christ plainly, positively, pointedly, and persuasively.

Giving a Clear, Scriptural Presentation

Personal evangelism is a three-way conversation among God, the soul-winner, and the person with whom you share. In the conversation, techniques and programs can have a useful purpose, providing that the soul-winner recognizes any technique's dangers and limitations. Perhaps the deepest danger of a system of presentation is the depersonalization of the soul-winner and the prospect. Personal evangelism can become impersonal if one is tied to a plan.

An elementary preparation for soul-winning is to know some Bible verses which tell the way of salvation. The soul-winner will need to make these Bible verses personal. It is not necessary to know all verses before trying to help others to become Christians; yet, the more Scripture one knows, the better one can present the truth. Some have had success in winning others to Christ by knowing and using personally only the one great verse, John 3:16.

An Outline by J. B. Leavell, Sr.

One of the simplest, most easily remembered scriptural outlines of "God's Way of Salvation" was written by J. B. Leavell, Sr., many years ago:

(1)—Salvation Needed
    (1)—All have sinned (Rom. 3:23)
    (2)—Sin brings death (Rom. 6:23)
(2)—Salvation Provided
    (1)—Sins may be cleansed (1 John 1:7)
    (2)—"Whosoever will" may be saved (John 3:16)
    (3)—Salvation is a free gift of grace (Eph. 2:8)
(3)—Salvation Accepted
    (1)—Through repentance and faith (Acts 20:21)
    (2)—Repent or perish (Luke 13:3)
    (3)—Believe or be condemned (John 3:18,36)

This simple outline, with its familiar references, can be committed to memory in a few minutes. These verses may be marked in the soul-winner's Bible. A copy of this outline or a similar one drawn up by the soul-winner can be written or pasted on the flyleaf of the soul-winner's Bible for quick reference.

The Roman Road

We next suggest an outline which has been called "The Roman Road." Paul's letter to the Roman Christians presented some basic truths of the gospel of Christ. The soul-winner can use Romans as a convenient and logical method to share the gospel with another person.

    (1)—Human sin: "For all have sinned, and come short of the glory of God" (Rom. 3:23).

    (2)—Sin's penalty: "For the wages of sin is death; but the gift of God is eternal life through Jesus Christ our Lord" (Rom. 6:23).

    (3)—God's provision: "But God commendeth his love toward us, in that, while we were yet sinners, Christ died for us" (Rom. 5:8).

    (4)—Response of faith: "That if thou shalt confess with thy mouth the Lord Jesus, and shalt believe in thy heart that God hath raised him from the dead, thou shalt be saved" (Rom. 10:9-10).

    "For whosoever shall call upon the name of the Lord shall be saved" (Rom. 10:13).

    (5)—Christian commitment: "I beseech you therefore, brethren, by the mercies of God, that ye present your bodies a living sacrifice, holy, acceptable unto God, which is your reasonable service. And be not conformed to this world: but be ye transformed by the renewing of your mind, that ye may prove what is that good, and acceptable, and perfect, will of God" (Rom. 12:1-2).

An Outline by W. W. Hamilton, Sr.

Dr. W. W. Hamilton's tract "How May I Be Saved and Prove It?" has a simple but very effective outline. On the tract there is a picture of the "hand in faith." Each finger of the hand bears one of the five letters F-A-I-T-H. Each finger also bears one of the five words in the following outline.

    (1)   Repent (Luke 13:5)
    (2)   Believe (Rom. 10:4)
    (3)   Receive (John 1:12)
    (4)   Confess (Matt. 10:32)
    (5)   Obey (John 14:15)

These five passages of Scripture are sufficient to lead almost any honest seeker to accept the Lord Jesus Christ. An earnest Christian can begin his endeavor to win souls with this short outline only. His successful experience will inspire him to search for and memorize many more helpful passages of Scripture.

An Outline by Austin Crouch

Dr. Austin Crouch's admirable book *The Plan of Salvation* outlines the following five steps which the soul-winner must take to lead a soul into salvation:

Step 1—Show him that he is a sinner and lost.

Step 2—Show him that he cannot save himself.

Step 3—Show him that Christ can save him.

Step 4—Show him that Christ will save him on two conditions.

Step 5—Show him the duty of a believer in Christ.

Appropriate passages of Scripture are cited in Dr. Crouch's elaboration of these five steps. His outline of the steps in soul-winning is simple to learn, scripturally true, and quite complete.

An Outline by the Home Mission Board

Several years ago the Home Mission Board developed a presentation for the Lay Evangelism School. This outline can be committed to memory and used effectively to present Jesus Christ.

(1) God loves you. He offers you a full and meaningful life. See 1 John 4:9; 1 John 5:11; John 10:10; John 3:16.

(2) This life is made possible by Christ's death and resurrection. See Romans 5:8; Romans 4:25; Ephesians 1:7; Galatians 3:26; Romans 8:14; Philippians 4:19.

(3) You enter this life through a spiritual birth. See John 3:3; John 3:1-8; James 2:19; Ephesians 2:8-9.

(4) Failure to turn yourself over to Jesus Christ is sin. See John 3:18; Romans 5:12; Romans 6:23.

(5) This life becomes yours when you turn from sin and accept Christ as your Lord and Savior. See John 1:12; Acts 3:19; Romans 10:9-10.

In whatever outline that is used, the soul-winner should present the plain, unvarnished facts about the sinfulness of sin, the need of every soul for salvation, the offer of salvation through Jesus and Jesus alone, the necessity of repentance, and the effectiveness of faith in

Jesus Christ's death as the atonement for sin. Nothing can take the place of these essentials, and no one of them can be omitted. Nothing is so impressive to the unsaved person as that the soul-winner know these basic facts and is able to share scriptural truths.

Understanding the Desired Decision

A clear understanding of exactly what mental reaction a soul-winner desires to excite in the unsaved person's mind is helpful toward presenting effectively the plan of salvation. What functions of the sinner's mind should be excited into action?

Students of the human mind say that men relate themselves to the outside world through the intellect, the emotions, and the will. All three of these functions of the mind must be brought into action if the sinner is to become a Christian.

Intellect

Some people believe that the method of becoming a Christian is entirely a matter of the intellect. It is true that there must be an intellectual understanding and acceptance of some things. There must be a belief. "He that cometh to God must believe that he is, and that he is a rewarder of them that diligently seek him" (Heb. 11:6). Therein lies one value of teaching from the Bible such an outline of the plan of salvation as has been suggested heretofore. An infant whose intellect has not been developed sufficiently cannot experience conversion to Christ. One of the essential elements of conversion to Christ is repentance, which is a changing of the mind. "Come now, and let us reason together" (Isa. 1:18) is God's approach to the sinner's heart. The intellect of the sinner must grasp the truth before the sinner can be saved from his error.

Emotion

Other people would contend that there is no place for emotion in genuine religion. But there must be emotional excitement for anyone to become a Christian. Can a man fall in love with the girl who is to be his wife without some emotion? No! Neither can a man fall in love with God through Christ without some emotion. How can a man be patriotic toward his country without some emotion? It can't be done. Neither can a man be loyal and faithful to God in Christ without emotion. Let no soul-winner listen to the discrediting of any Christian experience because there was an element of emotion in it.

Will

The ultimate psychological basis of conversion is not in the intellect, the emotion, or the two combined. The ultimate basis of conversion is the will. Feeding the intellect and stirring the emotions lead to the moving of the will to repentance and faith.

Some people are inclined to identify religion with pure emotion; other people confine religion to pure intellectualism. Both should be used in order to reach the real objective.

The will is the basis of sin; therefore, it must be the basis of conversion. According to Jesus, if a man wills to become a murderer, he is already a murderer in his heart. Therefore, he must will to repent of the sin of murder and must will to trust God to save him from that sin, if he is saved. The experience of the prodigal son illustrates this. He might have wept streams of tears and uttered soulful sighs in a great emotional upheaval while in the hog pen, but that would never have gotten him out of the pen. He might have made an intellectual inventory of all the things in his father's house, but that would have been of little avail if his mental process had stopped there. Both this emotional upheaval and this intellectual inventory conspired to move his will to say, "I will arise, and go to my father." Upon saying that, he was soon on the road toward father and home.

In trying to win a soul, the soul-winner should present the plan of salvation with the definite purpose of leading that soul to will to repent of sin and to will to believe on the Lord Jesus Christ.

Introducing Another Person to Jesus

Winning others to Christ is the most exciting experience in the entire range of Christian service. Every true child of God may experience it if he wills. Have you ever experienced the romance of it? Have you ever introduced two persons, watched them fall in love, helped them get married, and rejoiced with them as they lived happily together? Soul-winning is like that. The soul-winner introduces a lost friend to Jesus. The friend watches his lost friend respond to the gracious love of Christ and rejoices to see him begin to enjoy eternal life through Christ the Savior, the Lord. The soul-winner's task is to bring someone face to face with Christ. Christ must be presented clearly, lovingly, and prayerfully. Only Christ can save.

No Other Way

Simon Peter declared to the Sanhedrin: "Neither is there salvation in any other: for there is none other name under heaven given among men, whereby we must be saved" (Acts 4:12). The soul-winner must concentrate on Christ. His task is that of declaring the love of God for the sinner as revealed in Christ and presenting this in so impressive a way that the sinner will change his mind from a love of sin to a love of the righteousness of God. This makes it imperative that Jesus shall be the heart and center of every presentation of a plan of salvation. The whole discourse must converge in him. Jesus is "the way, the truth, and the life." He is the Door. He is the Bread of life and the Water of life. He himself did not hesitate to say, "Bring him to me," "Come unto me," "Follow me," and "Abide in me." He is not only the center of the scriptural plan of salvation; he is *the* plan of salvation.

Conviction Through Vision of Christ

Genuine conviction for sin is not solely a conviction of being guilty of overt acts of wrong, such as lying, stealing, impurity, or profanity. Conviction by the Holy Spirit is for the sin of neglecting Jesus. Out of the sin of neglecting Jesus come all others as results. A vision of Jesus is used of the Spirit, not only to convict one of having broken God's law but also of having rejected God's Son. It is not only a conviction of sin committed, but also a conviction that sin may be canceled through Christ. Upholding Jesus before a sinner's eyes does more than convince him of his lapse of morality; it also reveals to him his lack of spirituality.

It was a vision of the Lord on his throne which made Isaiah cry out, "Woe is me! for I am undone" (Isa. 6:5). It was at the feet of Jesus that Simon Peter fell when he cried, "Depart from me; for I am a sinful man, O Lord" (Luke 5:8). It was a vision of Jesus which made Zacchaeus confess his dishonesty. It was the purifying presence of Christ which made the sinful woman weep while she anointed the feet of Jesus with ointment. By watching the matchless grace of Christ while in torture's grasp, the thief on the cross was constrained to cry, "Lord, remember me when thou comest into thy kingdom" (Luke 23:42).

Seeking to Secure a Decision

The soul-winner presents the gospel of Christ with the objective of securing a decision. One must keep in mind that the emotions can be aroused and the intellect can be stirred, but the lost person has to experience his or her will. The soul-winner must respect the freedom of the human will. One can persuade another, but each individual must respond either positively or negatively.

The Respectability of Decision

God respects the dignity of each individual. He has created a human being with the capacity to rebel against him or to be open to him. God will not coerce a person to submit to him. He allows a person to exercise the freedom of the human will. This makes a person a unique creation and not a mechanical robot.

Though God will not force a person to decide for or against him, he will persuade graciously and earnestly. He persuades a person to trust him. He continuously invites an individual to respond positively to him. One of the hardest matters to comprehend is why a person refuses God's invitation.

Since God created human beings with the dignity of human freedom, the soul-winner must respect this gift. This does not mean that the soul-winner does not have to plead earnestly and gently, though. A Christian simply cannot assume a "take it or leave it" attitude toward a lost person after presenting Jesus as God's plan of salvation for him.

The Urging of Decision

With all earnestness the soul-winner should try to bring the unsaved person to a definite acceptance of Christ. The Lord's earthly ministry reflected an urgency about getting people to decide for him. Jesus permitted delay, but he never did encourage procrastination. The supreme objective for the soul-winner is the verdict, "I do repent and believe on Jesus."

With all earnestness the soul-winner should try to bring the unsaved man to a definite acceptance of Christ. "Sign on the dotted line" is what a salesman seeks to get his prospect to do. A lawyer addressing the jury has accomplished no good with his plea unless he gets the verdict in his favor. The aim of the soul-winner is for the verdict, "I do repent and believe on Jesus."

Trusting the Holy Spirit

Conviction and Conversion by the Spirit

No Christian in the world can bring a sinner to repentance of sin and faith in Jesus Christ without the working of the Holy Spirit in the sinner's heart. It is he who convicts the world of sin and righteousness and judgment. It is he who regenerates the soul. It is he who converts the sinner's heart.

Use of Human Agencies

It is also true that the Holy Spirit does not bring conviction, repentance, and faith to the sinner except through human agencies. The Spirit of God does not do for Christians what they can do for themselves. He stands by the soul-winner and carries on the work to success, taking up the task when the soul-winner's powers have been exhausted. The Christian must be the voice of God's Spirit to bring the lost man to a sense of his lostness. He must be the brush with which the Holy Spirit paints the picture of the Savior as the one great need of man in his desperate lostness.

Suggestions for Advanced Study

1. Work on developing your own approach in presenting the plan of salvation. Develop an outline on the following basic truths: God's Plan, Human Need, Christ's Provision, Human Response.

2. Compare in appeal and effectiveness the following types of evangelistic invitations: (a) the call to the front, (b) an invitation to an inquiry room, (c) the signing of decision cards, and (d) the request to hold up the right hand. List any other methods of invitations you may think worthy.

3. What methods can a soul-winner use in an interview with a lost man to help him bring his will into action, to say, "I will put my faith in Jesus Christ"?

References for Further Study

Chafin, Kenneth L. *The Reluctant Witness.* Nashville: Broadman Press, 1974.

Ford, Leighton. *Good News Is for Sharing.* Elgin, Illinois: David C. Cook Publishing Company, 1977.

Little, Paul E. *How to Give Away Your Faith.* Downers Grove, Illinois: Inter-Varsity Press, 1966.

Pleklser, Robert J. *Redeemed? Say So!* New York: Harper and Row, 1977.

Rinker, Rosalind. *You Can Witness with Confidence.* Grand Rapids: Zondervan Publishing House, 1962.

Stott, John R. W. *Our Guilty Silence: The Church, the Gospel, and the World.* London: Hodder and Stoughton, 1967.

Watson, David. *I Believe in Evangelism.* Grand Rapids: William B. Eerdman's Publishing Company, 1977.

17

The Soul-Winner's Helpful Equipment

Study to shew theyself approved unto God, a workman that needeth
not to be ashamed, rightly dividing the word of truth (2 Tim. 2:15).

On a hunting trip in the mountains, a Christian man was successfully
calling up a wary wild turkey. A mountain youth heard the turkey
yelping and ran down the mountainside to see the hunter shoot the
bird. Of course, he ran the wild gobbler away. The exasperated hunter
was on the verge of loosing his tongue against the thoughtless lad,
but he restrained his temper. He engaged the boy in conversation.
He found that the young fellow was already a whiskey-drinking, swear-
ing, and rough-hearted sinner. He took out his New Testament from
his hunting trousers and tried to lead the youth to Christ. The young
mountaineer was more interested in the fact that the man carried a
pocket New Testament in his hunting clothes than he was in becoming
a Christian. The soul-winner lost his turkey and also failed to win
the lost boy. Many months later the youth sent a message to the
hunter, stating that he had become a Christian and had joined a church
there in the mountains. He said he could never get away from the
fact that a hunter from the city had a New Testament in his hunting
clothes and tried to teach him how to become a Christian in spite
of the turkey episode.

The correct equipment enabled the hunter to win the boy. It is as
sensible to go hunting without a gun as to go day by day expecting
to win souls but not having some equipment to help. The carpenter
has his tools; the dentist has instruments; the painter has his brushes;
and the soldier has his weapons. The soul-winner's equipment is both
material and spiritual. Let us examine some items in the soul-winner's
equipment.

210

Thoughtfully Preparing a Prayer List

The reader will recall that at Pentecost there were three preeminent factors in the activities of the Jerusalem Christians: prayer by the 120, personal witnessing by the rank and file of the church, and preaching by Simon Peter. Successful soul-winners must begin as they began, with prayer. Importunity should match opportunity.

Specific Prayer

The first item of equipment for a soul-winner should be a carefully and prayerfully prepared list of specific names of unsaved people for whom to pray.

The value of such a prayer list cannot be overestimated. It gives a definiteness to one's praying and leads to a definiteness in one's personal work. It is a constant reminder of the Christian's duty toward the lost, as well as a constant reminder of the lostness of those who have not believed on Christ. It is a spiritual challenge to the Christian's soul. It is a silent sentinel to warn against indifference concerning the fate of those who are going directly toward their doom. It produces more persistent and more importunate prayer.

Suggestions for Making a Prayer List

A simple list of names is a splendid start; yet the list can be made up in a more helpful way. It should be given a title of the soul-winner's own choosing. We suggest such titles as "One Win One" or "Stars for My Crown" or "White Already unto Harvest" or "Fishing for These Men." The list should have a margin on both sides. The left margin should contain the date when each name was inscribed. The right margin should be left blank until the one who is named there has accepted Christ; then the date of acceptance and profession of faith by that one should be recorded. At the bottom of the list there should be a pledge of consecration to pray for these persons and a place for the signature of the soul-winner.

S. M. Sayford, who was transformed from a worldly, godless man into a consistent soul-winner, was led to Christ by a traveling salesman named Edward R. Graves who came regularly to Mr. Sayford's store,

---

WHITE ALREADY UNTO HARVEST

Date   Date
enrolled   won

James Westmoreland
Mrs. Will Eustice
Mabel Fulbright
Whitman Walters
John Bigelow
Ruth Whitlock
Sara Murphree

It is my purpose to pray daily and seek conscientiously to lead these friends to Christ.

Psalm 126:6

Signature _____

---

representing a New York paper bag manufacturing concern. On one visit Mr. Graves gave Mr. Sayford a tract, and, on the next visit, another one. Later he asked Mr. Sayford for the privilege of putting his name on a prayer list. In a private office he produced the prayer list and asked Mr. Sayford to write his own name on it. The merchant's hand trembled as he wrote, and at the same time conviction smote his heart like an arrow. On Mr. Graves' next visit Mr. Sayford became a Christian. Mr. Sayford won C. K. Ober to Christ; C. K. Ober won John R. Mott to Christ. Dr. Mott has been the means of winning scores and hundreds.

Sources for Securing Prayer List Names

Possibly there is someone who says, "I do not know any unsaved persons for whom to pray." The names for a prayer list can be gotten from many sources. There is no lack of names. The enrollment of any Sunday School will reveal many who are out of Christ. A religious census of any community will startle any soul-winner by the large number of unsaved there. A walk down any well-known street looking for the lost will bring to mind enough names for a good long list. Find out if the policeman or the fireman are Christians. Find out about the paper boy, or the bus driver, or the grocer, or the merchant and his clerks, or the mechanic at the garage; and see your list grow.

Easy Reference to Prayer List

The prayer list should be kept where it can be seen easily at the time of prayer and where it can be referred to easily when time affords an opportunity to do some personal work. Some people pin the prayer list to the flyleaf of the Bible; some put it just over the study desk; some put it on the mirror; and some put it within the billfold.

Continually Carrying a New Testament

Probably it was miserably hot in the desert between Jerusalem and Gaza, and sand was flying into the eyes of the travelers. But heat and flying sand do not stop a real soul-winner or an earnest seeker after Christ.

"Understandest thou what thou readest?" asked Philip, the layman evangelist, of the Ethiopian treasurer (Acts 8:30).

"How can I, except some man should guide me?" was his sensible answer (v. 31).

"Philip opened his mouth, and began at the same scripture, and preached unto him Jesus" (v. 35). The truth is that today unsaved men are not often found reading the Scripture, as was the Ethiopian. Therefore, it is all the more important that soul-winners know how to open up scriptural truth to those who do not know Christ. The successful experience of those who have tried using the Bible in winning others to Christ universally teaches that this is true.

The Most Effective Instrument

The New Testament is the most effective instrument in soul-winning. There is no reason why every Christian cannot always carry a pocket New Testament everywhere he goes. It is easy to do. It is no heavier than a knife, but it is sharper than a two-edged sword. It is no larger than a compact such as ladies carry in their purses, but is more efficacious for giving one the beauty of holiness. It is no larger than a man's billfold, but it contains more wealth. Besides being handy for Bible-reading by the soul-winner, it is useful beyond comparison when accidental opportunities for soul-winning present themselves.

Advantages of Carrying a New Testament

The alert soul-winner who carries a New Testament will find it more and more useful with practice. It will be advantageous in visitation evangelism, in conversational evangelism, in pen-and-ink evangelism, in accidental opportunities for evangelism, and in the fellowship of prayer-partner evangelism.

1. Breaks down opposition.—One of the values of carrying a New Testament is that it breaks down opposition and criticism from the unsaved individual who would say in his mind that his own opinion is as good as that of the Christian.

2. Inspires confidence in the soul-winner.—To see a soul-winner carrying his New Testament convinces the lost man of the soul-winner's sincerity about the matter.

3. Inspires self-confidence.—The soul-winner needs that self-confidence which will enable him to pursue his efforts to win another without hesitation. When he is teaching another a Bible truth, he knows he is on solid ground and can go forward with assurance.

4. Avoids being sidetracked.—Furthermore, the use of the New Testament in soul-winning avoids the danger of having the whole subject sidetracked by the lost man as so many unsaved people are anxious to do. They bring into the conversation every imaginable extraneous topic. The soul-winner who keeps bringing the topic of discussion back to the Bible truth which is visibly before them is sure to keep the main issue to the forefront.

5. Prevents argument.—And again, the New Testament in the hand is the best possible prevention against argument. If the soul-winner allows himself to be drawn into argument, the battle is certain to be lost. "Thus saith the Lord," written in the Bible, does not allow further room for argument.

Skillfully Using the Sword of the Spirit

An unsaved student in a university was having breakfast in the home of one of his college friends. He talked freely with the mother of his friend of his ambitions to become a lawyer, to become wealthy, to advance in the political world, to attain fame and fortune. The soul-minded mother in that home was quiet and thoughtful while he talked.

Upon leaving the home that morning, the visitor shook hands with the mother. As he did so, she left a note in his hand but never said a word. He put it in his pocket and opened it after he had reached the privacy of his own room in the college dormitory. He read, "For what is a man profited, if he shall gain the whole world, and lose his own soul?" (Matt. 16:26). The truth pierced his heart like a sharp sword. Conviction for sin and conversion to Christ were the results. She was skillful in using the "sword of the Spirit."

God's Sharp Sword

The author of Hebrews describes in the following graphic terms the efficacy of the Scripture in reaching the hearts of men: "For the word of God is quick, and powerful, and sharper than any two-edged sword, piercing even to the dividing asunder of soul and spirit, and of the joints and marrow, and is a discerner of the thoughts and intents of the heart" (Heb. 4:12).

As an illustration of how God's Spirit uses the words of the Bible to win men to Christ, consider the testimony of Toyohiko Kagawa of Japan. When Mr. Kagawa was asked what passage brought him to a decision for Christ, he quoted Matthew 6:28-29: "And why take ye thought for raiment? Consider the lilies of the field, how they grow; they toil not, neither do they spin: And yet I say unto you, That even Solomon in all his glory was not arrayed like one of these." He saw in this statement that if God loves nature, he must also love human nature, even though it has fallen into sin. He surrendered to God through faith in the Christ who taught such a beautiful love. Thus the Spirit transcended our thoughts about how to win others and used a verse of Scripture which none of us would have chosen to use in dealing with a Japanese person. The Word of God is indeed the "sword of the Spirit" (Eph. 6:17). The Spirit of God who inspired the Bible will use its words for daggers with which to pierce the unbelief and indifference of the unsaved.

A sharp sword can be used easily and successfully if the swordsman is skilled in its use. Let the soul-winner trust in the sharpness of the sword and thrust with all the skill in his power. One well-aimed shot is enough to kill a lion. One spear thrust into the heart will kill a tiger. One verse of Scripture is enough to begin. It is well for the soul-winner to recall that Paul began preaching immediately after his conversion; and he began by telling what he already knew. As he preached, he learned more. Men have been won to Christ by newly converted Christians who did not know so much as one verse of Scripture.

The soul-winner who is discouraged about trying because he knows only a few verses of Scripture should remember that in all likelihood, the one whom he desires to win to Christ does not know a single passage of the Bible. Depend heavily on the sharpness of the sword.

Pointers in Skillful Use

Skillful use of the Bible in soul-winning depends in a large measure on practice. One cannot learn how merely by reading a book any more than he could learn to use a literal sword by reading how. But pointers may be given which will help increase the skill of the soul-winner.

1. Beginning with a few verses.—Some group of verses such as those in the chapter which gives outlines of the plan of salvation can be learned in a few minutes. In the vast majority of cases, such a group will answer the purpose. Anyone can learn and use a small number of verses such as the following:

Must be saved in God's way (Acts 4:12)
Must repent and believe (Acts 20:21)
Must call on God (Rom. 10:13)
Must confess Christ (Matt. 10:32-33)

The persistent soul-winner will find himself studying more and more verses to use with the lost. Each experience will be different in some degree from all others. Different verses will appeal to different people. Problems will send the soul-winner back to the Bible to find a scriptural answer.

2. Answering arguments and solving problems.—If answers must be given to arguments, no answer is as effective as a quotation from the Scripture. Said D. L. Moody, "When men argue, I give them the Bible. When they say they do not believe the Bible, I just keep right on giving them the Word of God." It is no wonder that D. L. Moody is classed among the foremost soul-winners that America has ever produced.

An evangelist found a college girl, the daughter of a minister, who was exceedingly difficult to interest in the matter of becoming a Christian. She was a church member, but she expressly declared that she was not a Christian. She could glibly quote the Scripture about how to be saved. She blandly avowed that she was not interested in becoming a Christian. After making no headway in their conference, the evangelist sent her to the religious leader of the students. After a time the leader came back in despair, and the girl came back openly proud of her "victory" in resistance.

Finally the evangelist said, "Now go to your room, remembering that you are like the prodigal son, in the hog pen of pride and rebellion against God. The only thing in the world which will save you now is for you to say, 'I will arise and go to my Father.'" She laughed and left. But that night those words, "I will arise and go to my Father," kept ringing in her ears. At ten-thirty she asked her roommate to pray with her. By midnight she was in another student's room saying, "We must all say, 'I will arise and go to my father.'" By two o'clock she had led eight of her lost friends to accept Christ. The Scripture was the dagger point which went into her inner heart.

A young man, in his early attempts at winning others to Christ, spoke to an older man about his salvation. The older man, well versed in the extreme Calvinistic doctrine, said, "If the Lord wants me to be saved, he will convert me without any help from either of us." Quietly the young Christian produced his New Testament and read, "Behold, I stand at the door, and knock: if any man hear my voice, and open the door, I will come in to him, and will sup with him, and he with me" (Rev. 3:20). That one verse slashed the man's erroneous idea into shreds. The "sword of the Spirit" was effective. That man turned to Jesus, was baptized, and soon became useful as the superintendent of the Sunday School in his church.

The soul-winner should study the Bible as a salesman studies the catalog of his wares. He should know his Bible as an agent knows his prospectus.

3. Letting the lost person read the Bible.—Unsaved people usually are not accustomed to reading the Bible. For that reason it is more impressive to have them read from the Bible than to read to them. Get them to use the "Sword of the Spirit" on themselves, so to speak.

When the lost man reads for himself the living word of God, it becomes almost irresistible.

In a Southern college town a young lady from the Northwest came to hear the pastor preach, curious to see some "Southern emotionalism." She began to experience some of it herself when her heart was touched, and she began to realize her guilt in neglecting God's will in her life. A conference with the pastor ensued. Conversation revealed that she knew no more about the Bible than if she had been reared in the heart of some pagan land. The pastor placed the Bible in her hands and had her read Isaiah 53:4-6. He then asked her to read it, substituting the singular personal pronoun for the plural. She read: "Surely he hath borne MY griefs, and carried MY sorrows; yet I did esteem him stricken, smitten of God, and afflicted. But he was wounded for MY transgressions, he was bruised for MY iniquities, etc." The "sword" went straight to her heart. She burst into tears and said, "Do you mean that Jesus did that for me?" The next day she happily surrendered to Jesus. After telling the pastor of her newly found joy in her love for the Master, she said: "I can hardly wait until Christmas to go home. I have a brother there who never has heard that story."

4. Aiming toward the desired spiritual results.—In using the Bible as an instrument with which to win others to Christ, it is necessary, first of all, to quote passages which are most likely to bring conviction of sin. In the case of the Ethiopian eunuch, it was the verse "All we like sheep have gone astray; we have turned every one to his own way" (Isa. 53:6) which convinced him of his need of a Savior. The tenth and twenty-third verses of the third chapter of Romans are worth more in bringing one to a sense of his sin than hours of eloquence or logic.

If the unsaved one has reached the point of sincerely asking, "What must I do to be saved?" then the next mental and spiritual processes into which he should be directed are "repentance toward God, and faith toward our Lord Jesus Christ." It is helpful indeed to show this statement in Acts 20:21, where Paul sums up his whole gospel message into this irreducible minimum.

When one has truly and definitely put his faith in Jesus as Savior and Lord, it is timely and important that he be led to want to confess before men that he is a believer. The soul-winner should seek to win a soul to accept Christ, and then seek to lead that soul to begin a life of testimony and service. This duty can best be impressed upon the mind of the newly converted person by some verse of Scripture, such as "Whosoever therefore shall confess me before men, him will I confess also before my Father which is in heaven" (Matt. 10:32).

Discreetly Distributing Tracts About Salvation

A tract on the plan of salvation to place in the hands of an unsaved person for him to read is a valuable piece of equipment for the soul-winner to carry. This is especially helpful if the interview cannot be followed through until a decision for Christ has been made. It is always possible to secure concise, scriptural leaflets on how to be saved. One of these, carried in the pocket or folded into the pocket New Testament, often proves to be of great value. They may be carried in the automobile and wisely used when stopping at filling stations or on other occasions.

The best tract in the world is an inexpensive copy of the Gospel of John. These can be secured from book stores for a few cents each. A certain businessman kept these in his office. The businessman asked a boy about his relation to Jesus Christ. As the boy was leaving, the man said, "You have brought me a message. Now let me give you a message which I want you to read." The boy took the copy of the Gospel of John, promising to read it. The Holy Spirit used it to its intended purpose. You remember that the Gospel of John was written "that ye might believe that Jesus is the Christ, the Son of God; and that believing ye might have life through his name" (John 20:31).

Humbly Depending Upon the Holy Spirit

Jesus, the master soul-winner, said: "The Spirit of the Lord is upon me, because he hath anointed me" (Luke 4:18). The one phase of spiritual equipment without which no Christian can ever lead another to accept Christ is the presence and power of the Holy Spirit. Perhaps all too many Christians are like the men of Ephesus (Acts 19:2), who did not know that the Holy Spirit had been given. The Christian must plant and cultivate, but the Holy Spirit must give the increase.

Worldwide Sphere of the Spirit's Work

Jesus said that it was better for him to leave the world so that the Spirit might come (John 16:7). At first thought it is hard to understand how it was better for the world for Jesus to go away. Then we remember that Jesus was in only one place at a time. But the Holy Spirit can be present and active at the same time in all churches, in all nations, in all hearts the world over, wherever he is admitted. Like the amplifier of the radio which multiplies the volume of the speaker's voice so that it can be heard around the globe, the Holy Spirit takes the words of Jesus and so amplifies them that it is possible for all people everywhere to hear.

The Witness and the Spirit Linked Together

Jesus links together the witnessing of the soul-winner and the work of the Holy Spirit. "But when the Comforter is come, whom I will send unto you from the Father, . . . he shall testify of me: And ye also shall bear witness, because ye have been with me from the beginning" (John 15:26-27). The American Standard Version footnote explains that the Greek word which is translated "Comforter" is "Paraclete." "Paraclete" literally means one who is called alongside. The Holy Spirit stands beside the soul-winner, waiting for him to do everything humanly possible to win the unbeliever to Christ, but ready to carry on to completion the work in the sinner's heart.

When the back wheels of an automobile stick in a mudhole, the wheels spin only the faster when the engine is raced. Presently someone stands along beside the car to push and urges the driver to "step on the gas." When the engine is racing at full speed, he gives a push, and the automobile leaps forward. Just so, the Paraclete stands along beside the soul-winner and gives that extra push of power which brings success. In this day when people depend on manpower, money power, and machine power, let every Christian learn to depend on the power of the Holy Spirit of God.

The Power of the Holy Spirit

How may I have the power and presence of the Holy Spirit? This is a question which oftentimes harasses the Christian who is sincerely desirous of winning others to Christ. It is reasonable to believe that a Christian gains the presence and blessing of the Holy Spirit exactly as he gains the presence and blessing of God the Father and God the Son. One finds Christ through faith. A Christian has God in him and God with him by trusting God. Likewise, the fullness of the power of the Spirit of God comes according to one's faith. Every successful winner of souls needs to trust the Holy Spirit implicitly for his power to accompany the use of the Scripture in winning others.

Illumination by the Spirit

The soul-winner must trust the Holy Spirit to illuminate the scriptural truth, without which the unsaved mind cannot understand its spiritual content. "But the natural man receiveth not the things of the Spirit of God: for they are foolishness unto him: neither can he know them, because they are spiritually discerned" (1 Cor. 2:14). Without the Spirit's illumination, the Scripture is to the unsaved man as a stained-glass window is when viewed from the outside—neither the beauty nor the connection can be seen. The Holy Spirit takes the unsaved heart inside where he can see to an advantage; then he shines upon the truth so that one may see its unity, its divinity, and its sufficiency. The Holy Spirit illuminates the central character of the Scripture, the Lord Jesus Christ, glorifying him in the beauty and radiance of God's grace.

Suggestions for Advanced Study

1. Learn particular verses or passages in the Bible which were immediately effective in the conversion of (a) Augustine of Hippo, (b) Martin Luther, (c) John Wesley, (d) Toyohiko Kagawa, and (e) some other worthy Christians whom you may know.

2. Write a sentence for each of the following phases of a well-equipped soul-winner, giving your appraisal of the value of each of them: religious training, experience, knowledge of the Bible, a prayer partner, Christian character, personality, compassion, and concern for souls.

3. Philip won the Ethiopian treasurer while riding in a chariot. Do you know of instances of conversions in "modern chariots," such as on horseback, on a subway or bus, on a train, on a bicycle, in an automobile, or in an airplane?

18
The Soul-Winner's Wisdom

Behold, I send you forth as sheep in the midst of wolves: be ye therefore wise as serpents, and harmless as doves (Matt. 10:16).

Why not help brighten up heaven? None of the thirteen major inventions of the last century affected civilization more than the incandescent lamp which has so splendidly brightened the earth. But brighter than any electric light is Christ in heaven, who is made radiant by his redemption of sinners. Every soul redeemed by him adds to his glorious radiance. "And they that be wise shall shine as the brightness of the firmament; and they that turn many to righteousness as the stars for ever and ever" (Dan. 12:3). To turn a sinner to righteousness is to brighten up heaven the more. Yet it takes wisdom to do it.

Jesus knew the necessity for wisdom when a soul-winner meets difficulties, for he knew there would be difficulties. Jesus knew that the spirit of the world is ever against soul-winning, for it obscures from the sinner's sight the Savior of the soul. Jesus knew that the spirit of the flesh is another dread enemy to put difficulties in the pathway to Christ and salvation. Likewise, Jesus knew Satan. Behind the program of worldliness and fleshly living there is the archenemy of the soul, the old devil, Satan. It is his satanic purpose to keep every possible individual from accepting Jesus Christ as Savior. He hates God. He knows that the best way to hurt the heart of God is to lead God's beloved people away from Christ. He will always be dogging the footsteps of every sinner who is interested in becoming a Christian. Despite the devil and all his difficulties, the faithful soul-winner can confidently say, "If God be for us, who can be against us?"

In speaking of difficulties, it is necessary to remind soul-winners continually that they will not win to Christ everyone whom they ap-

222

proach. Yet they will win some. The same message may be the savor of life unto life for some, and the savor of death unto death for others. It is not the soul-winner's responsibility if sinners refuse Christ; but it is his responsibility to present Christ as wisely and winsomely as possible. It is also the soul-winner's responsibility to foresee difficulties as far as possible and learn to deal deftly and wisely with them.

The soul-winner is reminded continually that the greatest difficulty in winning others is within the soul-winner's own heart and life. All the principles mentioned in the chapter on "The Soul Winner's Self-Discipline" may be recalled. Indeed, there are "fightings and fears without and within." Yet truth is stronger than falsehood; light overcomes the darkness; and the gospel is the power of God unto salvation to every one who believes.

Intelligently Recognizing Personality Difficulties

The successful experience of salesmen, solicitors, and agents teaches that the personal approach is the best method of winning others. Personality is an indefinable thing, but it is one of the most dynamic forces which we have. All Christians should consecrate their personalities to their widest possibilities in winning others to Christ.

Just as no two soul-winners are alike, so no two lost persons are likely to have identical personalities or identical problems. A soul-winner finds a freshness, a challenge, and a thrill in every approach to a new personality about his relation to Christ.

The Approach of Jesus

Nineteen times it is recorded that Jesus stopped to talk personally with individuals. He dealt with all manner of problem people, the rich and the poor, the men and the women, the rulers and the social outcasts, the Greeks and the Romans, the Pharisees and the Sadducees, the moralists and the criminals.

Jesus had no cut-and-dried method of approach to all unsaved, but met each as a unique personality with unique problems.

Knowledge of Each Personality

Since no two personalities are identical, it is extremely wise to study each personality as carefully as possible. Some sinners love gross sins;

some harbor pride or prejudice; and many have misguided ideas about how to be saved. In a casual meeting with an utter stranger on the street or on a plane, one should urge him then and there to repent of his sins and accept Christ as Savior; with him it is possibly then or never. But when trying to win a personal friend, it is better to ask for an immediate but private conference, in which the whole matter can be talked through and prayed through. The soul-winner might seek from interested relatives and friends to know the background, personality traits, and other details about the one he is trying to win.

A zealous but misguided college student rushed up to a Jewess and tried to persuade her then and there to accept Christ. The Jewess was steeped in all the traditions of her religion and prejudices against Jesus. The attempt to lead her to become a Christian ended in pitiful failure, of course. The roommate of the Jewess, far wiser in soul-winning, sought daily to live the Christian life before her. From time to time they conversed about the merits of the claim of Jesus to be the Jewish Messiah. By infinite patience, consummate tact, and unfailing prayer, the girl swept away the prejudices of the Jewess against Jesus and won her to a glorious faith in him as Savior.

A soul-winner led two young men to Christ within a few months of each other. His methods of getting to their difficulties were as different as day is from night. The first was the know-it-all type, a freshman in college. He said he could not accept so much emotionalism and could approach the subject of Christianity only from the intellectual standpoint. The soul-winner launched into a discussion of whether regeneration is subjective or objective. He talked about the authenticity of the Lukan account of parthenogenesis. He spoke of the Aramaisms and the Hebraisms therein. He sought to get the college freshman to discuss the archaeological import of the Rosetta Stone, the moralities in the Code of Hammurabi, the discovery of the Oxyrhynchus papyri, and the plenary inspiration of the Scripture. The young fellow stumbled and sputtered through all of this, but finally succumbed when he was asked about his eschatological predilection, whether it was postmillenarian or premillenarian. He broke down and confessed that he knew nothing of this, but he knew he was a guilty sinner before God. He was soon on his knees, making a confession of his sins. Within six weeks he made a public confession of faith in Christ.

The other young man could not be won by such horseplay as that.

He was of the quiet, morose, introspective sort, and, withal, mean of spirit and dissipated in life. The soul-winner won his confidence through many kindnesses to his sick father. His mind was turned toward Christ by earnest, serious conversation. His heart was touched and won by love.

The difficulties in the way of these two young men had to be removed by exactly opposite methods, each according to his own personality. Winning them required wisdom, applied psychology, knowledge of human nature, and prayer for heaven's guidance to know how to approach each individual and to remove his difficulties.

Scriptural Help for Every Type

There is a scriptural answer to every spiritual problem. There is a Bible truth to solve every spiritual puzzle. There is a scriptural key with which to unlock the heart of every particular type of personality. It is highly important to study some of these different types and to find one or two scriptural references which might suit each of them.

The stubborn (Prov. 29:1)
The skeptical (John 7:17)
The drifter (Heb. 2:3)
The backslider (Jer. 2:19)
The procrastinator (2 Cor. 6:2; Heb. 3:15)
The half-interested (Rev. 3:15-16)
The inconsistent church member (Eph. 4:1,17)
The one unwilling to surrender (Luke 13:3)
The worldly minded (1 John 2:15-17)
The wicked (Rev. 21:8; Isa. 55:7)
The moralist (Rom. 3:10,23)
The atheist (Ps. 14:1)

This list is in no way complete, either in enumerating all the different types or in suggesting all the verses of possible use with them. It merely contemplates individual searching of the Scripture to find the truths suitable for individual needs.

Boldly Dealing with Timeworn Excuses

Unsaved people today, just as in the days of Jesus, begin to make excuses. Any soul-winner meets the same ones time and time again. They become timeworn and hackneyed and foolish to the Christian;

yet many unsaved people believe that they are genuine reasons and original with them. One difficulty the soul-winner may have to face is with himself. It is difficult to exercise Christian patience when such an oft-exploded excuse as "hypocrites in the church" is offered by an otherwise sensible man as his reason for not accepting Christ as his Savior.

Excuses Answered Only by Scripture

There is no more perfect way to shatter these excuses than to answer them by appropriate Scripture quotations. Comparatively there are only a few of these oft-repeated excuses, and a verse or two will be enough to wipe out almost any one of them. We shall give the excuses which are more frequently met, and only one or two of the many verses available for erasing each difficulty from an honest mind. By using these and other verses, the soul winner will grow more and more effective in showing the shallowness and the fallacies of these obstacles.

(1) I am afraid I cannot hold out (John 10:28-29; Heb. 7:25).

(2) There are too many hypocrites in the church (John 21:21-22; Rom. 14:12).

(3) I do not feel like it now (Jer. 17:9; Rev. 3:20).

(4) I am not a bad sinner (Rom. 3:10-23; John 3:17-18,36).

(5) I am too great a sinner (1 Tim. 1:15; Luke 19:10).

(6) There is plenty of time (Isa. 55:6; Prov. 29:1).

(7) I do not believe in a hell (Luke 16:23-26; Rev. 21:8).

(8) I do not believe the Bible (Matt. 5:18; 2 Tim. 3:16).

(9) God is too good to send anybody to hell (Ezek. 33:11; 2 Pet. 3:9).

(10) I will try to become better (Matt. 9:12; Isa. 1:18).

(11) I will accept Christ someday, but not now (Gen. 6:3; 2 Cor. 6:2; Heb. 2:1-3; Rom. 5:6-8).

(12) I cannot give up evil habits (Luke 13:3; Heb. 7:25; 1 Cor. 10:13).

(13) I cannot forgive enemies (Matt. 6:12; 18:21-35).

(14) I am doing the best I can (John 3:3,17-18).

Excuses Often Camouflage for Sin

Excuses are frequently mere camouflage for excesses and inconsistencies in life. Particularly is this true in the case of the excuse of "hypocrites in the church." One who hates hypocrisy would be attracted to Jesus above all persons, for it was Jesus who taught the world the hatefulness of hypocrisy. So often it is hypocrisy which makes the unsaved man give this excuse for not accepting Christ.

At a large conference of students there was one boy who came with the others, but he claimed to be seriously troubled with doubts about the reality of a God. The campus minister talked and prayed with him, to no avail. His pastor was there and sought to dissolve his doubts, but met no success. Fellow students tried in every way to help him over his difficulty. The teacher of the class in soul-winning in the conference met the boy and obtained a private interview with him. The boy outlined his doubts about the reality of God, his skepticism about the genuineness of the Bible, and his abhorrence of the hypocrites in the churches. The leader listened with long-suffering patience, and then abruptly broke in by asking him, "Old fellow, come clean with me now! Which is it that is in your life, stealing money, gambling, or impurity of conduct?" The boy's head dropped, his bold doubts vanished like a mist; and his sad confession of guilt came pouring out of his heart. His sympathetic listener knew how to point him to One who could cleanse his heart of its sin and stain.

Patiently Overcoming Personal Prejudices

William Borden, a young millionaire who was graduated from Yale University in 1909, led to Christ every unsaved member of his class before their graduation. He was a master in the art of overcoming prejudices. Of course there was prejudice aplenty for him to overcome. He would go to the rooms of his unsaved classmates, study with them, talk with them, laugh with them, wrestle with them, and then pray with them. Of course, it is not possible for everyone to use this exact method. But prejudices must be recognized and overcome before one can lead another to Christ.

Methods Necessary with a Jew

A taxicab driver told a soul-winner that he was a Jew. The Christian replied: "That makes me interested in you. The best friend I ever had was a Jew." From that he went on to tell the driver about Jesus, the Jew's greatest friend. Usually it takes long friendship and Christlike living to overcome the inborn and inbred prejudices of Jews against

Christ. Argument never wins. It is helpful to interpret the books of Matthew and Hebrews, showing how Jesus fulfills all Old Testament prophecies concerning the Messiah. Successful witnessing requires the cultivation of the person's confidence.

Overcoming Erroneous Religious Views

In dealing with such as are misled by erroneous views, it is necessary to know much about their beliefs. In anticipating a conversation with Unitarians, Seventh-Day Adventists, Spiritualists, Russellites, Mormons, or Christian Scientists, it would be advantageous to write to some religious book store to get pamphlets on their beliefs and learn how to show them the points of agreement as well as the errors of their ways. There are splendid books concerning the beliefs of all these and other sects.

Carefully Clearing Up Conscientious Doubts

One of John Bunyan's immortal pen pictures is that of Doubting Castle. Doubting Castle holds in its dismal dungeon many who are genuine but unhappy Christians as well as multitudes who are without Christ.

Reality of Doubts

"Except I shall see in his hands the print of the nails, and put my finger into the print of the nails, and thrust my hand into his side, I will not believe" (John 20:25), said "doubting Thomas." The number of "doubting Thomases" is not as large as the number of excuse makers, but it is a very real group whose doubts may be very genuine. While there are some who would cover up their moral delinquencies by parading their intellectual difficulties, there are others who would be most happy to have their doubts dissolved.

Cause of Doubts

Doubts are usually symptoms of something underneath the surface. The wise spiritual physician will study the symptoms to determine the real cause of the trouble. The symptoms cannot be removed without finding and removing the cause.

1. Sin.—In a large number of cases, sin in the life brings doubts. These doubts are the natural reactions of a guilty conscience which is trying to shift the focus of attention.

2. Inactivity.—It may be idleness in the kingdom program which brings doubts. The doubts of Thomas about the resurrection of Jesus came because he had cut himself loose from the other apostles and was not present that Sunday night when Jesus appeared unto them. Satan does not overlook an opportunity to drop the seed of doubt into the soil of an idle brain.

3. Fighting God's call.—Often when God is calling a sinner to repentance and faith, he is also calling that one to do some definite task in the kingdom program. Many a young man has become a doubter in this way because he sinned against God's call to the ministry.

4. Seeds of skepticism.—Many are doubters because the tares have been sown in the fields of their immature thinking by others who are skeptics or infidels.

5. Adversities.—Some doubt because of the coming of adversities into their lives. They wrongly blame these on God instead of recognizing the evil work of the devil in these adversities, or instead of realizing that often these troubles come as the fruit of one's own life.

It is plainly seen that if the cause of these doubts can be found and eradicated, then the pathway is clear for casting aside every doubt which is an obstacle in the way to Christ.

Antithesis of Doubt

The antithesis of doubt is faith. After removing the cause of doubt patient perseverance in a clear-cut plan for building up faith in God must be exercised. This, too, requires thought, prayer, zeal, skill, study of the Scripture, and love.

Deftly Dealing with Various Ages

It is as helpful to know the psychology of various age groups for winning them to Christ as it is for teaching them. An intelligent approach to adults, a winsome approach to youth, and a wise approach to children may be made by one who studies to show himself approved unto God as a soul-winner.

Difficulty of Winning Adults

Adults have developed prejudices. They have gone further away from Christ than youth. They have become more hardened in sin every year of their lives. They must become trustful and believing and loving, like little children, to be converted.

The greater difficulty in winning adults demands greater earnestness in seeking them for the Savior. The nearer a blind man walks toward a precipice, the more frantic should be the effort to rescue him. The lesson of the two thieves who were crucified with Christ should apply here. One thief was saved, so soul-winners should never despair of anyone. One thief was lost, so no one should ever presume. Soul-winners should never give up trying to win older people; yet they should keep in mind the fact that it becomes more and more difficult with every passing day for an adult to become a Christian.

No Clever Tricks for Winning Adults

There are no clever tricks by which older people are to be won. They require more spiritual power, more Christlike influence, and more instruction in the way of life. The approach through their emotional nature is less open. The appeal to them must go more largely through their intellectual nature. Older people watch more critically for inconsistencies in the lives of the church members. Some church member is the key to the heart's door of almost every unsaved adult.

Appeal of Christ to Youth

Youth is a glorious time for making the surrender to Christ. A very wise man said many years ago, "Remember now thy Creator in the days of thy youth, while the evil days come not, nor the years draw nigh, when thou shalt say, I have no pleasure in them" (Eccl. 12:1).

1. Christ's love for youth.—Jesus had a flair for youth while he was upon earth. The statement "Then Jesus beholding him loved him" (Mark 10:21) was true in many more cases than the one of which this was said. When the genuine love of Christ for youth is properly presented, this love will beget a love in return.

2. Appealing characteristics of Christ.—Youth should be easier to win to Christ than adults because the Savior has every manly, heroic, and lofty characteristic to inspire the ideals of youth. Youth finds in Jesus all the fearlessness, self-restraint, magnanimity, loyalty, endurance, and sincerity that may be wished to inspire the highest idealism. The soul-winner who knows youth and who knows Christ can present these qualities to youth so that they will be led to repent of their poor sinful ways and to throw themselves at the feet of the soul-saving, character-building, and destiny-determining Son of God.

Youth may be won best by Christians of their own age group. The unsaved young men and women will listen to their own friends much more quickly than to their elders. Every effort should be made by church leaders to encourage and to train youth to win their own companions and friends to the Lord Jesus.

Delicate Task of Winning Children

Jesus loved little children devotedly. He blessed many of them and commanded that they should be brought to him. He did not say, "Suffer little infants to come unto me," as some denominational groups say. Nor did he say, "Suffer only the adults to come unto me," as some misguided parents and church leaders seem to say. Jesus knew that in childhood one may be brought to repent and believe with far more ease than later in life. Jesus could never encourage anyone to wait another day in unbelief and sin before coming to him for salvation. Little children should be won to Christ.

1. Two dangerous extremes.—In dealing with little children, there are two extremes to be prayerfully avoided. First, there is the dangerous extreme of saying that a child is too young to become a Christian or that the child does not know enough to become a Christian. Jesus did not command little children to grow old in order to be converted. On the contrary, he said that children naturally have the correct mental and spiritual attitude for conversion. Older people must become as little children, or they cannot enter the kingdom of heaven. Most people who are saved are converted when young. It is said that among any one thousand conversions of the average type, only about twelve will be people twenty-five years old or above. A majority of them will not have passed fifteen years of age. About four hundred of them will be children who have not reached the age of twelve.

A wise example of how to deal with a child of tender years is that of the pastor of a great city church who was continually besought by his eight-year-old boy for permission to join the church. The father talked and prayed with the boy, rejoicing in his interest in his salvation, but fearful about his son's joining the church at so tender an age. After some time the brave little fellow said positively, "Father, I am going to join the church this morning." The father took the boy into the church office, knelt beside him in prayer, and prayed thus: "Heavenly Father, thou didst send Jesus to us, and he commanded that little children be brought unto him. Here, Father, is my boy, thy boy. I bring him unto thee. He is thy boy, and this is thy church. Approve of his coming into the church, or prevent it, dear Lord. I commit him unto thee."

The other extreme to be avoided in dealing with children is that of herding them into the church in groups, when their only motive is to go with the other children. This has been done too often. No one is wise enough to know exactly when a child is old enough and knows enough to experience a genuine conversion to Christ. Yet there are some things which they should know and which older people can be sure that they know. Children should not be urged into church membership until they have experienced a personal sense of their sinfulness before God. Also, they should experience a change of attitude toward sin through repentance. And assuredly, they should know the experience of trusting Jesus Christ to be their Savior. Until a child has given satisfactory answers to questions about these things, he should not be urged to unite with the church.

2. *True conversion necessary.*—Children have not gone as far away from God as older sinners have. Therefore, their conversion experience need not be as dramatic as that of a grown person. Yet the elements in the conversion of a grown person and that of a child are identical. Every child who has reached the point of knowledge of right and wrong is a fit object of prayer and personal work. He should be led to repent of sin and to put his trust in the Lord Jesus Christ. It is worth every effort to win him while young. Any child is worth a whole series of evangelistic services in the church.

Prayerfully Cultivating Qualities That Are Winsome

A halfhearted attitude does not win souls, whether it be in the pulpit or in private interview. A discouraged young preacher, talking to Spurgeon about his failure to win converts, said, "I do not expect somebody to be converted every time I preach." Immediately Mr. Spurgeon told him that a Christian tries to win another to Christ; he should confidently expect to win him and be genuinely disappointed if he does not. One must woo with the determined purpose to win.

There are definite elements which must characterize the wooing if one is wise in winning others to Christ.

Sincerity of Soul

The Christian who wins souls must have some of the genuine sincerity of Jonah, who cried, "Yet forty days, and Nineveh shall be overthrown" (Jonah 3:4). Jeremiah lamented, "Behold, and see if there be any sorrow like unto my sorrow" (Lam. 1:12). Isaiah pleaded, "Let the wicked forsake his way" (Isa. 55:7), with such ringing sincerity in his voice that it could not be mistaken. Amos earnestly warned, "Prepare to meet thy God." Peter passionately preached, "Repent, and be baptized every one of you in the name of Jesus Christ for the remission of sins" (Acts 3:38). Jesus sobbed as he most sincerely said, "O Jerusalem, Jerusalem, . . . how often would I have gathered thy children together, even as a hen gathereth her chickens under her wings" (Matt. 23:37). There could be no doubt about the sincerity of the soul of General William Booth when he stood before Queen Victoria. The queen asked him if there was anything which she could do for him. He replied, "Your Majesty, some people's passion is money, and some people's passion is fame; but my passion has been men."

Enthusiasm of Spirit

The word *enthusiasm* is derived from two Greek words meaning "God in us." God in one's heart gives a divine interest and eagerness in the matter of winning the souls of others. Spiritual enthusiasm is magnetic and attractive to the unhappy heart of an unforgiven sinner. The legend is told of John Vassar, how he sought to win to Christ a woman whom he accidentally met in a hotel lobby. As he passed out of the hotel, the woman's husband came up and asked her what the stranger was saying to her. She told him that John Vassar was trying to lead her to become a Christian. "Why didn't you tell him to mind his own business?" asked her husband. "Ah," said the lady, "if you had heard him, you would have thought that he was minding his business." That was enthusiasm in action.

Persistency of Purpose

There is a wise and forceful persistency by which the soul-winner should press on toward getting a decision for Christ. Most unsaved people come to the point of decision and then falter. It is exceedingly dangerous to let a lost soul turn back. That is the time to press for an immediate commitment to Christ. Hold out the hand and ask the faltering man to grasp it, thereby signifying his decision. Get him on his knees before God, if possible. While bending the body prostrate before God, it is easier for one to bend his will to the goodwill of God in Christ.

The danger of getting up to the point of decision and then turning back is illustrated by the experience of Aaron Burr while he was a college student. It is said that a revival was sweeping through the student body, and Burr was almost persuaded to become a Christian. He consulted a professor, telling of his inclination toward committing his all to Jesus Christ. The professor thought he should appear thoughtful and scholarly, so he said, "Mr. Burr, you are in an abnormal state of mind, being affected by this great wave of emotion which is sweeping the campus. You are a man of intellect. Why not wait until this has passed away and then clearly think through your religious problem?" Aaron Burr said that was exactly what he would do. And never again did anyone ever hear of Aaron Burr being concerned for one single moment about his relationship to Jesus Christ.

Tenacity of Faith

Never give up a lost soul until he is dead. Trust God; "never give up prayer" (1 Thess. 5:17, Moffatt). Believe that God's word will not return to him void. God instructed Isaiah to preach until the hearts of the people were fat, their ears heavy, and their eyes shut. A soul-winner must be willing to do the same. "He that goeth forth and weepeth, bearing precious seed, shall doubtless come again with rejoicing, bringing his sheaves with him" (Ps. 126:6). Soul-winners can cling to God's "doubtless." No case was hopeless to Christ, the master Soul-Winner.

Suggestions for Advanced Study

1. Study the masterpieces of art to see how many people are pictured as believing Christians and how many as rejecting Christ: (a) Hoffman's *Christ in the Midst of the Doctors,* (b) Da Vinci's *The Last Supper,* (c) Ruben's *Christ on the Cross,* and (d) Michelangelo's *The Last Judgment.*

2. Why did the early Christians use the fish as their sign and symbol (Greek, *ichthus*)? Organize a band of "Christian Fishermen."

3. Study Acts 13—28, and determine what percentage of people with whom Paul dealt might have become Christians.

References for Further Study

Chamberlain, Eugene. *When Can a Child Believe?* Nashville: Broadman Press, 1973.

Ingle, Clifford, ed. *Children and Conversion.* Nashville: Broadman Press, 1970.

Green, Michael. *You Must Be Joking: Popular Excuses for Avoiding Jesus Christ.* Wheaton, Illinois: Tyndale House, 1976.

———. *Faith for the Nonreligious.* Wheaton, Illinois: Tyndale House, 1979.

Starkes, M. Thomas. *Today's World Religions.* New Orleans: Insight Press Incorporated, 1978.

Stott, John R. W. *Our Guilty Silence: The Church, the Gospel, and the World.* Grand Rapids: William B. Eerdmans Publishing Company, 1969.

A Bibliography on Evangelism

Background

Autrey, C. E. *The Theology of Evangelism.* Nashville: Broadman Press, 1966.
————. *Basic Evangelism.* Grand Rapids: Zondervan Publishing House, 1959.
Bader, Jesse M. *The Message and Method of the New Evangelism.* New York: Round Table Press, 1937.
Borchert, Gerald L. *Dynamics of Evangelism.* Waco: Word Books, 1976.
Coleman, Robert E. *The Master Plan of Evangelism.* Old Tappan, New Jersey: Fleming H. Revell Company, 1963.
Dillistone, F. W. *Revelation and Evangelism.* London: Lutterworth Press, 1948.
Dobbins, Gaines S. *Evangelism According to Christ.* Nashville: Broadman Press, 1949.
————. *Good News to Change Lives: Evangelism for an Age of Uncertainty.* Nashville: Broadman Press, 1976.
Drummond, Lewis A. *Leading Your Church in Evangelism.* Nashville: Broadman Press, 1975.
Fackre, Gabriel. *Word in Deed: Theological Themes in Evangelism.* Grand Rapids: William B. Eerdmans Publishing Company, 1975.
Finney, Charles G. *Revival Lectures.* Oberlin, Ohio: E. J. Goodrich, 1868.
Ford, Leighton. *The Christian Persuader.* New York: Harper and Row, 1966.
Green, Michael. *Evangelism in the Early Church.* Grand Rapids: William B. Eerdmans Publishing Company, 1970.
Havlik, John F. *The Evangelistic Church.* Nashville: Convention Press, 1976.
Hunter George G., III. *The Contagious Congregation: Frontiers in Evangelism and Church Growth.* Nashville: Abingdon Press, 1979.
Leavell, Roland Q. *Preaching the Doctrines of Grace.* Nashville: Broadman Press, 1939.
McDill, Wayne. *Evangelism in a Tangled World.* Nashville: Broadman Press, 1976.
McGavran, Donald A. *Understanding Church Growth.* Grand Rapids: William B. Eerdmans Publishing Company, 1970.

Miller, Herb. *Evangelism's Open Secrets.* Saint Louis: The Bethany Press, 1977.

Sangster, W. E. *Let Me Commend.* New York: Abingdon-Cokesbury, 1948.

Smith, Bailey. *Real Evangelism: Exposing Subtle Substitutes for That Evangelism.* Nashville: Broadman Press, 1978.

Stott, John R. W. *Christian Mission in the Modern World.* Downers Grove, Illinois: Inter-Varsity Press, 1975.

————. *Our Guilty Silence.* Grand Rapids: William B. Eerdmans Publishing Company, 1967.

Sweazey, George E. *The Church as Evangelist.* New York: Harper and Row, 1978.

————. *Effective Evangelism.* New York: Harper and Row, 1976.

Sweet, W. W. *Revivalism in America.* New York: Charles Scribner's Sons, 1944.

Whitesell, F. D. *Basic New Testament Evangelism.* Grand Rapids, Michigan: Zondervan, 1949.

Watson, David. *I Believe in Evangelism.* Grand Rapids: William B. Eerdmans Publishing Company, 1976.

Warren, Max. *I Believe in The Great Commission.* Grand Rapids: William B. Eerdmans Publishing Company, 1976.

History

Bloesch, Donald. *The Evangelical Renaissance.* Grand Rapids: William B. Eerdmans Publishing Company, 1973.

Drummond, Lewis A. *The Awakening That Must Come.* Nashville: Broadman Press, 1979.

Evans, W. Glynn. *Profiles of Revival Leaders.* Nashville: Broadman Press, 1976.

Scharpff, Paulus. *The History of Evangelism.* Grand Rapids: William B. Eerdmans Publishing Company, 1966.

Stoeffler, Ernest F. *The Rise of Evangelical Pietism.* Leiden, Netherlands: E. J. Brill, 1971.

Methods

Barnette, Jasper N. *The Place of the Sunday School in Evangelism.* Nashville: Broadman Press, 1945.

Brooks, W. Hal. *Follow-Up Evangelism.* Nashville: Broadman Press, 1972.

Caldwell, Max L., comp. *Positive Evangelism Through the Sunday School.* Nashville: Convention Press, 1978.

Chamberlain, Eugene. *When Can a Child Believe?* Nashville: Broadman Press, 1973.

Chafin, Kenneth L. *The Reluctant Witness.* Nashville: Broadman Press, 1974.

Chaney, Charles L., and Lewis, Ron S. *Design for Church Growth.* Nashville: Broadman Press, 1977.

Coggin, James E., and Spooner, Bernard M. *You Can Reach People Now.* Nashville: Broadman Press, 1971.

Feather, R. Othal. *Outreach Evangelism Through the Sunday School.* Nashville: Convention Press, 1972.

Fish, Roy J., and Conant, J. E. *Every Member Evangelism for Today.* An updating of J. E. Conant's work *Every Member Evangelism.* New York: Harper and Row, 1976.

Fish, Roy J. *Giving a Good Invitation.* Nashville: Broadman Press, 1974.

Ford, Leighton. *Good News Is for Sharing.* Elgin, Illinois: David C. Cook Publishing Company, 1977.

Green, Michael. *Faith for the Non-Religious.* Wheaton, Illinois: Tyndale House Publishers, Incorporated, 1976.

————. *You Must Be Joking: Popular Excuses for Avoiding Jesus Christ.* Wheaton, Illinois: Tyndale House Publishers, Incorporated, 1976.

Hogue, C. B. *I Want My Church to Grow.* Nashville: Broadman Press, 1977.

————. *Love Leaves No Choice: Life-Style Evangelism.* Waco: Word Books, 1976.

Ingle, Clifford, ed. *Children and Conversion.* Nashville: Broadman Press, 1970.

Ishee, John, ed. *Is Christ for John Smith?* Nashville: Broadman Press, 1968.

Kennedy, James D. *Evangelism Explosion,* rev. ed. Wheaton, Illinois: Tyndale House Publishers, 1977.

Lindgren, Alvin J. *Foundations for Purposeful Church Administration.* Nashville: Abingdon Press, 1965.

Little, Paul E. *How to Give Away Your Faith.* Downers Grove, Illinois: Inter-Varsity Press, 1966.

Moore, Waylon. *New Testament Follow-Up.* Grand Rapids: William B. Eerdmans Company, 1963.

Neighbour, Ralph W., Jr. *The Touch of the Spirit.* Nashville: Broadman Press, 1972.

Neighbour, Ralph W., Jr., and Thomas, Cal. *Target-Group Evangelism.* Nashville: Broadman Press, 1975.

Price, Nelson L. *I've Got to Play on Their Court.* Nashville: Broadman Press, 1975.

Read, David H. C. *Go and Make Disciples.* Nashville: Abingdon Press, 1978.

Schaller, Lyle E. *Assimilating New Members.* Nashville: Abingdon Press, 1978.

Sisemore, John T. *The Ministry of Visitation.* Nashville: Convention Press, 1954.

Young, J. Terry. *The Church—Alive and Growing!* Nashville: Broadman Press, 1978.